Living Positively
One Day at a Time

Living Positively One Day at a Time

Power thoughts for each day of the year

Robert H. Schuller

Fleming H. Revell Company
Old Tappan, New Jersey

Library of Congress Cataloging in Publication Data

Schuller, Robert Harold.
 Living positively one day at a time.

 1. Devotional calendars. I. Title.
BV4811.S366   242′.2   81-8563
ISBN 0-8007-5068-3   AACR2

INTRODUCTION

In writing this devotional, I have tried to capture the key thoughts and powerful scripture verses that have helped me grow in my faith, to have the courage to discover God's potential within me.

As I keep a favorite Bible verse, Proverbs 3:6, before me, I know that "in everything I do, if I put God first, He will crown my efforts with success."

My prayer is that *LIVING POSITIVELY, One Day at a Time,* will connect you to the one who has been my North Star, my Iron Pillared Friend, and my constant inspiration as the greatest possibility thinker that ever lived. That ideal is Jesus Christ!

As you read these daily thoughts, be sure to record and reflect upon your feelings by writing in the blank spaces. I have found that physically autographing a note, writing a letter, or signing a document, makes me more committed and more involved.

God Loves You and So Do I!

Robert Schuller
Garden Grove, California

CONTENTS

Dear heavenly Father—we thank you for this beautiful new year filled with many fantastic surprises!

As we stand before the unchartered waters of a new year, we are filled with a sense of urgency and expectancy. For with You as our Captain to guide us, we can face vast unknowns confidently, and fierce storms courageously.

Help us, O Lord, to turn our scars into guiding stars upon which we can set our sights. Help us to navigate from our strengths and not from our weaknesses. Help us to set our goals on Your limitless possibilities, rather than on our own limited abilities.

Give us the courage, O Lord, to leave the sheltered bay and face the high seas unafraid. For with You, Eternal Father, at the helm of our lives, we know that we can face our tomorrows with enthusiasm, confidence, courage, and great anticipation of many exciting adventures.

It is in You and Your almighty power that we anchor our hopes. We love You and we praise You! Amen.

Robert A. Schuller

Living Positively
One Day at a Time

Get Enthusiastic About Tomorrow—Today!

Key-In To Enthusiasm

"Indeed, the Lord will give what is good."

Psalms 85:12

If you know you are being led into a vital and exciting life filled with new possibilities and dynamic potential, you can be enthusiastic about tomorrow—today! You'll get so excited you can hardly stand it! The key to enthusiasm is to know that there is a fantastic tomorrow waiting for you.

If you want to be enthusiastic, really enthusiastic, it's very simple. Enthusiasm comes when you set goals. When you make commitments to a God-inspired dream and you give it all you've got, that produces enthusiasm! But when you hold yourself back and are not totally committed, you create an emotional blockage which restricts the flow of natural, godly enthusiasm.

Repeat this positive affirmation out loud:

THERE IS A FANTASTIC TOMORROW WAITING FOR ME!

Right now, open your heart to God. Pray that He will give you a wonderful dream for this new year. Then promise Him that you will totally commit yourself to the realization of your dream. Begin your commitment now by putting your dream in writing.

Self-esteem, rooted in God's call, generates enthusiasm for God's work.

Key-In To Enthusiasm

"God at work in you will give you the will and the power to achieve His purpose."

Philippians 1:6

The word *enthusiasm* comes from two Greek words:
En Theos—"In God"
How can we be in God?
First, God tells us He *needs* us. So, He recruits us.
Next, He says, "I'll *lead* you into a dream, a project, a calling, into my work. It's going to be very exciting and very fulfilling." When He guides you to make a decision to attempt the impossible for Him, He will not desert you to failure, but He will give you the supply and the strength to succeed!
Sister Theresa had a dream one day. She told her superiors, "I have three pennies and a dream from God to build an orphanage." "Sister Theresa," her superiors chided gently, "you cannot build an orphanage with three pennies. With three pennies, you can't do anything." "I know," she said smiling, "but with God and three pennies, I can do anything!"

With God's help, I can do anything!

Key-In To Enthusiasm

"For I know the plans that I have for you," declares the Lord, "plans for welfare and not for calamity to give you a future and a hope."

Jeremiah 29:11

Have you made your resolutions yet? It's not too late. I believe in New Year's resolutions. I really believe some people's lives are changed through revolution, some through evolution, and many through resolution.

I met a waiter in the restaurant the other day. "Well," I asked, "did you make your resolutions for the new year?" "No," he replied, laughing, "I'm still celebrating."

Let's stop just celebrating, and let's set some goals. What areas of your life can be improved? What great opportunities or dreams has God given to you today? He has amazing plans for you. The sky is the limit to what God can do with your life this year. As you pray, He'll lead you to do something beautiful. Follow Him in trust and acceptance. It's that simple.

Be sure that God will get you so enthusiastically involved in His work that you'll have no time for depression. A mind that's busy with God's work is too full of exciting ideas for negative thoughts to find entrance!

With God's help, write down five resolutions for the new year.

_____   _____

_____   _____

_____

> **Thank you, God, for leading me to do something beautiful!**

Get Enthusiasm

"The righteous will live by faith."

Habakkuk 2:4

You may think to yourself, "If I make the commitment to the dream that is coming into my mind now, I might fail." Of course you will fail unless you depend on God! You can be sure of one thing, when you get God's call, it will always be humanly impossible to do it alone. God always leads us into a commitment that will force us to feed upon Him constantly or we will face failure.

When God gives you a dream, it will be so big that you'll have to remain dependent on Him. It's His way of keeping you humble. How does possibility thinking deal with the problem of humility? Simple! *You possibilitize until you get an idea from God that is big enough for God to fit in*—so big that if you don't remain totally dependent upon Him, there's no way you can ever succeed!

He'll *lead* you—and then He'll *feed* you! If you're led—you'll need to be fed! God feeds only when we agree to follow where He leads! If you wait to follow His leading until you can be sure of His feeding—He'll never show you. For He feeds—only when our needs grow as a result of following where He leads. That's Faith!

Lord God, I will follow Your leading and trust You to take care of me.

Get Enthusiasm

"Giving thanks to the Father, who has qualified us to share in the inheritance of the saints in light."

Colossians 1:12

What's the cure for depression? The answer is simple: Get enthusiastic about life! And how do you get enthusiastic? Enthusiasm must rise from an emotional state of inner health which we define as self-esteem. And within the Lord's Prayer there lies a key that can unlock the inner door of enthusiasm.

The Lord's Prayer has been the single most significant prayer ever prayed in any religion throughout the centuries because it deals with the deepest negative human emotions that could restrict or constrict the spirit of enthusiasm—with depression being the result.

The first negative emotion it deals with is the inferiority complex—the lack of self-respect, self-esteem, self-confidence, and self-worth. That all time, classical, deep-rooted, emotional human ailment is conquered in the opening lines of the Prayer when you say, "Our Father Who are in Heaven, hallowed be thy name."

IF GOD IS MY FATHER, I AM HIS SON—I AM SOMEBODY! I belong to His righteous royal family! The opening sentence of the Lord's Prayer provides the basis for authentic self-esteem.

God is my Father—that makes me somebody special!

Get Enthusiasm

"And you will seek me and find me when you search for me with all your heart."

Jeremiah 29:13

Do you earnestly seek enthusiasm? I believe the word *seek* can be translated as the word "drive." What qualities solidify into the kind of drive that motivates one to success? In other words, what prompts a person to strive for success in marriage, education, business, or in recovering from a physical illness or disability? During my 25 years as a pastor, I've learned what the letters in this word *drive* stand for. I want to share with you the motivational key to success and achievement locked in the letters of this word *drive*.

D—**Dedicate** yourself to God's plan.
R—Be **responsible** enough to carry out that plan.

I —Stand on your **integrity** and honesty and God will be with you.
V—Have **vision**. Only God knows the good that can come from what you do for Him.
E—Get **enthusiasm**.

When you are pursuing a God-given idea, you will never run out of energy because God will keep you enthusiastic. The word *enthusiasm* translates, "God in me." With God in you, you can never lose. You will never become so discouraged, so defeated, or so tired that you will want to quit.

> **"But seek first His kingdom and His righteousness; and all these things shall be added to you." Matthew 6:33**

Get Enthusiasm

"Wait for the Lord; be strong and let your heart take courage; yes, wait for the Lord."

Psalms 27:14

I remember my father as one of the most quiet men I've ever met in my life. Many times during the more than 50 years of my parents' marriage, I remember my mother saying to him, "Tony, why don't you say something?" Even on the quietest of evenings, my father would maintain his calm, serene silence. "Why don't you say something?" my mother would prompt. "What shall I say?" my father would reply. I don't think I've ever heard anything more often during my life than that exchange between my parents.

A year after my father passed away, I remember my Mom saying, "Oh, how I miss your father." "Mom, why do you miss him so much?" I asked. "You know, Momma, when he was here, he didn't do much talking." "That's true," she argued, "He would sit there for hours and never say anything. But I knew he was there."

Today God is my silent father—sometimes He is even more silent than my human father. Sometimes I want to say to my Heavenly Father, just as Momma said to Dad, "Father, say something." And sometimes He remains silent. But when He does speak, I listen. He gives me dreams to which I become dedicated. Then I am responsible, maintain integrity, keep looking ahead with vision, and allow His enthusiasm to permeate my life.

> **I believe in the sun, even when it is not shining. I believe in God, even when He is silent.**

Get Enthusiasm

"Then Moses said, 'Dedicate yourselves today to the Lord—in order that He may bestow a blessing upon you today.'"
Exodus 32:29

Dedication is the core of all human enthusiasm. It is synonymous with commitment. One of the problems of today's society is that people don't want to make commitments. Why? Because to commit yourself to a goal means you must close the door on all other options. The committed person leaves no alternatives. He eliminates options. To become dedicated, you must first realize that God has a dream, a plan, an idea for your success. Hence, dedication begins in prayer. Real drive is born when you begin seeking God's will, God's way and God's word.

In the psychology of motivation there are many theories as to what motivates people. Adler said motivation is born of the will to power. Frankl says it springs from the will to find meaning. Fromm says motivation arises from the will to love. And Maslow says the will to self-actualization is the root of motivation.

But in possibility thinking we say that motivation comes from the will to self-dignity, self-esteem and self-love. No matter what line of thought you subscribe to, no motivation is more powerful than that which springs from the will to do what you believe God wants you to do.

It takes guts to leave the ruts.

Get Enthusiasm

*"The Lord is my light and my salvation; whom shall I fear?
The Lord is the defense of my life."*

Psalms 27:1

If I understand what God wants, then I know what I am
attempting to achieve is right and God is on my side.

There is an enormous amount of enthusiasm present
when you realize that what you are seeking to accomplish is
sanctioned by God because you know you are acting with
integrity and honesty.

Only a person with integrity can be totally enthusiastic. If
you lack integrity, you don't dare to be committed or enthusiastic. The dishonest person cultivates a subconscious emotional shield to protect himself from the kind of spontaneity
that will "let the cat out of the bag." He is afraid of exposing
his own true motives. A person who lacks integrity can
never be genuinely enthusiastic, spontaneous, bubbling, natural, or free. Hence he can never develop the tremendous
drive that motivates the honest person.

> **Dear Lord, please give me a purpose I can
> live for, a self I can live with and a faith I
> can live by.**

Get Enthusiasm

"I can do all things through Christ who strengthens me."
Philippians 4:13

I encourage you today to set exciting, challenging enthusiasm producing goals. I want you to pick a goal, and dream a dream, because God has more in store for you than you could dare to imagine.

But why should we dare to set goals? Why should we put ourselves in such a publicly vulnerable position? Why should we dare to expose ourselves to the possibility of an "ego-blow-out?" The answer is simple:

If we get an idea we're sure originated with God, we know that we'd never be able to live with ourselves knowing we didn't try simply because we didn't want to be embarrassed by our failures. To fail to try for fear of failure is the ultimate selfishness—especially when we have every reason to hope to succeed.

"I can do all things through Christ Who strengthens me" (Philippians 4:13).

I've learned something about that Bible verse. I used to think it meant that I could accomplish anything I set out to do. But sometimes I found that I tried and failed. Those were the times, I learned, when I was not trusting God enough. So to compensate, I took the opposite approach. I trusted God, His message is, *"You've got to give it all you've got and you've got to trust Me for all I am. Then together we'll win."*

Working *with* God, what goals will you make today?

> **I can fulfill my God-given dream if I'm**
> **willing to strive to arrive.**

Keep Enthusiasm

"And do not be conformed to this world, but be transformed by the renewing of your mind that you may prove what the will of God is, that which is good and acceptable and perfect."
Romans 12:2

The key to keeping enthusiasm at a peak is dynamic energy! And there are two forces of energy—positive and negative.

Negative energy is energy that grows out of negative thoughts and negative feelings.

It's amazing how many people live their lives with an energy output that is stimulated from a negative source. But the end result is high blood pressure, nervous breakdowns, ulcers and heart trouble.

In contrast to negative energy there is positive energy. Whether literally climbing a mountain, or climbing your mountain of obstacles, success depends upon positive energy that enables you to stay with it! Energy that is positive is energy fed with enthusiasm!

When we are in God and God is within us then we have His ideas. His ideas are full of possibilities and these possibilities stimulate us with great positive expectations! And that feeds our enthusiasm. Show me a person who's really dynamic and alive with exciting energy and I'll show you a person who's turned on by God's ideas!

God's ideas generate positive energy.

Keep Enthusiasm

*"They are like trees along a river bank bearing luscious fruit
each season without fail. Their leaves shall never wither, and
all they do shall prosper."*

Psalms 1:3

Negative energy leaves you with fatigue, but positive energy leaves you with a great replenishment of fresh energy. Positive energy becomes a self-propagating force that knows no end. You achieve a new peak experience and from the new peak experience you become so exhilarated you are confident that you can do even more than you thought!

You see a new peak so you begin to reach for the next peak. When you reach that peak you receive a larger vision. Soon you have a success cycle going that nothing can stop. Each new achievement only intensifies your energy capacity because it whips up more enthusiasm! That's the key!

Positive energy is energy released through enthusiasm that comes from the dynamic commitment to ideas that hold within themselves great possibilities and great potential to help people. So enthusiasm is positive energy!

Here's how positive energy produces more enthusiasm! Your enthusiasm gets you going and you start climbing! As you start climbing, you have a peak experience and when you have a peak experience you aim at a higher peak and you get enthusiastic about that! Enthusiasm is a positive, self-propagating, dynamic self-expanding energy!

> **My enthusiasm lifts me higher, and my
> success becomes self-perpetuating.**

Keep Enthusiasm

"The greatest among you shall be your servant."
                                        Matthew 23:11

Enthusiasm is positive energy that flows out of a positive thought or a positive idea.

So how can you begin? Very simple. Seek God's plan for your life through prayer. The answer will come in the form of an idea. A possibility idea will keep your enthusiasm up if it has 3 qualities within it!

The first quality is *integrity*. There can be no enthusiasm in anything unless it has total integrity. If you are not totally honest, you cannot be enthusiastic because the subconscious mind builds a protective shield against the deeper emotions.

The second quality is *extra-ordinary*. If the idea is only something you did yesterday and is commonplace it will not turn you on. The reason is that stimulation that produces enthusiasm only comes from an idea that challenges you to grow. The capacity to be extra-ordinary—a little more than you did before and a little better.

The third quality is this: *Will your idea bring you ego fulfillment through sacrificial involvement with others?* Will your dream help other people, thereby giving you a sense of personal accomplishment?

> **Dear God—please give me an extra-ordinary idea so that I can help others.**

Keep Enthusiasm

"Tomorrow I will stand at the top of the mountain with the rod of God in my hand."

Exodus 17:9

When you stand at the top of the mountain you can see a new dream in your new vision. You enjoy a peek into the new tomorrow, a glimpse of greater things that God has in store for you. And this peek from the peak will add new momentum to your enthusiasm.

The Bible says that God blesses faith and that God cannot bless the doubter. Unless you have the faith to climb the mountain you will never be able to see the fertile valley beyond. There is no way.

So what really happens to the peak experience after reaching the top of the mountain? You begin to dream greater dreams. The dream gives rise to desire, the desire gives rise to the daring-to-do, the daring-to-do gives rise to the deciding-to-begin! The deciding-to-begin gives rise to the deciding-to-try seriously.

Some of you may be afraid to begin. You don't think you can finish. You're thinking, "Can I make it all the way to the top?" Here's a great concept: *Just decide to begin and then decide to keep going.* Don't worry about the top, just decide to keep going past the point of no return.

LORD, RIGHT NOW I DECIDE TO BEGIN
THE FOLLOWING PROJECT:

Beginning is half done.

Keep Enthusiasm

"Truly, truly, I say to you, unless you are born again, you cannot see the kingdom of God."

John 3:3

How can you have an enthusiasm generating peak experience? There is no way it can happen without the kind of dynamic, religious experience we call, "establishing a relationship with God." That is the key.

The other day I received this letter from a woman. She said, "Dear Dr. Schuller: As a child, and as an adult, my life has been one of turmoil. Two years ago, I attempted suicide and failed. I was on the verge of a nervous breakdown. Because I wasn't able to sleep well, I was awake early on Sundays when your program, the Hour of Power was shown. At first I watched the program simply because I needed anything to keep my mind occupied to hang on!

"Then, as the weeks passed, I found myself, an unbeliever, drenched with tears as the Lord spoke through you, Dr. Schuller. One evening when I was in a desperately low state, I knew that if I didn't get help, I was going to die. I spoke to God, even though I wasn't convinced that He existed. My prayer was very short. I simply told God I couldn't make it on my own. The amazing thing is, He heard me and came to me. Something happened! Now, I awaken in the morning and praise God for giving me breath for one more day rather than hurting because I lived one more day. I have grown to love Jesus more than words can express. I even care about myself!"

I am born again—I am brand new!

28

Keep Enthusiasm

"He gives me the sure-footedness of a mountain goat upon the crags. He leads me safely along the top of the cliffs."
                                        Psalms 18:33

Have you noticed how some people seem to be constantly excited and enthusiastic about their lives? They seem to experience one success after another. Their achievement level continues to escalate and climb. How do you explain it?

Knowingly or unknowing these persons have tapped into a vital principle that I call the *"Peak to Peek"* principle. They have discovered a peak experience that gives them the vision of greater things they can accomplish.

A peak experience is a positive experience that affirms to you who you are and leaves you with an awareness that you are more than you ever thought you were. It then becomes a self-congratulatory experience that affirms to you your positive potential.

List some peak experiences you have had before:

_____

_____

_____

> **God is with me and will lead me from peak to peak.**

Keep Enthusiasm

"And we know that God causes all things to work together for good to those who love God, to those who are called according to His purpose."

Romans 8:28

My producer, Michael Nason, has a young daughter named Tara. Tara suffered from a brain injury which left her without the capacity to walk. In fact, it left her deaf, dumb and blind. It looked like she would be a vegetable all her life. Now, some five years later, she can see, she can hear, she can speak perfectly, but she cannot walk.

A few days ago, her dad called with exciting news. For the first time Tara got on her hands and knees and began to creep. He said, "She held herself up for about 30 seconds on her own; on her hands and knees." Tara experienced a new vertical dimension as she raised her head to see things from a perspective she's never had before. So this "Peak" experience was a "Peek" experience for her. From being cradled in the arms to crawling on the floor, to creeping on all fours—all are peak experiences!

From the "peaks" you listed yesterday, what "peek" experience did you have?

_____

_____

_____

> **I will take what I have, and God will help me to use it for His glory.**

Use Enthusiasm

"My help is from the Lord who made the mountains! And the heavens too! He will never let me stumble, slip, or fall. For He is always watching, never sleeping."

Psalms 121:2-4

There are times when I run into problems and God's voice isn't clear to me at first. Even in the dark times, however, I know He's there and because of that I never give up. I keep on driving until one way or another the objective is accomplished. You will find, as I have, that enthusiasm dispells discouragement as swiftly and surely as the rising sun spreads its golden fingers across the dark sky.

A student who was so discouraged he wanted to quit college once said to me, "Dr. Schuller, I'll never make it. Finishing school is simply an impossible goal for me." Just as he finished speaking, these words shot like a thunderbolt into my mind. "NEVER BELIEVE IN NEVER" I told him.

To those who say, "I'll never walk again," I say, "Never believe in never." If you are saying, "I'll never get out of here," or "I'll never succed in this marriage," I say, "Never believe in never." There was once a day when the Romans had completed the act of crucifying and burying the Lord Jesus. When they rolled the mammoth stone in front of the tomb, I'm sure they thought, "That's the end of that. We'll never be bothered by Jesus again."

"Never believe in never!"

Dear God, because of your love, I will never believe in never.

Use Enthusiasm

"And He has said to me, 'My grace is sufficient for you, for power is perfected in weakness.' Most gladly, therefore, I will rather boast about my weaknesses, that the power of Christ may dwell in me."

2 Corinthians 12:9

If we focus our energies and attention on our problems, we will only be crisis managers. But if we focus on solutions, we can use our enthusiasm to maintain creative leadership.

When faced with uncertainty, you have three choices: You can pack up quick. You can back up, regroup and reorganize—a tactic that is sometimes necessary. Or you can rack up a new victory and climb to a higher level of success remembering, "that the power of Christ dwells in me."

Right now, focus on solutions to your problems. Ask Christ to help you. Write your solutions down here.

1.) _____

2.) _____

3.) _____

When faced with a mountain I will not quit!

Use Enthusiasm

"Your old ones will dream dreams, and your young ones see visions."

Joel 2:28

If you have a dream, you have everything! Conversely, if you have everything but don't have a dream toward which to aspire, all your material possessions amount to nothing. *Challenging dreams that come to us from God are the very life form of human energy.*

A person is alive when enthusiasm flows through him. And genuine enthusiasm comes from a total commitment to an exciting goal. Today as I realize my dreams have not merely come true but have extended far beyond what I could have ever imagined, I understand the truth of Alfred North Whitehead's principle. He said, "Great dreams of great dreamers are never fulfilled; they are always transcended."

What dream has God given you?

_____

_____

_____

Dream a new dream!

Use Enthusiasm

"And looking upon them Jesus said to them, 'With you this is impossible, but with God all things are possible!' "

Twenty-five years ago I had a dream. I had a beautiful wife and two lovely children. And I had a relationship with God. I had a faith—a belief in a person named Jesus Christ who, 2,000 years ago, claimed to be the Messiah. I believed then, and I believe more strongly today, that this beautiful Jewish young man, this dynamic positive thinker, was the Messiah promised by God through the Old Testament prophets. I believe Jesus was born, that He died on the cross, and that He rose again on Easter morning! I believe more today than ever that Jesus is alive—more alive than you or I.

Some of you may ask, "How can that be?"

Very simply. Our total aliveness is diminished by the degree to which we expose ourselves to negative thoughts and emotions. Fear, anxiety, worry, guilt, jealousy and self-pity all diminish our life and vitality. None of us are totally alive all the time.

But I believe Jesus was. I believe He is! And I believe He communicates His aliveness to us through a variety of means, persons and moods. He loves us. Our best ideas will come from Him if we will only seek Him. And if we will follow His ideas, we can literally move mountains. We can achieve the impossible!

With God—it's possible!

Use Enthusiasm

"And He said to me, 'It is done. I am the Alpha and the Omega, the Beginning and the End. I will give to the one who thirsts from the spring of the water of life without cost.'"
Revelation 21:6

When you tap the spring of God's energetic flow, you have emotional power. That means power to feed enthusiasm, power to think positive thoughts, power to push negative thoughts out, and power to maintain peace under enormous pressure.

You can have stamina unlimited! When you've tapped the spring, you don't trust your own strength! That's a reservoir! You can't just depend upon business associates, friends, or family. That's a well. You have the mountaintop spring! You are connected with Almighty God!

Stop running away from opportunities and possibilities! Run toward fulfillment, actualization, and success!

Thank you God, for your fountain on the mountain.

Use Enthusiasm

"Listen to me . . . put your trust in the Lord your God, and you will be established. Put your trust in His prophets and succeed."

2 Chronicles 20:20

Tom Lasorda, manager of the Los Angeles Dodgers, has a story that he likes to tell. He was a manager in the minor leagues in 1971, when his team lost seven straight games.

Defeated and exhausted, Tom's losing team headed for the locker room. A few minutes later he walked in and found all the players sitting around, dejected, with their heads down. "Hey, get your heads up!" Tom yelled. "I don't ever want to see you fellows with your heads down again. Just because you lost seven games doesn't mean you're not a great team. You're going to start winning! As you know, according to a recent poll, the greatest team to ever play in the major leagues was the Yankees in 1927. And they lost nine straight games!"

Suddenly heads went up and expressions changed. It was the turning point. The team started winning, and by the end of the season they were the champions!

A few days later Mrs. Lasorda asked, "Tommy, are you sure the Yankees lost nine games in a row?"

"How would I know?" Tom answered. "I was only a year old. But it made the point. The team had to believe in themselves. They had to believe they could do it!"

> **What I believe determines the decisions I make.**

Use Enthusiasm

"Let your light shine before all in such a way that they may see your good works, and glorify your father who is in heaven."
Matthew 5:16

I had the honor of participating in the commencement activities at Pepperdine University, in Malibu, California. There were probably a hundred or more students who received their B.A. degree that night. The average age of these college graduates was close to forty.

Among the graduates was a sixty-seven-year-old mother of ten children and grandmother of twenty-seven grandchildren. When that enthusiastic determined woman stepped onto the stage to receive her diploma, an older man and several children jumped up from their seats and began to applaud. "You did it, mama!" they screamed. "You did it, grandma!" When the newly graduated sixty-seven-year-old grandmother met me afterward, she gave me a big hug and said, "If it hadn't been for my faith and your possibility thinking, I wouldn't have made it." She was so proud of herself. And her family was proud of her, too.

What a beautiful illustration of God's reward to the person who's made the decision not to fail anymore, but to choose to be a success for the glory of God! That's using enthusiasm! That's what you call self-esteem! God wants you to succeed!

> **I will never be too young or too old to live enthusiastically for God.**

Share Enthusiasm

"Go therefore and make disciples of all the nations, baptizing them in the name of the Father and the Son and the Holy Spirit."

Matthew 28:19

God leads you because He needs you! More than yourself, He wants you to succeed. Why? Because God really needs you to accomplish His plan. As you commit yourself to His plan, He'll lead you to do something special and significant where you are.

> I have no hands but
>   your hands to do my
>   work today.
> I have no feet but your
>   feet, to lead men on
>   the way.
> I have no tongue but
>   your tongue to tell
>   men how I died.
> I have no help but your
>   help to bring men to
>   God's side.

"Present your bodies a living and holy sacrifice, acceptable to God, which is your spiritual service of worship." Romans 12:1

Share Enthusiasm

"So when they had finished breakfast, Jesus said, to Simon Peter, 'Simon, do you love me more than these?' He said to him, 'Yes, Lord; You know that I love you!' He said to him, 'Feed my lambs.' "

John 21:15

God needs you! That is the basis of authentic self-esteem. Self confident people who are tuned into God have so much enthusiasm that they can share it with others. God needs you—whoever you are, wherever you are, in whatever situation you find yourself.

Perhaps you're in a hospital bed today and you have just undergone major surgery. You may not know what the future holds. But God has a word for you today.

He is saying, "I will bring people to your bedside—doctors, nurses, visitors, other patients. You can be my voice to them. Yes, you in your broken, bleeding, unhealed state can be an inspiration to the people you see every day. Please love them, for me."

God, with your help, I promise to share myself and you with at least this one person today:

_____

Bloom where you are planted.

Share Enthusiasm

"And if, as my representatives, you give even a cup of cold water to a little child, you will surely be rewarded."
                                                          Matthew 10:42

I derive great personal fulfillment from my ministry. But it only results to the degee that I give of myself as a pastor by helping people. I had a beautiful experience recently. I paid a hospital visit to a friend who was eighty-two years of age and had been a member of my church for eighteen years. It was a cold and rainy night and I selfishly wanted to stay at home by the cozy fire. But my friend was very sick, so I drove to the hospital. As I entered his room, I saw his lips trembling and his eyes filling with tears.

"Hello, Bob," he whispered softly. We prayed together and talked about heaven. Before I left the room, I took both of his feeble hands and said, "What can I do for you?" "Bob," he said, "just keep on being my friend. Just keep on loving me."

I found my ego fulfillment as I gave him my love and received love in return. I knew when I left that hospital that I had shared my enthusiasm and helped somebody who's coming to the end of the road. It was the perfect feeling of self-esteem. I helped someone who needed help. In that moment I realized my peak: *a Child of God.*

You can experience that wonderful feeling of redeemed pride which is real humility. Although it sounds like a contradiction, you will get that ego fulfillment safely when it results from sacrifice.

**Lord, please show me who you would like me
to share my enthusiasm with today.**

Share Enthusiasm

"If you cling to your life, you will lose it, but if you give it up for Me, you will save it."

Matthew 10:39

You may know the story of Sadhu Sundar Singh, a well-known convert who became a missionary in India.

One day, Sadhu Sundar Singh and a Buddhist monk were traveling up a steep mountain on their way to a monastery. A blizzard threatened their lives as the chilly, icy winds blew through their thin clothes. "We must hurry because darkness is falling," the monk said. "The weather is bad and if it gets any worse we will soon freeze to death."

Suddenly they heard a cry for help. About twenty feet in front of them was the dim form of someone lying in the snow. "We must help," Sadhu exclaimed. "We cannot help," said the monk. So the monk went on while his companion, the Christian convert, insisted on helping his fallen brother.

If he must die, he would die saving someone. The figure in the snow was a man with a broken leg, so the Christian made a sling out of his blanket and dragged the dying man like a team of dogs pulling a sled. Finally he saw the blinking lights of the monastery. Now he was sure he could make it. Suddenly he stumbled and fell over something hidden beneath the snow. He brushed off the white powder and saw the frozen body of the Buddhist monk. Sadhu's life had been spared because he helped someone in need.

Do unto others as you would have them do unto you.

Share Enthusiasm

"Much is required from those to whom much is given, for their responsibility is greater."

Luke 12:48

We are hearing volleys of folly from the valley, while positive-thinking people who have it all together don't have time to parade, fight, or argue, because they are so busy pursuing their exciting dreams and projects. If we are so busy achieving, succeeding, and watching our dreams come true, we can easily forget to speak from the peak!

Successful achievers have a responsibility for leadership in the world. We cannot surrender leadership to loud losers.

What is the fee of success, the price tag of achievement? *"Unto whom much is given, much will be required."* Look at all the corruption in the world. Somebody needs to counteract all those negative ideas and that somebody must be you!

Stop being silent! When you hear loud negative voices, put a smile on your face and speak out with enthusiasm! Tell them the truth! Tell them they have only two choices: to be negative or to be positive; to make commitments or to play it loose. The only choice that produces any lasting hope, love, and peace is in the relationship with God, your creator. He has done a lot for you, hasn't He?

Speak from the peak!

Share Enthusiasm

"Fix your thoughts on what is true and good and right. Think about things that are pure and lovely, and dwell on the fine, good things in others. Think about all you can praise God for and be glad about."

Philippians 4:8

How do you speak from the peak? You speak *positively.* You give an idea or a dream that corrects the problem.

The man of La Mancha, Don Quixote, only looked at the good. He was not unaware of the bad, but he didn't talk about it. He talked about good and ignored the evil. He kept talking about good, so people would become good. For if they became good, the bad would be self-correcting! He had the positive approach.

In the stage play *Man of La Mancha,* Don Quixote was accused of being crazy. "Who's crazy?" the man of La Mancha asks. "Am I crazy because I see the world as it could become? Or, is the world crazy because it sees itself as it is?"

The man is crazy who fails to lift the rest of the world. The person who paints only the dark picture spreads sickness, because people believe it. They become depressed and lose their own strength to resist.

The only sane person is a positive-thinking person with a redeeming idea. Because he gives the world a star, a dream, and a positive idea. He tells the world, "You are beautiful!"

Dream the impossible dream!

Share Enthusiasm

"But Jesus told him, 'Anyone who lets himself be distracted from the work I plan for him is not fit for the kingdom of God.'"

Luke 9:62

A good friend of mine, Ralph Showers, had an inner call to build a ranch for mentally retarded adults so they could be taught to have meaningful jobs and have tremendous self-esteem. He had no money, but he had a call! He had a conscience. He couldn't turn his back on the idea. Today, in Arizona, a ranch for the mentally retarded brings tremendous joy to many young adults.

Real courage produces inner strength. The Bible uses the word *bowels*—the innards—to signify real courage in the deepest part of you. Mountain climbers have it. They are willing to take risks. They know they'd rather die trying to do something than live turning their back on God's call.

There are millions of people who have sold their minds and hearts out to all sorts of negative thinking. They put down people who have dreams. They put down people who have high hopes. If you want to be a climber, you have to have the courage to face that kind of crowd. Don't let them get under your skin. Just keep going—climb your mountain!

The heart of a climber is driven by a call. He's driven to seek a great cause. He's driven by a conscience to be faithful to that call. And he's driven by a courage to climb and share his God-given enthusiasm with others.

Better to try and fail than never to try at all.

Love Is A Decision

Love Elevates

"Casting all your cares upon Him for He cares for you."
1 Peter 5:7

If you put yourself down, that proves you do not love and respect yourself as you ought to. *REAL LOVE ELEVATES!* It lifts you above and beyond your circumstances.

I remember a day many years ago when my daughter, Sheila, was at a very low point emotionally. A heartbreaking relationship left her with a deep negative self-image. One morning I asked her, "Sheila, what do you really want out of life?" With tears streaming down her face, she poured out her heart.

"Dad, I guess all I really want is a home like the one I was raised in." She paused for a moment and as I gently brushed the tears from her cheeks, I cried too. "You know," she continued, "I don't care if I have a husband who's rich or famous. All I want is a man who will treat me like a *precious gem.*"

As we wept together, I shared her inner anguish and lovingly assured her, "Sheila," I said, "that is a noble dream. God will give you someone like that."

All persons whether they are young and strong, or bent-backed and old—need somebody who will treat them like a precious gem. God does that for us. He sees you as "a pearl of great price"—A PRECIOUS GEM!

**Dreams start coming true when somebody
cares about you!**

Love Elevates

"Love always protects, always trusts, always hopes, always perseveres."

1 Corinthians 13:7

The greatest power and influence in a human life is the power of love. You can travel around the world and meet Christians in every country. And when you talk to them about their faith the conversation will quickly focus on the life and person of Jesus Christ. When you ask them what Jesus means to them, you will get many different answers because Christians have different concepts of Jesus Christ.

But if you listen at a deeper level, you will conclude that they all agree about one thing: *Christ Is Love!* The essential quality about His life was *He was love incarnate.* And that makes the difference! What really sets Jesus Christ apart from all the other religious teachers and leaders is the quality of life that is evidenced in the word, *love!*

He lived it! He died because of it! And He rose again in it! The quality of love makes all the difference in the world.

If you choose to put love at the central core of your life, you will find a rising power within you that will change everything! Just as the spring sap rises through the seemingly dead twigs of a tree to press off the last dead leaf that has refused to drop in the winter's storms until the new bud forces it to fall, so the rising love within you will cause you to find inner fulfillment that will give you the emotional maturity and security to handle your problems in a way that they will suddenly disappear.

Christ is love—may His love live in me!

Love Elevates

"When someone becomes a Christian he becomes a brand new person inside. He is not the same anymore. A new life has begun!"

2 Corinthians 5:17

There is no dessert like a baked souffle. When the mixture comes together and is put in the right heat, with the right tender touch, the delicate dessert rises and rises and rises. A good souffle is never flat. It always rises and puffs. When you see it, it's like seeing a person who's come to full blossom—full bloom where all of the possibilities now rise to their crown and glory. *Love is the souffle of life!* Love gives life its lift—its beautiful puff!

There is nothing in the human creation like a Christian who has the rising warmth of the love of Jesus Christ. Love causes something to rise within you and it brings out your potential—your hidden possibilities! There is nothing that can do it like Jesus Christ when He comes to you and enters your life.

But, souffles don't just happen. They are planned. Love isn't a chance, it's a choice. *You don't fall into love, you get a call to love.* When we say, "God loves you," it isn't an accident, it's a promise. Think of it. If love isn't a choice, love is meaningless. Love has no meaning unless the person has the freedom to choose to love or not to love.

Love is the souffle of life!

Love Elevates

"And having chosen us, He called us to come to Him; and when we came, He declared us 'not guilty,' filled us with Christ's goodness, gave us right standing with Himself, and promised us His glory."

Romans 8:30

So many lives are empty and without love. I've counseled many people with this problem and said to them, "But your father loves you and your mother loves you!" And they reply, "My parents had no choice, they had to love me. I was their child."

When somebody comes to you who is not a blood relative and he sees you and treats you like a beautiful gem, precious, and unique, then you suddenly realize, *"I have been chosen to be loved!"* It's not a chance, it's a choice! And something happens at a profound level then and there. That experience with love begins to put the souffle into life.

Many of you are going to have an experience with God through Jesus Christ as you never had before. You will begin to sense that your life is changing; there will be a rising within; there will be an uplifting; there will be a warmth; there will be a souffle!

God wants you to know that you are beautiful. He will treat you as you are—a unique, unparalleled human being unlike anyone who has ever lived before. This was why Jesus came. God made you and Christ died for you on a cross. That means His love for you isn't a chance. It's a choice! It isn't love unless you have the freedom to choose not to love.

I have been chosen to be loved!

Love Elevates

"The spirit's seal upon us means that God has already pur-chased us and that he guarantees loving us to Himself."
Ephesians 1:14

Let me share with you my favorite story of the little boy who built a sailboat. He took it to the lake and pushed it in, hoping it would sail. Sure enough a wisp of breeze filled the little sail and it billowed and went rippling along the waves. But suddenly before the little boy knew it, the boat was out of his reach even though he waded in fast and tried to grab it.

Some time later, the little boy was downtown and walked past a second hand store. There in the window he saw his boat. So he went in and said to the proprietor, "That's my boat. I made it. See." And he showed him the little scratches and the marks where he hammered and filed. The man said, "I'm sorry, Sonny. If you want it, you have to buy it." The poor little guy didn't have any money, but he worked hard and saved his pennies. Finally, one day he had enough money. He went in and bought the little boat. As he left the store holding the boat close to him, he was heard saying, "You're my boat. You're twice my boat. First, you're my boat 'cause I made you. And, second you're my boat 'cause I bought you!"

God feels that way about you! You are His—twice His. First you're God's child because He made you. And, second, you are His because He bought you—on the cross!

> **God made me—God bought me—I belong to Him!**

Love Elevates

"And we know that all that happens to us is working for our good if we love God and are fitting into His plans."
                                                    Romans 8:28

During the summer months, I always take time for travel, study and lecturing abroad. One year in July Mrs. Schuller and I were ministering to thousands of pastors in Korea when we received a call that our 13-year-old daughter, Carol, had been in a tragic motorcycle accident in Sioux City, Iowa. As it turned out, we spent about nine weeks with Carol Lynn, in the hospital.

One of the things that we learned as a family was how much love people have for us. God's love became very real to us through cards, letters, gifts, flowers and other beautiful expressions of concern. Mrs. Schuller and I would take shifts, sitting by Carol's bedside; and, it was during all hours of the night or day, that we would read the mail.

What impressed the nurses most were the cards, pictures and gifts from celebrities. Even President Jimmy Carter sent her a two-page telegram. But the biggest surprise was when the phone rang and the raspy voice at the other end of the line said, "I want to talk to Carol Schuller." It was obviously the voice of John Wayne. On an autographed photo to Carol, he wrote, "Dear Carol, Be Happy—You're Loved!"

Love is the happiest feeling in the world! Even your greatest sorrow can become gladness if love is in it.

Be happy—you're loved!

Love Elevates

"For I am convinced that nothing can ever separate us from His love. Death can't and life can't. The angels won't, and all the power of hell itself cannot keep God's love away."
Romans 8:38, 39

What do you really want to accomplish? Riches? Fame? Power? Do you really know? Well, I think I do. Everybody, at the deepest level, wants to be happy. *You want happiness!* But how do you get there? *By having love at the core of your life. You will be happy if you are surrounded by love.*

How can you get that kind of love inside of you and around you? Will you get there if you keep living the way you are living now? Are you really headed in the right direction? Are you living the right way?

You can get the kind of love inside of you and around you that can make you happy in sadness. You can find the love that will make you happy even in grief. You find that love when you have a direct line to Jesus. You need a spiritual umbilical cord between your immortal soul and Jesus who is alive at this very moment. He comes into your life if you let Him. No person is too small for His love. You're surrounded by it right now. You can feel it. Take it in, accept it. It'll be the most precious thing you ever did.

Dear Lord, by faith I take you into my life and accept the love you have for me.

Love Liberates

"Dear friends, you have been given freedom: not freedom to do wrong, but freedom to love and serve each other."
                                                    Galatians 5:13

When real love elevates then a second thing naturally occurs—*LOVE LIBERATES*.

No one is more imprisoned than the person held captive by his own negative self-image. When you elevate someone above that negative self-image, you set his mind and his spirit free. Many people who lack self-esteem do not dare to love. They're afraid that if they experience real love, they will lose control over those who are a source of their emotional nourishment, and so they hold on too tightly.

One of my most delightful memories as a small child on our Iowa farm is of the days in the spring when we would receive our little baby chicks. I used to take the soft, fuzzy, newly hatched little things and rub what felt like silky fur against my cheek. Sometimes I would squeeze too tightly because I loved them so much and I didn't want them to get away. "Don't hold so tight," my father warned. "But I love it so," I protested. "If you love it so much," he said, "you have to let go."

Let go and let God!

Love Liberates

"For when you are deadened to sin you are freed from all its allure and its power over you."

Romans 6:7

For nearly two thousand years, the cross has been the symbol of the Christian religion. Many people misunderstand its meaning. They say it is a depressing thing. But the cross is a symbol of freedom. It reminds us that God loved us so much that He died to forgive us and redeem us.

God's love doesn't manipulate, it liberates.

In the jungles of Thailand, once a wild elephant is made captive, hunters tie the end of a long chain around the elephant's foot. The other end is tied to a huge banyan tree. The great elephant will pull with all its strength, but it can't budge the banyan tree. Finally, after struggling for days and weeks the elephant surrenders to the chain.

At this point, they take the elephant and chain it to a little iron stake by a circus tent. The elephant never attempts to pull away because it still thinks it is chained to a banyan tree. The elephant never realizes how easily it could achieve freedom.

God's love tells you that you are not chained to a banyan tree! Your problem is not insurmountable! Your problem is not a banyan tree; it is only a stake. What problem have you allowed to trap you?

_____

_____

> **Real love sets you free to give, free to be what God wants you to be!**

Love Liberates

"There is no fear in love; but perfect love casts out fear."
                                                        1 John 4:18

Yes, perfect love casts out fear. And most of our fears stem from the imperfections of our love.

Possessive love produces anxiety and fear. This love says: I love him, or I love her, or I love my children because I derive emotional strength from them. Possessive love can be very destructive. One of its by-products is jealousy, whereas real love seeks to liberate the potential and the possibility in someone, not to possess them.

I am thinking of a woman who is now deceased. She loved me like an adopted son, after her only son was killed in the war. I loved her dearly, but she always expected me to share all my time with her and her alone. Her love was a very possessive love. She loved her son and her husband in the same way. When her son became engaged to a beautiful girl, she broke up the relationship. This possessive mother caused the breakup of her son's marriage.

Possessive love is the mother of jealousy, and jealousy is a form of fear! It's the emotional reaction of someone who feels threatened. Imperfect love—you can see the kinds of fears that are generated by such possessive love.

Pray right now that God might reveal to you if you are loving someone too possessively. And ask Him for the strength to change your imperfect love into His perfect love.

I won't be afraid, Lord. I'm trusting in your love.

Love Liberates

"Love does not act unbecomingly; it does not seek its own."
1 Corinthians 13:5

Exploitative love is another form of imperfect love. It produces a variety of fears of different levels. It is seen in the professional who loves a client becauses he represents a very important account.

Dr. William Havender, a prominent ophthalmologist, once gave the following illustration to a group of graduating medical students:

"Three stone workers, depending upon their viewpoint, look upon their job in different ways. One worker sees his job as carrying stones; another sees it as building a wall; the third sees his job as creating a cathedral to the glory of God. As doctors, you have the same attitude. If you see your job as carrying stones, you will then see your patients as complaining crocks, indigent invalids, sick scoundrels and poor protoplasm.

"A second attitude is you can see your work as the futile patching up of worn out bodies.

"But if you believe that there is a God and every human being is one of his unique and special creatures, then you will look upon each person as a cathedral."

How are you loving those around you today? Is it in an exploitive way? If so—with God's help, begin to make changes. Learn the joy of perfect love!

Grandma Clark's Birthday 1901

I am creating a cathedral to the glory of God.

Love Liberates

"We are saved by grace through faith, not of ourselves; it is a gift of God. Not of works, lest any one should boast but only because of the shed blood of Jesus Christ."

Ephesians 2:8

A third form of imperfect love is *judgmental or conditional love.* This form of love says: I will love you *if* you lead a clean life. I will love you *if* you will obey all of the commandments. I will love you *if* you agree with my theology or my politics. Many children grow up learning to love judgmentally. They get the idea that Daddy and Mommy love them only if they are good. Christ doesn't say, "I'll give you love if . . . ." Jesus Christ says, "I love you!" period.

Many people can't buy that because, at a very profound infantile level of their mind, they cannot believe in nonjudgmental love. They only accept judgmental love. They think God really won't love them unless they live a pure, sinless life. They say: "When I am good God is loving me. When I am sinning, He isn't." And that produces all kinds of fears.

Imperfect love is judgmental; perfect love is nonjudgmental. Perfect love seeks to liberate the potential that is within the individual and to give him liberty to be himself!

I'm free to be me!

Love Liberates

"So Christ has made us free."

Galatians 5:1

Imperfect love can also be *manipulative.* I counseled with a girl once who was having a love affair with a young man. They had been going together for months, yet he constantly put her down just to build himself up. Finally, she understood what was happening. He claimed to love her only because she fed his ego.

He had somebody to show off like a trinket and a toy, but not as a genuine person. He was expressing what I call a destructive or manipulative love. It was destroying her potential.

Many fearful persons today were childhood victims of manipulative love. But God's perfect love liberates us from this. First He elevates you beyond the guilt that could give you a negative self-image, which would cause you to lose all self-confidence and render you woefully and totally ineffective.

THEN HE SETS YOU FREE TO BECOME THE PERSON YOU WERE MEANT TO BE.

I am free!

Love Liberates

"Be full of love for others, following the example of Christ who loved you and gave Himself to God as a sacrifice to take away your sins."

Ephesians 5:2

Where do you get this kind of perfect, liberating love? We get it from our Ideal One.

The late Ozzie Nelson used to tell this story about his son, Ricky:

"Ricky was just a young boy when his friend, Walter, came over to spend the weekend with him. I got off work a little early so I could play with the boys. We went into the backyard and started throwing a football around. I was getting really good when Ricky said, 'Hey, dad, you're great!' And Walter piped in and exclaimed, 'Gee, Mr. Nelson, you've got a pretty good arm, but not as good as my dad.' When it came to dinner time, I carved the roast with thin even slices. Walter enthused, 'You carve the roast pretty good, Mr. Nelson, but you should see my dad do it!'

"Well, I couldn't wait for Walter's mother to pick him up so I could find out about this super-dad! When she came to the door I said, 'Hi! I'd sure like to meet your husband. He must be something else!' 'Oh, no' she said, 'Has Walter been talking about his dad again? You see, Walter was only three years old when his dad was killed.'"

That little boy had an Ideal One who lived within him. His image of his father gave him courage.

My Ideal One died before I was born—at Calvary! His name is Jesus! That's where I get my love.

> **I have decided to follow Jesus.**

Love Motivates

"I am aware of all your good deeds—your kindness to the poor, your gifts and service to them."

Revelation 2:19

When somebody really cares about you, elevates and liberates you, then you are motivated to believe you can do something wonderful! As George Kennedy, the famous actor, once said, "You dare to believe you can give something back." A dear friend of mine, Mary Crowley, said recently, "God never puts you down; but He never lets you off." He liberates you so that you can do His work. He motivates you so that you can make your contribution.

When Jesus Christ liberates us from guilt through salvation, we begin to believe that with God on our side, we can win at life. Once you're freed from the sins that would tie you down, trap and oppress you, you can really soar. You don't have to make it on your own power. When you slip, stumble and fall, there is someone who really loves you and He wants to help you. He will lift you up and set you free to become all that you can be.

Everybody needs someone who really cares for him. When you receive Jesus Christ, He treats you like a precious gem. His love motivates you.

What work will you do with Him as your friend today?

_____

_____

_____

You're saved so you can serve.

Love Motivates

"And in the morning you will see the glory of the Lord, for He hears your grumblings against the Lord."

Exodus 16:7

First of all, *Love motivates us to have the courage to forgive.* You will not love long if you cannot forgive quickly. That includes my love for God. Forgive God? Yes. There are people today who are atheists because at the deepest level they are really angry at God.

Maybe as children they cried out and didn't get what they thought God should have given them, so they became angry towards Him. Or perhaps they experienced a crisis in a personal relationship and they cried out to God, asking for something but God appeared to be silent. They've never really brought themselves to a point where they are willing to forgive God and start over again.

When you forgive, you are not saying that the other party has done anything wrong. Forgiveness means you are able to *accept* what comes your way. It's easy to forgive somebody if they are guilty and they repent, but it's not easy to accept some things that life puts before you. That kind of forgiveness takes courage. Exercise the courage to forgive with your love for God as you pray this prayer.

Dear God, I confess that I have blamed you for my circumstances and not accepted what has come my way. I forgive you right now for _____

I am striving for acceptance with joy.

Love Motivates

"Be kind to each other, tenderhearted, forgiving one another, just as God has forgiven you because you belong to Christ."
Ephesians 4:32

Some of you may harbor a resentment against a husband, wife, child, teacher, or maybe an employer. You just don't dare to forgive. Part of it is the fact that if you really forgave that person, you'd have to swallow your pride. Only brave people dare to be humble! It takes courage to love. It takes courage to forgive because you run the risk of rejection, ridicule and scorn from those whose scales of justice are too heavy and scales of mercy are too light. But love motivates courage!

Dear Lord, please give me the courage to be humble. Help me not to fear rejection and ridicule, but to honestly forgive these people:

_____   _____

_____   _____

_____

Help me, Lord, to let go of myself!

Thank you, God, for courage that forgives.

Love Motivates

"The one who serves best will be the leader."

Luke 22:26

Secondly, *Love motivates us to serve.* The world today offers self-assertiveness as the key to happiness. Self-assertiveness says: "I will be number one. Nobody's going to make a doormat out of me. I'm going to make sure that I get my credit. Don't say I'm egotistic. I just have a positive self-image."

Self-assertiveness can be very constructive, if it is under the control of Jesus Christ. Indeed there are some people who are so shy, so retiring, so bashful that in fact they should be a little more assertive. And it is true that some of you have to learn how to say no without feeling guilty.

However, self-assertiveness without the humility of Jesus Christ, is the most dangerous thing in the world. You will come across as a self-aggrandizing, self-serving, self-seeking, ego-tripping bully. You will only create problems and unhappiness for yourself.

The beauty of being under God's love is that He motivates us to serve others—not ourselves. Jesus said: "If any man wants to be first, let him be last." (Luke 9:48) There is no greater happiness than that which comes when you serve those around you.

With God's love, I'm looking outward—not inward!

Love Motivates

"If any one be my disciple let them deny themself, take up their cross, and follow me."

Luke 14:27

Third, *Love motivates us to live self-sacrificial lives.* How can we handle ourselves in such a way that we become an inspirational act to those around us?

It's simple: Take the "I" in your life, put a line through it, and turn the "I" into a cross. St. Paul said: "It is no longer I who lives, but Christ who lives in me." (Galatians 2:20) Which is a way of saying that he committed sanctified suicide. Jesus said: "Except a grain of wheat fall in the ground and die, it can bear no fruit." (John 12:24) This is not self-assertive or self-destructive. It's self-sacrificing!

Repeat this prayer: "Lord, I lose myself in loving and helping people who need me so that in helping others, I forget myself."

Now try this exercise:

"I" will live my life in love today.

Now put a line through the "I", and let the cross symbolize who really lives through you!

It's no longer I that lives, it is Christ who lives in me.

Love Motivates

"And so, dear friends, I plead with you to give your bodies to God. Let them be a living sacrifice, holy—the kind He can accept."

Romans 12:1

Christianity is accepted by many people as a good way of life; a nice philosophy; an interesting set of ethics; a basically wholesome moral system; culturally quite refined. It is accepted, but not understood.

Do you want to understand it? This is what is involved: I say to Jesus Christ, "I'm willing to sacrifice myself, my pride, my honor, and my name. And I want you to live in me and through me. I will die, Jesus, so you can live in me and through me. I will die, Jesus, so you can live in this brain, thinking my thoughts; in this face, smiling at people; in this heart, loving the lonely; and I will never expect any credit."

That's understanding Christianity and that's power! You can have this power. He's the power that comes from the force of love—your love for God! It's the power that comes when you sacrifice all to Christ. For only then can He really live through you!

The trouble with a live sacrifice is that it keeps crawling off the altar. Please keep me on the altar, Lord, tied with your bonds of love.

Love Motivates

"Your love is already strong toward all the Christians throughout your whole nation. Even so, dear friends, we beg you to love them more and more."

1 Thessalonians 4:10

I read a story years ago in a book entitled, *Try Giving Yourself Away*. A young girl, about fifteen years of age was sitting alone in the corner of a train depot. A mother with two crying children and an armload of packages entered the train station and sat near her. Before the woman could get settled into her seat, the teenage girl ran over to her. "Can I take care of your two children while you go out to get something to eat?" she asked. Startled, the mother said, "Oh, thank you, that would be wonderful."

A little later the mother returned looking relaxed and refreshed. "Thank you so much," she said. And the young girl enthused, "Are you catching the next train?" "Yes," she replied, "as soon as I can get everything together." "Let me help you," the young helper said. And then she gathered all of the lady's packages and headed towards the train. Then she turned and went back into the train lobby and sat down.

She wasn't seated more than ten minutes when she spotted another mother with children. Again this young girl walked over and volunteered her help. She continued this all day, drifting from mother to mother. She knew the joy of motivating love!

Love makes the world go round!

Love Demonstrates—A Commitment

"Let me add this, dear friends: you already know how to please God in your daily living, for you know the commands we gave you from the Lord Jesus Himself. Now we beg you— yes, we demand of you in the name of the Lord Jesus—that you live more and more closely to that ideal."

1 Thessalonians 4:1-2

Perfect love is willing to make a commitment. Imperfect love is playing it cool—not willing to make permanent, binding, lasting commitments. There is a lot of that kind of love today.

There are many people today who say they have a loving relationship and so they live together. But they are not ready to get married. Now that's living without commitment to continuity. That's imperfect love.

Perfect love seeks to make a commitment—to care for better, for worse, for richer, for poorer, in sickness and in health. To love when my skin is tight and beautiful and when it is old and wrinkled.

Noncommittal love is cheap love, it doesn't cost much. Perfect love always calls for costly commitments to care—always.

I am committed!

Love Demonstrates—A Commitment

"He has done this through the death on the cross of His own human body, and now as a result Christ has brought you into the very presence of God."

Colossians 1:22

Commitment is the key and that's why the cross of Jesus Christ is so important. It's God's commitment to love you for better, for worse, for richer, for poorer, in sickness and in health till death brings you face to face with Him.

God gives perfect love! Perfect love is not possessive. Perfect love is not judgmental and it does not manipulate. Perfect love encourages. *Perfect love makes the commitment,* and the commitment is the high price.

One of the reasons that we have such a problem in our society is that there are not enough people who understand that *perfect love calls for an unconditional commitment to continuity. "I will love you always. I'm willing to pay the price."* That's why the cross of Jesus Christ is not a negative symbol, but a positive symbol of our faith. The cross is perfect love!

I invite you to meet Christ. The Christ who makes a commitment that He will love us today and tomorrow and forever until we come to stand before Him. When you've got that kind of love, what can you really be afraid of?

The cross is perfect love!

Love Demonstrates—A Commitment

"For the free gift of eternal salvation is now being offered to everyone, and along with this gift comes the realization that God wants us to turn from Godless living and sinful pleasures and to live good, God fearing lives day after day."

Titus 2:11, 12

It takes a great deal of courage to love because when you really love someone, you become emotionally involved and that means you've made a choice! *You have made an emotional commitment.* Now you are committed to something and you run the risk of being rejected.

People often ask me, "Dr. Schuller, why isn't there more love in the world?" And my immediate reply is, "You are asking the wrong question. The right question to ask is, 'Why don't more people dare to love?'" It takes courage to love because when you love you get involved! You are liable to be swept away, and before you realize it, you've made a deep commitment!

There are many people, today, who are afraid of marriage. They offer several reasons for living together. But, at a deeper level, they are afraid of marriage because they are afraid to make a commitment to continuity. *It takes courage to love!* Ultimately, love leads to a commitment to continuity.

Jesus Christ demonstrated a commitment to continuity. His love never ends.

I'm going to dare to love!

Love Demonstrates—A Commitment

"Since Christ suffered and underwent pain, you must have the same attitude He did; you must be ready to suffer, too. For remember, when your body suffers, sin loses its power."

1 Peter 4:1

People have said it through the years and I affirm it today—Hubert Humphrey had great courage! People who fight a terminal illness, and keep on fighting bravely, have courage! I have always admired their perseverance. I have always admired their faith. But I used to say, "Why do you call it courage? What's so brave about it? Perseverance? Yes. Tough? Of course. But courageous? But why do you say it's courage when somebody's fighting cancer?"

It's courageous because a person who fights a brave battle with a terminal illness is making a commitment! There can be no courage unless there is a choice between alternatives. The person who is fighting a terminal illness is making a choice between two alternatives. One is to overdose and slip away quickly. The other is to hang in there as bravely and optimistically as possible until God stops the heartbeat. When you're faced with alternatives, you choose the one where the personal price is high but the rewards in terms of inspiration to those around you is high. That's courage! That's loving to the point of commitment!

Set your goal and pay the toll!

Love Demonstrates—A Commitment

"Yes, we live under constant danger to our lives because we serve the Lord, but this gives us constant opportunities to show forth the power of Jesus Christ within our dying bodies."
2 Corinthians 11

I have never met Charlotte Valente, but I read about her in a story told by a hospital worker.

By the age of six, Charlotte had been in and out of the hospital 85 times. She has a rare disease in which her bones break very easily. She had over 200 fractures by the time she was ten, but she was a delightful little girl, always smiling and very positive.

Charlotte couldn't walk because by the time she reached puberty the disease arrested itself and her normal development had been permanently distorted. She would probably never weigh more than fifty pounds in her entire lifetime.

Charlotte went on to high school and graduated. Then she picked a university that had ramps equipped for the handicapped. She was accepted and graduated four years later Cum Laude! But Charlotte did not stop there! She went on to law school and passed the state bar exam. All 50 pounds of her! That's courage!

Courage is the back side of love! It's the other side of the coin. somebody who loves life enough to want to live every minute no matter how costly it may be! Somebody so much in love with life that he will fight everyday through the pain of chemotherapy and radiation. Somebody who loves God enough to believe that He will never abandon you!

Diane Miller's Birthday was today

**Through Christ, I can have courage—the
back side of love!**

Love Demonstrates—A Commitment

"Right now, God is ready to welcome you. Today He is ready to save you."

2 Corinthians 6:2

I have good news for you! Many of you may not have had a happy life. Some of you were born into an unfortunate home situation or you went into a bad marriage situation. You feel you've been manipulated, you've been abused, and you are very unhappy. Now you think life is tough and cruel. Listen!

I studied piano when I was a little boy and my mother was my teacher. When it came time for my recital, my mother made me practice the conclusion of my music until it was perfect. She used to say, "Look, Bob, you can make a mistake in the beginning or in the middle. The people will forget it, if you make the ending glorious!"

Make the ending glorious! I don't know what kind of childhood you had. I don't know what kind of life you had. But I know where you are now! And where you are now, Jesus is present. Take Him into your life and the ending will be glorious!

Love is a decision! You can decide right now!

Love Demonstrates—A Commitment

"Little Children, let us stop just saying we love people; let us really love them, and show it by our actions."

1 John 3:18

At the heart of Christianity is a valve called love. And you open the valve with a decision. Love is a decision! And it requires a commitment! That is what Christianity teaches.

"Deny yourself, take up a cross, and follow Jesus!" Look for people who are hurting and try to help them. That's what drives us in the ministry! I look at you and I wonder, "What's your problem? How can I help you?"

Christianity is Christ being accepted into my heart; into my mind; into my life; and then flowing through me—out of me, reaching the people who need my love.

Pray now that God will show you how you can help others that you come into contact with on a daily basis. Write down what He tells you and commit yourself to the task.

_____

_____

_____

_____

_____

Put strong wings on weary hearts!

Iron Pillared People

Saving Power

"So you see, our love for Him comes as a result of His loving us first."

1 John 4:19

CHRIST IS MY IRON PILLARED FRIEND. He can be your iron pillared friend too.

Years ago when Jesus was talking to the people of His day, the Pharisees gathered around Him and began to look at Him with interest, listening keenly to His words. They didn't know quite what to make of this Man. So Jesus finally confronted them, "What do you think of Christ?" He asked.

Today my answer would be, "Christ is my iron pillared friend."

In psychology, we talk about attachment bonding. Attachment bonding refers to relationships that meet our deepest emotional needs and provide a basic source of positive emotional reinforcement and replenishment. First my wife and then my children are vitally important attachment bonds to me. But even above my wife and children is the attachment bond between the single, solitary man called Robert Schuller and a Man known in history as Jesus of Nazareth.

Between Jesus and me is an invisible cord through which I receive the spiritual and emotional nourishment I need. This God-given sustenance is translated into faith to live by, hope to live for and love to give away. Jesus Christ is my closest friend. He is my source of faith, hope and love.

Jesus loves me, this I know.

Saving Power

*"Then He took the children into His arms and placed His
hands on their heads and He blessed them."*

Mark 10:16

When we begin to examine the character of Jesus Christ,
one thing rings increasingly true:

Jesus treated people beautifully.

In the world of His day, it was not uncommon for people
to treat each other like trash. Unfortunately, 2,000 years
have not had much effect in changing human nature. Part of
the problem with human relations, which is resulting in the
moral decline of Western civilization, is that persons are
often treated like things. They are treasures to possess; trin-
kets to play with; tools to use; toys to enjoy and discard.
Often you hear Freudian slips that reveal how we look upon
the fellow members of the human race today. For instance,
there is a tendency for some people to refer to other persons
in animalistic terms such as "chick," "fox," or "turkey."

But people are not animals—they're persons! Jesus
treated every person as if he or she were a beautiful gem of
infinite worth and irreplaceable value.

Whether He was speaking to a harlot, a thief, a crooked
politician or a saint, Jesus treated that person as a beautiful
human being. By the very nature of His character He in-
fluenced people to see the good person that they could become. He urged us to treat one another with respect and
dignity. He lived by the commandments and He taught a
higher spiritual ethic. "Do unto others as you would have
them do unto you."

Jesus treats me beautifully.

Saving Power

"I am the way, and the truth, and the life. No one comes to the Father but by me."

John 14:6

Jesus made some fantastic claims. He said He was the Messiah, the Promised One, the Son of God. In His day the Jewish people anxiously awaited the day when God would come into this world incarnated in flesh. This belief was the heart of Jewish faith and religion.

The Pharisees, the religious leaders of His day, were astounded and indignant when He revealed to them who He really was. "I am the resurrection and the life." "I am the good shepherd; the bread of life; the door, if any man enter in, he shall be saved."

Undeniably Christ claimed to be God incarnate. When we examine that incredible claim, we are faced with three possibilities:

(1) *Christ was mentally deranged and suffering delusions of grandeur* or
(2) Perhaps, *he was deliberately lying,* or
(3) *Jesus was telling the truth, and He is indeed the Messiah!*

When we look into history, we find no evidence that Jesus was ever ill in mind or body. When we examine His character we find it impossible to believe that a man of His nature could ever be a liar.

Therefore, the only thing we can reasonably believe is that He was telling the truth and He is the Son of God, the Christ.

I believe in Jesus—His character affirms his claim!

Saving Power

"Pilate replied, 'But you are a king then?' 'Yes,' Jesus said. 'I was born for that purpose. And I came to bring truth into the world.'"

John 18:37

When you respect a person's character and examine a person's credentials and both check out without a flaw, then check out his life. What were his commitments? Did he practice what he preached? Consider the commitments of Christ's life.

Jesus committed Himself totally to His calling. During His lifetime He told His followers, *"If I be lifted up, I will draw all men unto Me."* Just as He foretold, He died on a cross—not because He was tricked, trapped or cornered, but because *He chose to die.* His death was not a suicide. It was a sacrifice.

Jesus was given capital punishment for a crime that, in the minds of the religious leaders of His day, was among the worst offenses a person could commit. This crime was looked on with such severity that if you committed it, you got the death penalty then and there. What crime was that? Jesus was charged with blasphemy. He dared to claim that He was the son of God!

So that's what the trial was all about. Pilate asked Jesus very forthrightly, "Are we misunderstanding you? Tell us the truth. Are you Christ?" But even when given the chance to deny His duty and save His earthly life, Jesus stood fast; and for His commitment He died.

> **For Jesus, the cross was not an ego trip—it was an integrity trip!**

Saving Power

"How we praise God, the Father of our Lord Jesus Christ, who has blessed us with every blessing in heaven because we belong to Christ."

Ephesians 1:3

I remember when I took my 14-year-old daughter, Carol, to make a hospital call on a special friend of ours named Tara Nason. Tara is the ten-year-old daughter of our producer, Michael Nason. When Tara was only a little girl, she suffered a fall which resulted in brain injury.

Today Tara Nason cannot walk or use her hands. She spends her days in a wheelchair. But she has a fantastic mind and can speak clearly.

When we called on Tara in the hospital, Carol sat down in the chair beside her and they began to talk. Both girls had permanent injuries, for Carol had lost her leg in a motorcycle accident.

A little wistfully, Tara said she wished she could walk. And Carol agreed it would be wonderful to have her own leg back. But then they began to talk about Jesus and how much He meant to them. They agreed that even if you have physical handicaps that keep you from walking or running, everything will be fine as long as your soul is in good shape. And when Jesus lives in your soul, you feel clean because you're saved and forgiven. And when He forgives you, you'll be happy. And if you're happy, you'll be a beautiful person to be around. And when you help others, they love you and your life is wonderful. "Isn't Jesus terrific!" they both exclaimed.

Every obstacle is an opportunity.

Saving Power

"Once you were less than nothing; now you are God's own. Once you knew very little of God's kindness; now your very lives have been changed by it."

1 Peter 2:10

Christ's character is beautiful. His credentials say He is the Son of God; and He backed His claim with a commitment that took Him to the cross and ended in conquest when He arose from the grave three days later. Even today He is accomplishing beautiful things in the lives of those who love Him. Eventually you must face the question He asks of you: *"What do you think of Jesus Christ? Will you accept Me as your Lord and Savior?"*

Are you a Christian today? A Christian isn't a perfect person; a Christian is simply someone who wants to become the beautiful person he was created to be. If you have never explored the world of possibilities that can be yours when you enter into a love relationship with Jesus Christ, there has never been a better time for you to begin than now. This beautifully different world can be yours when you ask Jesus to forgive you for your sins, and you accept Him as your Lord. When you do, you will discover a new world of beauty and wonder. He is simply waiting to love you.

JESUS CHRIST—YOUR IRON PILLARED FRIEND —GIVES SAVING POWER!

You can leave your rut and begin a new life.

Saving Power

". . . for all we need is faith working through love."
                                              Galatians 5:6

"You mean Jesus Christ is alive and real and communicates with you? You mean He gives you your ideas and your energy? If that is true, why doesn't He prove to me today that He is alive?" My answer must be this, "He does—every day."

Yet even more than that, *God wants us to trust Him.* If you knew all the answers and could prove God's existence through a mathematical equation, you would have a science, not a religion or a faith. Even science must maintain a bit of awe at the universe if it is to remain open and creative. You've probably heard the rhyme,

> "Twinkle, twinkle little star,
> I know exactly what you are
> An incandescent ball of gas
> Condensing to a solid mass."

To fully appreciate life, we must maintain a sense of wonder. There must always be some sort of mystery. God forbid the day we have no more unknowns, no more mountains to conquer, no more challenges. For when there are no more unknowns, there will be no room for faith.

I invite you to close your eyes. Face Him. Pray to Him. Talk to Him, He's alive. He'll hear you. This could be the moment of the beginning of a new faith for you. And a new faith will mean a new life! He can become the best friend you'll ever have in life or eternity! He will become to you what He is to me—*My Iron Pillared Friend.*

> **With God, yes! I shall try and give God a chance to work a miracle.**

Weighing Power

"The only way out is through faith in Jesus Christ; the way of escape is open to all who believe in Him."

Galatians 3:22

There is the story of a fellow who had dropped off a cliff and was plummeting toward the rocks below when he managed to grasp the twig of a tree that was growing through a crack in the granite cliff. Hanging there hundreds of feet above the sharp granite rocks and swirling white water below, he looked up into the clouds that hid the edge of the cliff from his sight and cried, "Help! Is anybody up there?" And out of the clouds came the words, "I am here." "Who are you?" he questioned. "I am your God," the voice replied. "Can you help me?" the man asked in a voice tinged with desperation. "Have faith," the heavenly voice commanded. "Let go." The man looked down at the jagged rocks, then looked up toward the clouds and shouted, "Is anybody else up there?"

There is no alternative to faith! Decision making is easy if the alternatives are clear. It's easy to see that there is no alternative to living by faith. Everyone must have faith in somebody or something.

> **God, I claim your promises. You promise that if I try, you'll help me win.**

Weighing Power

"Reverence for God gives you deep strength; your children have a place of refuge and security."

Proverbs 14:26

When you go to church on Sunday morning and sit in the pew, you have faith that the pew will hold you up and not collapse. You have faith that the roof of the building will not tumble in on top of your head. Every human being lives constantly by faith. If you didn't, you would spend every waking moment analyzing the negative harmful consequences that could befall you and never dare to engage in any kind of positive action. Can you be sure that when you get on the road that you will make your destination without being involved in a fatal car crash? No. When you board an airplane can you be absolutely sure that you will land safely? No. It is simply not possible to live without faith!

But what is the object of our faith? Whom can we believe? Where we feel we can safely place our faith is based largely on reliable evidence and our experiences.

What experiences and reliable evidence have increased your faith in God! List at least five:

_____

_____

_____

_____

_____

> **I believe!**

Weighing Power

"Jesus said, 'If you have faith as a grain of a mustard seed, you can say to this mountain, Move! And nothing will be impossible to you.'"

Matthew 13:31

I heard a story the other day of a man who encountered a bit of trouble while flying his little airplane. He called the control tower and said, "Pilot to tower, I'm 300 miles from the airport, six hundred feet above the ground, and I'm out of fuel. I am descending rapidly. Please advise. Over." "Tower to pilot," the dispatcher began, "Repeat after me: 'Our Father Who art in heaven . . .'"

What do you have left if you don't have faith? When your life seems to fall apart, all you have to cling to is faith. Faith—who needs it? I do. You do. Anyone does who wants to become an "iron pillared person." A person who stands strong in the midst of trials. Only God can transform a bruised reed into an iron pillar. How? By faith!

"I will make you into an iron pillar, a *fortified city*." Jeremiah 1:18

Weighing Power

"What is faith? It is the confident assurance that something we want is going to happen. It is the certainty that what we hope for is waiting for us even though we cannot see it up ahead."
Hebrews 11:1

I took a tour with the Air Force a few years ago, and they told me a story of a man who had no faith. He was an incurable cynic. He was trained to be a parachutist. On the day of his first jump, his instructors gave him one final briefing: "First of all, when we reach the correct altitude, we will push you out of the airplane. You must count to ten slowly and then pull the ripcord. If the chute doesn't open, pull this second cord and the auxiliary chute will open. Keep calm. You will float down to the ground and a truck will be waiting to pick you up."

When the time came for the parachutist to jump, he was a bit hesitant. But his instructors pushed him out of the plane and he began to fall. He counted to ten, but not as slowly as he should have. Then he pulled the ripcord, but the chute didn't open. Slightly unnerved, he pulled the second cord. But the auxiliary chute didn't open. Feeling totally exasperated, he said to himself, "I'll bet the truck won't be there, either!"

Iron pillared people have faith. *If you have faith, you have everything.*

I've got faith—I've got everything!

Weighing Power

". . . This is accomplished from start to finish by faith. As the Scripture says it, 'The one who finds life will find it through trusting God.' "

Romans 1:17

How does someone become one of those strong iron pillared persons who is able to provide sustenance and emotional strength to people? Is it their environment that shapes them? Is heredity the important factor?

If you keep abreast of the study of psychology, you have probably been reading, as I have, about a social phenomenon called "the invulnerables." Invulnerables are young people born and raised in emotionally deprived, financially impoverished, and culturally barren environments. According to predictions based on known psychological data, their situations should ensure them to be losers. Yet some of these children are positive, bright, constructive, all-together persons.

They seem to be invulnerable to responding negatively to the stimuli which should render them sullen, rebellious, mental cases. Instead they continually overcome their circumstances to become dynamic leaders and superachievers.

Just as there are forces that shape the personalities of children, there are forces that transform a weak, soft person into a strong, supportive person. *A dynamic, positive faith will turn anyone into an iron pillared person!*

> **Miracles never happen until you take aim at something that is humanly impossible.**

Weighing Power

"He grants good senses to the godly—his saints. He is their shield, protecting them and guarding their pathway."
                                                      Proverbs 1:7, 8

Iron pillared people don't fall apart when life falls in because they have the instinctive capacity to weigh the alternatives and see their options. At times I've heard people who are faced with a problem say, "I have only one choice." That's not true. In every situation you face, you will always have at least four alternatives:

1. You can quit.
2. You can back down and retreat.
3. You can pause and wait.
4. You can fight to hold your ground and advance, however slowly, toward your goal.

How are you weighing the options in your life? Where do you think faith weighs heaviest? Write down how you can put these alternatives to work in your present situation.

_____

_____

Marina's Birthday

JESUS GIVES ME WEIGHING POWER!

Weighing Power

"Dear friends, is your life full of difficulties and temptations? Then be happy, for when the way is rough, our patience has a chance to grow."

James 1:2

A while back, I visited two men in different hospital rooms, in different situations. Neither one would allow himself to be defeated although many would say either one had reason to be.

The first young man I visited was eighteen years old. Before his illness, he was a star water polo player. When he returned home from a successful European tour with his team, he collapsed with a backache. The doctors discovered a cancerous tumor in his spine. Cancer specialists told him he had two months to live. That was seventeen months ago. Twenty-five malignant tumors have sprung up in his body. Each one should have killed him, but each one died. He fought his illness with as much determination as he once used to win for his team.

The second man I visited was another dear friend—37 years old and he, too, had cancer of the spine. His spine was so deteriorated that it no longer supported his head, so the doctors drilled a steel crown into his skull to hold his head upright. When I sat down beside him he said, "The doctors give me five months to live. But since I found that Jesus Christ is real, I'm happy," he continued. "I have discovered Jesus and now He's my friend." Jesus has become an iron pillar of strength to him.

Iron pillared people have the power to weigh the alternatives. They could give up, but they choose to fight.

> **"I will not quit."**

Praying Power

"Always keep on praying."

1 Thessalonians 5:17

Once you have weighed your alternatives, then you need PRAYING POWER—*the power to ask the right questions to acquire the information you need to choose the right alternative.* Iron pillared people know what questions they must ask to help them make the right decisions.

Some of you may be familiar with a concept known as "two-way prayer." Whenever we need to make a decision regarding church business, we always ask three questions. First of all we ask, *"Would it be a great thing for God as we understand Him?"* If the answer to that question is "yes," then we ask a second question. *"Would it help people who are hurting now?"* If the answer is "yes," we move along to the third question, *"Is anybody else doing the job?"* If they are, then we cooperate. And if they aren't, we make the decision to follow through and turn the idea into a reality. Decision making is easy if your value system is not confused.

People who can't make decisions after they have the raw data they need, are usually suffering from an internalized contradiction of basic human values. To make the right decisions, all you have to do is translate your value system into the right questions. It's that simple.

Enter into two-way prayer now, and write down God's answers.

_____

_____

> The spring rains of God's inspiring blessings
> fall into my mind to give birth to a great
> dream.

Praying Power

"He will answer all my prayers."

Psalms 6:9

I saw a cartoon the other day dated the morning after Easter. Two Roman soldiers were standing by the empty tomb in Jerusalem. They were responsible for guarding the tomb, but the stone had been rolled away and the body was gone. One of the soldiers was scared stiff. The other soldier, in an attempt to comfort him said, "Oh, forget it. A hundred years from now nobody will know the difference."

Two thousand years have passed since Jesus Christ's resurrection, and it's made all the difference in the world—it's made all the difference in my life. Today I know I can find my strength in Jesus. I don't know how a dead body could be resurrected into a new state. But I understand one thing: *When I pray to Him I get results. He makes it possible for me to be strong enough for others to lean on me.* That's a beautiful feeling!

In the words of Dr. Glasser, "Everybody needs that one essential friend they can tell it to." Jesus Christ wants to be that friend to you. Draw close to Him and He will make you as strong as an iron pillar.

He lives today and can come into your life!

Praying Power

"Pray all the time. Ask God for anything in line with the Holy Spirit's wishes."

Ephesians 6:18

An iron pillared person is somebody who, when facing discouragement and personal disappointment, drops his head and retreats in prayer. But returns from prayer head held high, back straight and saying, *"I will not quit."*

An iron pillared person is someone who, when going through grief, sorrow and sadness, puts on a rainbow face. He finds the strength and hope to smile through his tears just as the sun shines through the rain. As he weeps, salty streams of tears roll down his face into an open smiling mouth.

Perhaps you're in a hospital right now and have gone through surgery. Maybe you've lost an arm or a leg and will never be the same again. God has a message for you. He can save you and make you into an iron pillar, a fortified city. You will not give in to self-pity. You will not look back and ask, "Why?" "Why" is the one question God will never answer. Even Jesus asked that question and God remained silent. After all, when you ask "why," you don't really want an explanation; you want an argument. You wouldn't be willing to accept the reason God gave you.

But God wants you to know that no matter how hurt you are, there is something you can do that no one else in the world can do. You can pull yourself out of your rut and start a brand new, beautiful life.

God has put a rainbow across my soul!

Praying Power

"And His name shall be the hope of all the world."
Matthew 12:21

I heard a story the other day of a Roman Catholic priest who was a weekly golfer. One day he needed an eagle in order to win the game. (An eagle, as you may know, is hitting the ball and getting it in the hole two strokes under par.) So the priest took a big swing, but it was an awful slice. Just as the ball was spinning out of control there was an enormous clap of thunder. As lightning struck the ball, it hit a tree and bounced off, angled off a fence, hit another tree and landed in the sandtrap. But then it bounced out of the sandtrap, rolled onto the green, curled twice around the hole and rolled in for an eagle. The pious priest looked up toward heaven and said, "Thank you, Father, but I'd rather do it myself."

Well, that's the way most of us are. We'd like to make our dreams come true all by ourselves because deep down, we want all the credit. But remember, *God can do great things through the person who doesn't care who gets the credit.* The truth is, all by yourself you can never accomplish the great things God has in mind for you. No matter who you are or where you come from, Jesus Christ will come to you. All you have to do is drop on your knees; blame yourself for your failure; aim your voice toward Him; and name His name. Simply say, "Jesus, I take Your name as my salvation. I name You as my Lord."

**God can do great things through the person
who doesn't care who gets the credit!**

Praying Power

"Commit your work to the Lord, then it will succeed."
Proverbs 16:3

The other day I boarded a plane and sat on the front seat right in front of the stewardess who walked up and down the aisle, then came back to announce that every seat was filled. "Well," she said, "if the seats are full, I guess we can go." So the door was closed. We were told to fasten our seat belts. Then all of a sudden, I heard a knock on the door directly in front of me. I was amazed, and apparently, so was she. The stewardess opened the door and standing there, looking quite embarrassed, was the captain!

We thought we had everything we needed for a successful flight. But how can you go anywhere without the captain?

How can *you* possibly become all that you were created to be if you don't acknowledge the Captain of your life? *Jesus Christ is my Captain.* This doesn't mean that I am perfect or sinless—far from it! But He loves me and I love Him. I try my best, but when I make mistakes He is always there to pick me up again and we keep going and never look back or quit.

Ultimately, whether you become a strong person or are weak; whether you are a success or a failure, all depends on the leadership of your life. Ask yourself one simple question: "Would I be a better person than I am today if Jesus Christ became my Captain?"

Jesus Christ is my Captain!

Praying Power

"Happy are those whose hearts are pure, for they shall see God."

Matthew 5:8

In this church ministry we have many iron pillared persons. One such person is Gail Bartosh. I remember her father used to say to me, "I wonder what will happen to Gail." Although no one ever said much about it, some thought Gail was mongoloid; others thought she was mentally retarded.

Today, Gail is one of the greatest workers we have in this church. Gail works in our day care center. She beautifully and lovingly cares for these little children of all nationalities, creeds and colors while their working mothers make a living for their families.

"You know, Dr. Schuller," she told me one day, "when I was a child I was taken from one doctor to another and none could agree exactly what was wrong with me. So finally I stopped seeing doctors, started praying and going to church and decided to develop the potential God has given me the very best I could."

And that is exactly what Gail Bartosh has done. She touches the lives of children daily and inspires them to be beautiful, brave and successful persons. She decided to make the most of what she had and she has become a fantastic human being.

> **You, too, can be a successful iron pillared person!**

Praying Power

"Wait on the Lord and He will strengthen your heart."
                                   Psalms 27:14

Once you have a strong will and have committed yourself to God's plan for your life, you are going to run into trials and difficulties at all points. At times all you can do is to be quiet and still and let Him work it out. There will be times when all the will power in the world won't bring you success. You need the miracle of still power which gives you the courage to wait on the Lord and stand by Him in prayer.

Be still before God, now, and as you write a prayer of praise, draw from His endless power.

_____

_____

_____

_____

_____

_____

_____

_____

"Be still and know that I am God."
Psalms 46:70

Paying Power

*"Then He said to all, 'Anyone of you who wants to follow me
must put aside your own desires and conveniences and carry
your cross with you everyday and keep close to me!'"*

Luke 9:23

Iron pillared people have WEIGHING POWER—they
know how to weigh the alternatives. They have PRAYING
POWER—they know what questions to ask. Then when
they've weighed the alternatives and know they have chosen
the best option, they must have PAYING POWER—the
power to make the commitment and pay the price.

Dr. Joseph Jacobs, a world famous chemical engineer and
personal friend, has learned as a possibility thinker something that every one of you must learn. Just recently he said
to me, "There is nobody in the world who is achieving anything that isn't running the risk of failure. The successful
person is the person who refuses to be defeated by his failures." Every person pays a price either in prestige, dollars,
energy, or emotional output.

In the entire history of baseball, there's never been a hitter
who batted 1000 all the time. There's never been a pitcher
who struck everyone out during his whole career. Everybody strikes out once in a while. The point is we can't let our
failures defeat us. We must be willing to pay the price to
succeed.

What price must you be willing to pay in order to achieve
your dream?

Make a commitment to your dream.

Paying Power

"Yes indeed, it is good when you truly obey our Lord's command, 'you must love and help your neighbors just as much as you love and take care of yourself.' "

James 2:8

An Hour of Power friend received one of our little crosses which says, "God loves you and so do I." She wore the cross around her neck, and when she went into the hospital for surgery, she found strength and comfort in its message.

Then, ten days after she was released from the hospital, one of her dearest friends called her and told her of a terrible problem. "I gave her assuring words over the telephone," she said, "but when I hung up I felt void and cold. My words simply weren't enough. I knew I had to do more.

"Then suddenly the thought entered my mind, 'Maybe I should give her my gold cross.' But the thought of giving it away nearly brought tears to my eyes. It was so special because it had carried me through that dark, painful time in the hospital. But I knew in my heart that the cross would mean even more to her because it was so valuable to me. So I went over to see her and told her how the cross helped me.

"When I put the little gold cross around her neck, tears slowly ran down her cheeks. Eight hours later she called me and I could hear the ecstasy in her voice. The problem had been solved by miraculous means. God truly answers prayer.

"As long as I live I'll never forget the joy I felt when I shared with her and gave her the encouragement she needed."

> **You must have the courage to become a supporting, spanning, sustaining beam.**

Paying Power

"A true friend is always loyal, and a brother is born to help in time of need."

Proverbs 17:17

No matter who you are, God promises, "I will make you into an iron pillar." God wants to make you strong because somebody, somewhere, needs to lean on you. Throughout our lives, we have an audience. Somebody is watching to see how you handle life's crisis situations. You can be sure that you will either be a source of strength to them or you'll convey weakness.

"A bell isn't a bell until you ring it. A song isn't a song until you sing it. Love isn't love until you give it away." And, I might add, *strength isn't strength until you lift somebody who's down. Somewhere, today or tomorrow, someone will need to lean on you. Do you have the strength to support them?*

If not, take these moments now and retreat in prayer. Pray that Jesus will make you strong enough to face the crisis situations in your own life, that in turn you can also support those who need to lean on you.

> **If God is going to use me to be a supportive iron pillar, I must be strong and successful for others as well as for myself.**

Paying Power

"Except a grain of wheat fall on the ground and die, it bears no fruit."

John 12:24

An iron pillar is of no value lying on the ground. It has no purpose until it rises into the sky and loses its identity by being welded onto the total mass.

Many people fail to become iron pillared persons because they are afraid to become involved. They are afraid to count the cost in terms of time, money, or emotional involvement, so they play it cool. Rather than become a pillar of strength that supports the very structure of the building, they prefer to remain seated in the balcony.

What have you avoided becoming involved in which you know will be costly in one means or another?

_____

_____

_____

_____

Today make that phone call, write that letter, or sign that contract. Make the commitment. Become involved!

> **Every iron pillared person must grow, develop and become strong enough to bear the burden of success.**

Paying Power

"And those who are peacemakers will plant seeds of peace and reap a harvest of goodness."

James 3:18

Yesterday I called on a lady in the hospital. "They say I'm terminal. They're not even giving me chemotherapy any more. Everything has failed," she said. "Mary Lou," I soothed, "if what they mean by this is correct, the word is not 'terminal,' it's 'transitional.' You're not going to die; you're going through a transition." "But everything seems so hopeless," she persisted. Taking her hands in mine, I assured her, "When everything else fails, get ready to meet God, because that's when God steps in. He's always there. He never fails. This isn't an end for you, it's a beginning." And then she smiled at me and squeezed my hand and said, "Thank you. That helps."

For a brief moment I had the most wonderful feeling. I had been her supportive beam.

It's important that you take the time to get involved and become that supportive beam, that lift, that so many people need. When you become an iron pillared person, life becomes more exciting than you can imagine!

> **Success is building self-esteem in yourself and in others through sacrifical service to them.**

Paying Power

"Let everything you do reflect your love of the truth and the fact that you are in dead earnest about it."

Titus 2:7

Iron pillared persons are persons who dare to dream risky dreams. A dream that doesn't hold the potential for failure isn't worth dreaming because it doesn't produce excitement and fulfillment. It is the potential element of possible failure that produces the tension that generates the energy to strive to accomplish the impossible.

When a dream comes to you, you must be willing to leave the shelter of the harbor where you have entrenched yourself. Some of you are still living in the harbor of self-grief. You are being self-indulgent by continuing to mourn the passing of a loved one and excusing yourself from life. You have to escape the rut you're in. Maybe you're lying in a hospital bed and you haven't gone to therapy when you should and you find yourself surrendering to sickness. Many of you are still stuck in a job that is absolutely meaningless to you. It offers no challenge, no future, no meaning, but you continue to stay simply because it provides a paycheck. If you're in a rut, it's time to start dreaming.

Pray for a new dream now. Write it down as an act of commitment. _____

_____

_____

_____

I must have nerve to aim for an impossible dream.

Paying Power

"All things are possible to those who believe."

Mark 9:23

The only difference between weak people and strong people is the ideas that grip them. Ultimately there are no great people, only ordinary people with extraordinary commitments to outstanding ideas. First you choose your dream and then your dream will shape your future and your life.

Did you know that you are a potential genius? Psychological studies have shown that child prodigies are not born, they are developed. Within you is incredible, untapped potential! "All things are possible to him who believes!"

My friend Dr. Everett Koop, Professor of Pediatric Surgery at the University of Pennsylvania School of Medicine, holds the record for the greatest number of successful separations of Siamese twins in human history. If it weren't for his firm belief in the sovereignty of God—that "with God all things are possible"—then he would never have dared to tackle the obstacles involved in such delicate surgery.

Greatness begins with ideas that start in the realm of the imagination. What great things could you accomplish if you truly believed God would strengthen you?

> **Aim for the highest, most exalted peak you can conceive of.**

Staying Power

"So be truly glad! There is wonderful joy ahead, even though the going is rough for a while down here."

1 Peter 1:6

Finally, *you need STAYING POWER. Iron pillared people just don't know how to quit!*

I was lecturing back East at a large convention. While waiting backstage for my name to be announced, a woman approached me and said, "Dr. Schuller, I know you have to be on stage in a minute, but there's a man I want you to meet. He is a quadraplegic and has had a leg amputated. He never had any religious training; but since he's been watching Hour of Power, he has become a Christian. He no longer gets drunk on Saturday nights, and he no longer talks about suicide. He dreams of the day when he can come and sit in his wheelchair in the front row of the Crystal Cathedral! I'd just love for you to shake his hand. It would mean so much to him."

We went quietly to the back stage entrance. There we found the man in a wheelchair. As the woman had described, he was a quadraplegic with only one leg. I greeted him and shook his hand, but he couldn't talk. He just started to cry. But as the tears flowed down his cheeks, he smiled. And as he smiled through his tears, I was reminded of a rainbow when the sun is shining through the rain. I saw a rainbow across his soul!

When it rains—stay and look for the rainbow!

Staying Power

"Whatever happens, dear friends, be glad in the Lord."
                                                    Philippians 3:1

I was in a distant city not long ago and as I lectured to the large crowd before me, I saw a very famous face in the front row. This man held the key position in one of the most powerful political posts in his state. Just recently I had learned of his defeat at the polls.

After the lecture, security ushered him and his wife backstage. He approached me and said, "Dr. Schuller, I had to hear you. I've been watching Hour of Power for a long time and I've made my commitment to Christ. That's why I failed at the polls." "What do you mean?" I asked. "Two weeks ago," he continued, "I was approached by a group of powerful political figures who could sweep 100,000 votes from a massive, organized segment of society my way or the way of my opponent. They asked me to make a commitment to them, but what they asked me to do was both unethical and immoral. I couldn't do it and I told them so.

"But," he added, "I'll tell you something, Dr. Schuller, I feel very good about what I've done!"

Succeed or fail, the bottom line of real success is self-respect. You need Jesus Christ because the pressures of the world are too great for you to make it alone. Let Jesus be your iron pillar and He will make you strong and honest enough to achieve true success.

JESUS GIVES ME STAYING POWER!

Staying Power

"You will give me back my life, and give me wonderful joy in your presence."

Acts 3:28

YES—JESUS CHRIST IS MY IRON PILLARED FRIEND! When Jesus came to the end of His life, He carefully *weighed* His alternatives. He wasn't cornered and tricked in the Garden of Gethsemane. He could have run, but He chose to die on the cross. Then He *prayed* His way through in the Garden. He said, "My God, all things are possible unto Thee. Not my will, but Thy will be done." Then He *paid* the price—He went to the cross. He carefully considered the price He had to pay. He *stayed* with His commitment to the very end when He cried, "Father, into Your hands I give my spirit."

Jesus is my iron pillar of strength because I know He is alive today. When I draw close to Him in prayer, I feel I am entering the walls of an impenetrable protective fortress.

Draw now into the saving arms of Jesus—into the walls of the impenetrable protective fortress where he will make you into an iron pillared person!

> I love Him. I try my best, but when I make mistakes He is always there to pick me up again and we keep going and never look back or quit.

Turn Your Scars Into Stars!

My Choice? Rejoice!

"Behold a little child shall lead them."

Isaiah 11:6

This scripture means more to me today as I look back over the summer when God truly *turned our scars into stars.*

My wife, Arvella, and I were in Korea when the call came that our daughter Carol had been thrown from a motorcycle while riding with her cousin from the farm. Her left leg had been amputated below the knee and further amputation would possibly be necessary. In surgery they failed to get a pulse beat or blood pressure, but through several blood transfusions, God saved the life of our little girl!

When we finally reached Carol's bedside in the Iowa hospital, there were no tears. Carol spoke the first words, "Hi, Dad and Mom," she cheerfully greeted us. "I think I know why this happened." Before we could respond, she continued, "I think God has a special ministry in my life for people who have been hurt like I have."

It's not what happens to you, but how you react to what happens to you that makes the difference!

Here was our thirteen-year-old daughter already choosing to react creatively to something she couldn't do anything about! When something happens to you that is out of your control and you feel there is nothing you can do about it, you can still do something. You can decide what your reaction is going to be!

> **There is no gain without pain, I must be making headway because I hurt—Hallelujah!**

My Choice? Rejoice!

"My heart is quiet and confident, O God. I will greet the dawn with a song."

Psalms 57:7

When we finally reached Carol's bedside, we had already seen three dawnings. The first dawning was from our plane over the Pacific; the second was over Denver, Colorado; and the third was in Sioux City, Iowa, twenty-two hours after the accident had occurred. Three dawnings in one day!

No matter how you are hurting, what your problem is, or what your pain may be, greet every day with a song because God is in the daybreak! God rides in every morning. And tomorrow will not be the same as yesterday.

The dawn was breaking as Mrs. Schuller and I walked into the Iowa hospital. Just before we reached the door, I said, "I don't know if I can step into that room without crying." I had cried as we flew over the Pacific. As the loud uncontrollable sobs came, I decided to turn my problem into a possibility. I vocalized the agony into "Alleluia, Alleluia." As I did, I found complete healing!

If you ever hurt so much that simple wet tears turn into an uncontrollable loud cry, give God a chance to turn the sorrow into a song. Simply say, "Alleluia, Alleluia, Alleluia."

I was filled with strength when I entered Carol's room. The pain had turned to praise! What can you praise God for today?

I will greet each dawn with a song—a song of praise to God!

My Choice? Rejoice!

"Trust in the Lord forever."

Isaiah 26:4

Carol was far from recovery when we comforted her in the Iowa hospital. In fact, doctors were prepared for further amputation. I discussed the probability with Carol and I shall never forget her answer.

"Dad," she said bravely, "no matter what, if they take my knee and thigh, it won't change God's plan for my life."

So what are your hurts? What worries or problems are you facing? Learn this promise today: Nothing that happens to you can change God's plan for your life one bit!

Only you can do that. You can choose to react negatively to what happens to you. You have that choice. Or, you can *turn your scars to stars* if you choose to react positively to the hurts of life.

How do you react positively? You choose and believe that somehow God is bigger than the hurt and he can turn the hurt into a halo.

What hurt do you have today? _____

_____

_____

Right now, choose to believe that God is in control, and somehow this hurt will become a halo.

> **I will not be a bitter person. I will be a better person.**

My Choice: Rejoice!

"O give thanks to the Lord, for he is good, for His steadfast love, endures for ever."

Psalms 136:1

Victor Frankl, an eminent Jewish psychiatrist, was standing naked and stripped before the Gestapo. They had taken his watch and then had seen his gold wedding band and demanded it as well. As Frankl took the wedding band off his finger to hand it to the Gestapo officer, a thought went through his brain. He said to his captors: "There is one thing you can never take from me and that is my freedom to choose how I will react to whatever you do to me!" That we all retain to the end.

How will you react to your hurts today?

You can react negatively and *CURSE* your hurts, blaming others or yourself. But when you seek to blame someone else, you only create the opportunity for new problems to be born.

You can *NURSE* your hurts, tenderly keeping them alive, indulging in self-pity, and asking yourself, "Why did this have to happen to me?"

You can even *REHEARSE* your hurts, going over them again and again. But this keeps the hurts alive rather than letting them heal.

Don't curse your hurts. Don't nurse them and don't rehearse them!

REVERSE them! Turn them inside out. Let the obstacle become an opportunity, the problem a possibility. The hurt becomes a halo. The scar becomes a star!

My problem is a new project.

My Choice? Rejoice!

"All things work together for good to those who love God and keep his commandments."

Romans 8:28

When we were waiting in the airport in Seoul, Korea, hoping to board a plane to get to our daughter's side soon, the pastor, with whom I had been ministering, quoted the Bible verse above. I had heard that text probably a thousand times, but now I heard it knowing that my daughter was seriously hurt. I didn't disbelieve it, I didn't doubt it, I didn't deny it, but I couldn't feel it.

And when you cannot feel it, then there's only one thing to do, believe it and hang on! The night turns into a dawning, eventually the pain is gone and healing takes place. Through it all, God has His time and His chance to show you how He can turn the worst burden into a blessing, the most horrible hurt into a halo, your scar into your star!

What hurt did you write down the other day? Today—even if you cannot feel it, *Believe!* with an open mind to God's healing power. Think of some possible ways this hurt could be a halo, this scar your star! _____

_____

_____

My difficulties will produce divine dividends!

My Choice? Rejoice!

"Cast your burden on the Lord and he will sustain you, he will never permit the righteous to be moved."

Psalms 55:22

When I toured the Royal Palace in Teheran, Iran, I couldn't believe its beauty and splendor. The grand entry is resplendent with glittering sparkling glass, seemingly diamonds or crystal. But when you look close, you discover it is actually small bits of mirrors. The guide explained how the architect planned for beautiful mirrors throughout the Royal Palace. However, when the shipment arrived, every mirror had been smashed in travel. The architect gathered the tiny pieces of mirror and put some glue on the wall and arranged the broken bits. He did this until he had an enormous distortion in reflections, sparkling with a rainbow of brilliant colors. Today, the Royal Palace is a dazzling brilliant display of prisms reflecting light.

I could think of only one thing, as I stood in awe at the spectacular palace, it was BROKEN TO BE MORE BEAUTIFUL!

And this can happen to you too! Those hurts you have won't destroy you. If you're broken, rejoice! God will make you beautiful too. God is the ultimate architect—the grand Creator. Let him arrange the broken pieces of your life. And, you can be a prism of light to those around you!

Break me, Lord, to be more beautiful!

My Choice? Rejoice!

"The Lord is near to the brokenhearted and saves the crushed in spirit."

Psalms 34:18

I believe that what happened to Carol through her accident and what happened to her mother and father was just this. We were broken to be more beautiful. I reread my original message from 1973, "Turn your Scars into Stars" and near the end of the text were these lines I'd written then.

"The truth is, the more I meet people, the more convinced I am that there is no great person doing a great work who has not been hurt at a deep level. In fact, I'm so convinced of it that as I deliver this message today in 1973, I offer this prayer, 'Dear God, hurt me more so that I can help people more.'"

Today I can tell you with joy in my heart that God answered my prayer!

What prayer will you offer God today? He can turn your hurts to halos, your scars to stars; or, he can break you to be more beautiful. And as you seek his plan, He'll work through you.

God hurt me more so I can help others more.

Play It Down And Pray It Up!

"My flesh and my heart may fail, but God is the strength of my heart and my portion for ever."

Psalms 73:26

I learned a valuable lesson in the midst of my daughter's accident. It's another way of turning your scars into stars. *Never underestimate the ability of a positive thinking person to get on top of a tough situation!*

I was on the jet plane coming across the Pacific from Korea to Los Angeles, and between my wife and I, we were using up a lot of Kleenex. Our little girl had lost her leg and she was thousands of miles away. I was lost in grief, when this amazing sentence came into mind. "Schuller, you're taking it too hard. Play it down and pray it up!"

Then the word came clearly from God, "Schuller, she didn't lose her hands. She can still play the violin. She can still play the piano. She didn't lose both legs, only one. She's no embarrassment to her Lord, or to her friends or to you. You're exaggerating the accident. Play it down!"

My experience illustrates how our first inclination as hurting people is to exaggerate a tragic element. For 27 years as a pastor, I've counseled and prayed with people in a variety of situations, and in every instance, the first reaction is to exaggerate the tragic element. Because of the reality of a tragedy, the safeguard that would normally keep you from exaggerating is down. It's tough, but being aware of this is the first step towards a healing experience.

> I will pray my situation up. Then God can begin to show me how to turn my tragedy into a triumph!

Play It Down And Pray It Up!

"Why be discouraged and sad? Hope in God."

Psalms 42:5

So we know that it's our first reaction to exaggerate a tragedy, hurt or problem. We find all the wrongs and make them worse. Many negative thinkers do this every day. They look for faults in a great idea. They anticipate failure in future plans. They make life miserable for themselves and others.

As possibility thinkers, we can choose to react. How? Positively! But when a real hurt cuts deep, be aware of the desire to blow it out of proportion. Play it down! Here's where faith in Christ saves us from ourselves. When we are hurt beyond our strength, or troubled past our own supply of peace, then faith is the key. Trust in the Lord and He will sustain you!

How do you trust when you can't see ahead? You first remove the crust. You take away the desire to exaggerate the tragic element. You ask God to give you the strength to resist this temptation.

You can do this right now. Simply write down whatever problems or hurts you have blown out of proportion. List the hurts you've elevated.

_____

_____

_____

Now go back and cross out these negative thoughts. Cover them up on paper and clear them out of your mind. Play it down!

> **I let go of the negative pulls and cling to the promises of God!**

Play It Down And Pray It Up!

"Have no anxiety about anything, but in everything by prayer and supplication with thanksgiving make your requests be made known to God."

Philippians 4:6

I've been inspired by the story of a Norwegian fisherman. He lived in a simple little cottage by the sea with his wife, Ingrid, and his two sons. Every morning the fisherman and his two sons would row until they were far enough out in the ocean to catch a nice load of fish. But one day the men lost all track of time and before they knew it the sun went down. They didn't know which way to go.

Suddenly off in the distance one of the boys saw a golden glow. It was a bright light from shore! Someone must have suspected that they were out in the black of the ocean. The three men rowed towards the glorious glow until it became a huge blazing fire that lit up the entire wharf. They were home!

As they stepped onto land, all that was left of the fire was a few smoldering ashes. And there stood Ingrid, his wife, and mother of his two boys, sobbing uncontrollably. "Ingrid," the fisherman cried out, "We're safe!" She broke down again. "Everything's gone," she lamented. "What do you mean?" her husband asked. "The cottage burned to the ground," she exclaimed. "Oh, but Ingrid, the fire that consumed our house saved our lives!"

Play it down and pray it up! What may be a tragedy to you now can possibly be tomorrow's triumph.

I know that every sunset is a move closer to a new sunrise!

Play It Down And Pray It Up!

"Call to me and I will answer you and tell you great hidden things which you have not known."

Jeremiah 33:33

So now you've played down the problem, you've looked objectively at the situation, and you've resisted the reaction to exaggerate. That's a great start to step into healing!

Now pray it up! How do you do that? By having "UP-PRAYERS." Look at what you have! Look for the hidden secrets in your hurt, the promised blessings yet to come.

Thank you, God, that Carol has only lost a leg and is still alive! Thank you that I'm healthy enough to find a new job! Thank you that I had a loving relationship with my husband for 30 years. Thank you, God, that you have given me faith!

Take the time now to write your "Up-Prayer." With God's spirit healing your hurts, you have so much to be thankful for! _____

_____

_____

_____

_____

> **Trying times are times to try more faith. I'm trying! Lord, You're helping!**

Play It Down And Pray It Up!

"I will praise the Lord no matter what happens. I will constantly speak of His glories and grace."

Psalms 34:1

All throughout the Bible we find people who have encountered tragedies and hurts. Yet God is faithful as they turn to Him. Let's look at a few of these lives and record their response to tragedy, and their prayers through pain.

Read:	*Their Problem*	*Their Prayers*
Psalms 57		
2 Corinthians 1:8-11		
Job 1:13-22/42:1,2;10		
Luke 1:26-37;46-56		
Acts 16:19-32		

I choose to praise God and I feel surrounded by His presence!

Play It Down And Pray It Up!

"It is God himself who made us what we are and gives us new lives from Christ Jesus."

Ephesians 2:10

As you pray up your problems—no matter how big or small, you'll find yourself becoming more and more in tune with God. Through Jesus Christ we have a direct line to God. He'll hear your prayers. They'll get through. And God's promises to those who know Him are overflowing. Look back at the lives of those you studied yesterday. They all received God's presence and peace through their pain. David, Paul, Job, Mary and Stephen were all heirs to God's promises. All they had to do was pray! Today we have the privilege to pray through Christ. He is our connection to God.

I've done a lot of talking with Jesus and I know he listens. I know he's turning my scars into stars! If anybody is near me when I come to the point in my life when I draw my feet into bed for the last time, I will say to that person only one thing, "When I die, play it down and pray it up! Because I know where I'm going and who will be there. His name is Jesus Christ."

> **As I am filled with praise, I am filled with hope!**

Play It Down And Pray It Up!

"They who dwell in the shelter of the Most High, shall abide in the shadow of the Almighty."

Psalms 91:1

I have a friend who's a pastor in Bali, and he told me the funny experience that happened to him the first time he came to America. In the Indonesian culture, people sleep directly on top of the bed. When he came to this country he was hosted in a private home. When it came time to retire, he went to his bed and saw only the lace bedcover lying neatly on top of it. He didn't realize the blankets were underneath, so he looked through all the closets and under the bed. It was cold and he couldn't figure out why they hadn't provided him with a blanket. Finally he just lay on the bed, cold and uncomfortable.

The next morning when his friends asked how he slept, he mentioned that he was cold without blankets. His friends were a little puzzled and finally realized what happened. They smiled and explained, "The blankets were right on top of the bed. You have to pull back the bed cover and crawl into it." They showed him upstairs to the bedroom. "See, you don't just lay on top, you have to get in it."

That's how you get the faith to play it down and pray it up. You have to get into the Bible. You have to get into a relationship with Jesus Christ. It's not enough to know about Jesus, you have to get in and snuggle up to Him.

I am ready Lord, and eager to get closer to You!

Don't Wrestle—Nestle!

"Bring every thought into the captivity of Jesus Christ."
2 Corinthians 10:5

As you pray up your problems to Christ, you will discover a hidden secret and that is, the more you get to know Jesus, the more you'll experience peace.

If you still have disharmony instead of harmony, then you still need to experience the freedom that only comes by discovering the captivity of your soul to Jesus Christ. At a deep level there is internal peace when Christ is controlling your thoughts. You don't have to wrestle through life. Problems, tragedies, hurts and failures don't have to trap you. Stop fighting these imprisoning feelings as you give in to the freeing arms of Christ. Don't wrestle—Nestle! You don't need to struggle through that disappointment any longer, rather snuggle close to God. Bring every thought into captivity to Him and He will free you.

What trapped feeling will you surrender to Christ's control today?_____

Now in prayer, let your every thought and entire being become captive to your Lord. He is bringing a new harmony, a beautiful healing, and a silent peace as you snuggle close to Him.

> **I am free from every binding, limiting and hurting thought as Christ takes control.**

Don't Wrestle—Nestle!

"For one who was called in the Lord as a slave is a freed person of the Lord, and one who was free when called is a slave of Christ."

1 Corinthians 7:22

How can you really bring every thought in captivity to Jesus? It's simple. You develop an emotional screen through which all your thoughts must be filtered. As thoughts come into your mind, you can know they come from Christ by asking the right questions.

First: Does this thought stimulate my faith?
Second: Does this thought generate hope and make me optimistic?
Third: Does this thought generate love?

If the thought coming to you filters through this screen and the answers are yes, yes, yes . . . then that thought must be of Christ! He is giving you a creative idea, an inspiring guideline, or a challenging dream! Receive it—Believe it!

When your thoughts are captive to Christ—you are truly free!

What thought has He given to you as you get closer daily to Him? _____

_____

Isn't it exciting to have uplifting thoughts? They're coming from Jesus Christ.

> I draw so much energy—producing enthusiasm
> for living when I allow Jesus to
> fill my life!

Don't Wrestle—Nestle!

"My grace is sufficient for you, for my power is made perfect in weakness."

2 Corinthians 12:9

Ray Lindquist, a very dear friend of mine tells about when he was a boy on a Nebraska farm. He placed a ladder next to the barn and carefully climbed up. He was going to look in the rain gutter and try to catch sparrows. But as he leaned over the rain gutter to grab a sparrow, he reached a little too far and the ladder slipped and fell. He hung by only his fingertips and his feet were dangling. "Help, help!" he cried out. Then he heard a strong voice, "Let go." He looked down and it was his father. His arms were only a foot below his feet, so he let go and dropped into his father's arms.

Your struggle can become a snuggle. Don't wrestle—Nestle! Let go and Let God.

If you were to let go of one area of your life right now and snuggle close to God, what would it be?

_____

_____

Why don't you nestle close to Christ in prayer now? He promises to generate his power through you. He can and will make you the beautiful person you're now believing you can be!

> **Whenever God takes something away, He always replaces it with more of Himself!**

Don't Wrestle—Nestle!

"The Lord will fulfill his purpose for me; thy steadfast love, O Lord, endures for ever."

Psalms 138:8

In your own reading of the gospels you'll discover that Jesus never called anyone a sinner. And you know why? It's because Jesus knew you don't change a bad person into a beautiful person by telling him he's a bad person. Never! You turn a person into a beautiful lover of God by putting something inside of him—and that is a dream that he can be a beautiful person someday!

There is a hurt in your life that Christ wants to heal. He wants you to be a more beautiful person than you already are. That's why he's filling your mind with new, glorious dreams. When you have an internal disharmony, it's because you really think you know yourself. But do you? Let me tell you. As you go deeper into your self than you ever have before, you'll strike the rich ore of faith in God. And, as you get closer to Him, you'll become the harmonious, beautiful, positive person He intended you to be. You'll find possibilities deep within you that you never knew existed. You may be surrounded by frustrations, obstacles and difficulties, but in the midst of it all, you'll receive thoughts that can lift you above the mess—and they're coming from Him!

**My life is being made more beautiful
every day as Christ lives within.**

Don't Wrestle—Nestle!

"Everyone who believes that Jesus is the Christ is a child of God . . . ."

1 John 5:1

Borham, the great Christian writer, wrote something years ago that impressed me. He wrote, "When I was a young man, I was invited to spend a weekend with my friend at his house. I'd never been there before and my friend said that the room right across the hall from me was off limits. Nobody was allowed in the room, he said, and I respected that. But one night I happened to be awakened, and I thought I heard something. I quietly opened my door and peeked out. The door to the forbidden room across the hall was open and the light was on. I saw someone in bed, and it was a young man. But the young man had the look of a totally mentally deranged personality. And kneeling at his bed, caressing that mentally deranged child's brow was the mother."

Borham said, "I never will forget the mother's words. She was crying and she said, 'I brought you into this world. I gave you life. I gave you food. I have washed you and I have loved you every day of your life. And you still do not know me.'"

God looks at you that way, if you have never given your life to Him. He looks at you with all His power to heal, if only you would give Him your hurts. He desires to know you better.

Don't struggle in life. Snuggle! Get close to God and he will get close to you.

> I am resting in the strong loving arms of my father—and He is restoring my life!

Don't Wrestle—Nestle!

"Fix your thoughts on what is true and good and right. Think about things that are pure and lovely, and dwell on the fine, good things in others."

Philippians 4:8

The secret of tuning our minds and thoughts in to God's channel is to come daily—moment by moment to Him. That's what it means to have your thoughts in the captivity of Jesus. You nestle continually. You snuggle throughout the day. Why? Let me explain.

On a trip to Thailand one summer I witnessed a native milking the poison from a cobra. It was incredible how this native would taunt and tease the cobra until the head went up and the snake began to hiss and throw himself to strike the native with deadly poison.

But the native was too clever. He knew exactly how to grab it at the back of the neck and squeeze under its jaws. First the mouth opened and the two ivory fangs were bared; then, with a finger, he would press the glands and the drops of white liquid fatal poison would ooze out into a small vial. He was able to sell the poison at a large price. It was used for antivenom purposes.

The native told me through an interpreter that three hours after he'd milked the cobra, the cobra would have venom again, enough to kill someone. And it is the same with negative thoughts. You and I have to milk the poison of our minds constantly.

We have to constantly eliminate our negative thoughts. The way we do that is by getting close to Jesus Christ.

> **Minute by minute, my clouded mind is being cleared by God's fresh breath of love!**

Don't Wrestle—Nestle!

"I am leaving you with a gift—peace of mind and heart! And the peace I give isn't fragile like the peace the world gives."
John 14:27

A few days ago you wrote down a feeling that seemed to imprison you. The following day you recorded a thought that you felt God had given you. Today list the fears, hurts, worries, or negative thoughts that keep plaguing you.

Now contrast these small problems with God's powerful response. Be in prayer as you listen to his ideas.

Problems   *God's Response*

Jesus Christ is generating his power, love and hope through your heart and mind now. Receive Him and live!

God gives me the ears to listen, the heart to feel and the mind to think of his beautiful plan for my life!

Jesus Christ—Superscar!

"When someone becomes a Christian, they become a brand new person inside. They are not the same anymore. A new life has begun."

2 Corinthians 5:17

Probably the most exciting thing about getting closer to Christ is that He is the one perfect example you can follow. As you study His life, you'll find that He was not only truly God, but He was truly human! And He went through every hurt, challenge and temptation that anyone could experience.

I'm reminded of the story of the boy who had to take a spoonful of castor oil. But before the boy's grandmother would give the child the medicine, she took it herself and said, "See, there is nothing to it. It is easy."

That's what God did when he gave Christ as our Savior. He took His own medicine physically. We bring a number of ills upon ourselves every day by misusing our freedom. We let negative thoughts creep in, or we exaggerate hurts, or believe in failure.

Christ never did that. Rather, He came and took the effects of our misused freedom. He suffered physically, as human flesh, to prove that we too can know God, and we too can turn our scars into stars!

> **My roots are tapped into the positive source of love—Jesus Christ. I am free to follow His plan!**

Jesus Christ—Superscar!

"Let not your hearts be troubled; believe in God, believe also in me."

John 14:1

When Archbishop Fulton Sheen was alive, he made a profound impression on my life. His words you are about to read inspired the slogan, "Turn your Scars into Stars." That slogan has helped me in my toughest moments and I know it's helping you today.

"Young people today and many others know Christ as the Super Star. They are beginning to know Him. But to me He is not that. The Super Star always has a star on his dressing room door. But He was not Super Star. He had no star above His dressing room door; as a matter of fact, He was thrown out into a garbage heap and crucified.

"What is Christ if He is not a Super Star? He is a Super Scar! For when He arose from the dead He had five hideous scars on hands, and feet and side. Believe me, there is a great deal of credit that is given to Thomas the Apostle. Sure, he was a doubter. Sure, he was a skeptic, but he had great worth and he bequeathed to us an excellent lesson, and that lesson was, 'I am not going to believe anyone, unless he can show me that he loves even to the point of sacrifice. If Christ brought God's love to this earth, then He has to show love even to the extent of giving His life. I want, therefore, to see some scars, some marks of love, and when I can put my finger into His hand, and my hand into His side, then I will not be incredulous, then I will believe.'

"This is Christ, the Super Scar. The one who was wounded out of love for us."

JESUS CHRIST SUPERSCAR—
The Christ we believe, the Christ we preach,
the Christ we love.

Jesus Christ—Superscar!

"And we all, with unveiled face, beholding the glory of the Lord, are being changed into His likeness."
2 Corinthians 3:18

Even to a possibility thinker, there are some things that are impossible. For someone to stand at the beginning of a day and say to the sun, "Today you shall not make your sweeping sail through the sky" is an impossibility. Or for someone to go to the seashore and draw a line in the sand at low tide and say to the sea, "Today you shall not rise above this line," is an impossibility.

The Roman soldiers put a stone in front of the tomb where Jesus was laid and said, "He shall never rise again!" That was an impossibility! And to say, "You will not change if you take Jesus Christ into your life," is an impossibility. The truth is, Christ rose and nothing can hold Him back! And anybody who takes Christ into his life is going to change! Seeds will sprout, seas will rise, the sun will sail! Christ is alive and is invading human lives, changing hearts, minds and personalities. It is impossible to receive Jesus Christ into your life as your personal Savior without being genuinely and beautifully changed.

In what ways have you changed since Christ has come into your life? _____

_____

_____

_____

> **Help me, Lord, to accept what I cannot change, and then I will change.**

131

Jesus Christ—Superscar!

"Peace, I leave with you . . . ."

John 14:27

Jesus Christ—Superscar, gives an indescribable peace. Some of you have never experienced this dynamic peace. It can happen! Somebody said to me, "Are you sure Jesus Christ is alive today?" And my immediate response was, "Of that I have no doubt. But I wonder, are you really alive today? Or is there a stone in front of your life that keeps you emotionally blocked from really enjoying life?" If there is, Jesus Christ can transform you. Here's how: I shall give you four simple words that you can easily remember.

First of all, *COURAGE*. He gives you courage when Christ comes in by faith. And courage eliminates fear which is the main source of man's anxiety and depression.

The second word is *CONFIDENCE*. When Jesus Christ comes alive into your life, you have confidence. And confidence eliminates anxiety, the second major emotional cause of human unrest.

The third word is *COMPANIONSHIP*. When Christ comes in you are saved from loneliness—that isolation of spirit! Companionship!

And the fourth word is *COMMUNICATION*. Communication is the capacity to be creative. To understand and to be understood.

I will see faces of people today, Lord, I will see your love in their life!

Jesus Christ—Superscar!

"If you do this you will experience God's peace, which is far more wonderful than the human mind can understand. His peace will keep your thoughts and your hearts quiet and at rest as you trust in Christ Jesus."

Philippians 4:7

When you get close to the superscars of Christ, He gives COURAGE! Real dynamic courage. "Peace I give to you," he promises. Everyone knows Christ was not afraid of death. If you eliminate the fear of dying, you eliminate the mother of all fears.

British annals had an interesting anecdote. There was a time in the West Indies when five ships were anchored in harbor. One was a British ship. Suddenly an unexpected storm came up. The British officer set his sail directly out into the mounting rolling waves. He sailed directly into the face of the storm. Two days later, battered and bruised, he returned to the harbor to find that the other four ships had been destroyed.

There is only one way to conquer a fear and that is to face it! If Christ is your Lord, you can face any fear without being afraid. Christ gives courage. He offers peace to you today. What fear do you need to face today?

Lord, I feel your mysterious, calm, quiet
assurance rising deep within my being.

Jesus Christ—Superscar!

"Therefore do not throw away your confidence, which has a great reward. For you have need of endurance, so that you may do the will of God and receive what is promised."
Hebrews 10:35, 36

The second thing the scars of Christ give is CONFIDENCE. Confidence eliminates the anxiety that comes from irresponsible liberty. Isn't it interesting that our society is one of the most anxiety plagued in history, and during a period when we have, supposedly, now more freedom than ever before. How do you account for it? When you have total moral freedom without any moral restraints, you are bound to inherit anxiety.

Tests have been made by psychologists of children in playgrounds. One test hypothesized that those who played in fenced areas would be oppressed later on. They would grow up feeling restricted. To test this, they gave a group of children total freedom. No fences! And guess what happened? The children became anxiety prone and huddled together and played in the center of the playground. They didn't dare run for fear they might run into danger. But when the fences were put up again, they ran across the playground with arms outstretched. Fences meant security!

The Ten Commandments are God's positive guides to good living. They are rules for happy living. When Christ comes into your life, you have a new moral consciousness. You have fences. You say, "I will be true to Christ and I will be true to God and therefore I will be true to my fellowman." And this is what gives you confidence.

I have peace with God. He has forgiven and forgotten my sins!

134

Jesus Christ—Superscar!

"Let us then with confidence draw near to the throne of Grace, that we may receive mercy and find grace to help in our time of need."

Hebrews 4:16

In one of my books I tell the story of Bozo, the famous Indian elephant in London. He was a beautiful animal—a big tender hunk of gentleness. One day though he went on a rampage and began to charge at the children. The circus owner knew the elephant was now dangerous and would have to be exterminated.

On the appointed date, Bozo was in his cage and three men with high powered rifles rose to take aim at the great beast's head. But just before the signal was given to shoot, a stranger walked up to the owner and said, "Sir, this is not a bad elephant. Give me two minutes alone in his cage."

The owner agreed. The brave man stepped into the cage and began talking to him in a strange language. Now the stranger walked up to the elephant and began to stroke his trunk. The beast tenderly wrapped his trunk around the feet of the man, lifted him up, and put him back down cautiously.

As he walked out of the door, the man said, "You see, he is an Indian elephant and understands only one language. He was homesick for someone who could understand him." The man's name was Rudyard Kipling.

Loneliness. The cure is to know that there is one companion who truly understands you. Jesus is that companion!

> You have never failed, Lord, to be my one
> essential, intimate friend.

Jesus Christ—Superscar!

"Pray constantly, give thanks in all circumstances, for this is the will of God in Christ Jesus for you."
1 Thessalonians 5:17, 18

All sorts of emotional problems happen when you feel you need companionship—you need someone with whom you can COMMUNICATE. Do you want a close companion, one you can communicate with?

Christ is so real to me. When I'm alone He is my constant friend. I find it very easy to pray and I do it all the time when I'm alone. He's there just like I know the pilot of an airplane is in the cockpit.

A few weeks ago I had to spank my little girl when she misbehaved. She ran off crying to her bedroom. After a few minutes, I peeked into her room to see her. She was cuddled in her bed with her arms wrapped tight around her favorite dolly. I stroked her hair and dried her tears and said, "Gretchen, I love you very much, but you needed that spanking."

Then she let go of her dolly and slipped her arms around my neck and hugged me. "Dear God," I whispered, "Thank you for my darling little girl."

Jesus Christ is alive and comes to you in prayer! He wants to be your Father. Some of you are hanging onto your own special doll, which is your substitute for the love you really seek from your Heavenly Father. It may be a new car, a hobby, or a new club membership. *But a dolly is never a substitute for a daddy!* Let Jesus Christ love you today!

God is showing me more of Himself—and that shows me more of myself!

Jesus Christ—Superscar!

"Let the peace in your heart which comes from Christ be always present in your hearts and lives, for this is your responsibility and privilege as members of this body."

Colossians 3:15

The scars of Jesus Christ are the stars of hope in your life! He has turned your hurt into a halo, your tragedy into a triumph, your pain into praise!

Take these moments to reflect upon this month. As you face your day, remember that no matter what happens to you, you can choose how you will react. As you play down the negative thoughts that creep into your life, you can discover the joy that comes from praying up your problems to Christ. People who aren't afraid of hurting, and seek the positive elements in every potential possibility are those in tune with Jesus Christ. You can snuggle next to Him without struggling through life. After all, he is the "Superscar." He cares, and knows who you are and why you hurt. And he died on the cross so you could come to experience the peace of God in your life today. He is turning your scars into stars.

Praise him now for all He's done, and what He will continue to do in your life.

I will allow nothing to rob me of God's gift of peace of heart and mind!

Discover Your Hidden Treasures

Believe in Hidden Treasures

"It is the glory of God to conceal a thing. And it is the glory of Kings to search things out."

Proverbs 25:2

God carefully, quietly, hides his most precious gifts so that we may become joyous "kings" by discovering them. It is a universal truth that the greatest most valuable treasures are hidden from clear view. The pearl is hidden within the oyster beneath the deep waters of the ocean. The diamond is buried deep within the earth. And the gold nuggets are concealed within the sides of mountains.

I believe that the solutions to our biggest problems—those concerning energy, economics, and natural resources are planted by God within the universe. Perhaps the materials we need to solve our problems are locked within the center of our own earth.

But the greatest of God's treasures lie neither beneath the sea, within the earth or in distant heavens. *God's greatest treasures lie within you and me—the resource of human creativity and potential!* Within you are gems of incredible value—pearls of great price. Do you believe it?

There is a goldmine of undiscovered gems waiting to be found. It is God's gifts within me!

Believe in Hidden Treasures

"For I know the plans I have for you," says the Lord, "plans to prosper you and not to harm you, plans to give you hope and a future."

Jeremiah 29:11

Hidden gems and riches are waiting to be unearthed even today. Billions of dollars in treasure lie waiting to be discovered. It was only 20 years ago that the golden Buddha was discovered in the city of Bangkok, Thailand. For years this huge, ugly, old concrete Buddha sat in the middle of town. People put empty cola cans on it and used it to hold packages while they changed the film in their cameras. Then one Buddhist priest took the old statue to his temple, but in the moving process it was cracked. Inside was found the world's largest chunk of sculptured gold standing 8 feet high.

What I want to share with you is far more valuable than discovering an ancient golden Buddha. The good news I have for you is that God has buried treasure inside your own life, your future, your destiny. You and I are like tiny acorns which hold the potential for becoming mighty oak trees.

What is your greatest treasure? Maybe it's to be slim and trim. Maybe it's to gain control of a habit that's been gripping you. Maybe you need to develop a talent you've been brushing aside. Whatever it is, you must begin to develop the treasures God has hidden in your life.

Today holds a sparkling diamond—It is my undiscovered potential shining through!

Believe in Hidden Treasures

"You made us a little lower than the heavenly beings and crowned us with glory and honor."

Psalms 8:5

How can you be sure that there are great treasures within you? You can know it because you yourself are a treasure! You are of great worth to God. He sent Jesus Christ to die to redeem you. Why? So that you would realize your value.

God wants every man to feel like a king, and every woman to feel like a queen because we are created in His image. We are descended from God Himself. We are of royal blood!

And God knows you will feel like a king or queen when you make a great discovery. That discovery is the riches He sees within you. He sees your royalness. He has hid a crown of gems for you to discover. There is no thrill like the thrill of making a great discovery.

God has made life exciting! He sees your untapped talents, your latent leadership, your budding beauty. You are a child of the King—the Master Creator! And you have His gifts—the same creative energy in you. It's from Him, and for Him. Discover it—and discover your heritage!

> **I am of royal blood. A crown of riches is mine today as I discover God's riches within me!**

Believe in Hidden Treasures

"I love those who love me and those who seek me will find me. With me are riches and honor enduring wealth and prosperity."

Proverbs 8:17, 18

God knew what He was doing when He created you. And he planned life in such a way that your greatest treasures are concealed waiting for you to discover them. When you make that discovery—you'll feel fantastic! You'll know your worth.

Nobody feels like a king just because he's born of royalty. Children of very wealthy people, who inherit their wealth rather than earn it, do not have the joy, self-esteem and self-respect of accumulating it through their own cleverness, self-discipline or hard work. Children born into wealth, fame or power are not as appreciative of their positions as those who start at the bottom, struggle, work hard and achieve the same things. God gives every human being unique opportunities to discover the true possibilities hidden within their character.

Treasure hunts aren't a thing for children or of the past. Treasures are hid in the opportunities God gives you every day. Look for them—and you will find them!

I am about to make a grand discovery—that God believes in me!

Believe in Hidden Treasures

"And the Lord will guide continually, and satisfy your desire with good things."

Isaiah 58:11

One of the great joys of any family, including ours, is the annual Easter egg hunt. At Easter, I take tiny chocolate eggs and hide them in the garden. I always hide a few of the candy eggs in rather obvious places so the children will be encouraged. Others are hidden in moderately difficult places so the children will stay motivated. Some are hid so carefully that they really have to think and work hard to find them. When the hunt is over, so is much of the fun. Wouldn't it be tragic if one child found all the Easter eggs and everyone knew there was nothing more to find?

We can be thankful that God has made us each unique with hidden potential that only we can find.

God gives us obvious talents to encourage us. What are yours? _____

_____

He also hides some of our potential talents under the surface. We have to work harder to develop them. What are yours? _____

_____

And God hides beautiful gems and potentials deep within us that we have to dream and believe will someday surface. What are yours? _____

_____

Remember, reality is in the dream. The search has just begun!

> **God is showing me the untapped riches deep within me. I believe I will strike gold!**

Believe in Hidden Treasures

"Happy is the one who finds wisdom and understanding, for the gain from it is better than gain from silver and its profit better than gold."

Proverbs 3:13, 14

Since there are great gems hidden within you, then only you can discover them.

I have found that there are basically three kinds of persons who are shaped by their philosophy of life.

First, there are the PLAYERS. Their basic philosophy can be summed up in the words, "Eat, drink and be merry; for tomorrow we die." Their lives are dominated by the pleasure principle.

Second, there are the STAYERS. These are the people whose basic philosophy is, "What will be, will be." They whine, "I can't change anything. Here is where I was born and this is my destiny." They are still in a rut. They prefer to take it easy and avoid risk and commitment.

Third, there are the PRAYERS. These people live by an entirely different philosophy. They say we cannot understand all aspects of our destiny under God. They realize that what happens to the inside of a person matters more than what happens to the outside. Values are more important than circumstances because the values you hold will inevitably affect your circumstances.

Have you an idea as to which of these persons will truly find life's concealed treasures?

I plan to find the treasures within me. And with God's help, I will succeed!

Believe in Hidden Treasures

"The good person out of his good treasure brings forth good."
Matthew 12:35

You must make a choice. What will you be? A player? A stayer? Or, will you be a prayer? This decision will be reflected in every facet of your life as you search for God's treasures.

Prayers are motivated by different things than stayers or players. What turns on the players and stayers is found in the simple line, "I quit!"

Prayers on the other hand are motivated by the principle, *"It's time to dream!"* They are the ones who first choose to believe that God has hidden treasures within their lives. Then they dream of what those treasures are. And you know what? Reality is in the dream! When you dream it, it is already a reality in the opening stage.

I invite you to become a prayer—a decision-making person, a dreamer of unseen riches, a believer in hidden gems! No matter who you are, you can discover the untapped talents and potentials within you when you decide to become a prayer.

Take time now to make this decision and sign your name as an official "prayer" in this new adventure called "treasure hunt."

I _____, commit myself to becoming a prayer, to actively seek and dream of God's hidden treasures within me and those around me!

> **I am ready to search, to work, and to believe
> in God's abundant riches!!**

Clue-in to Hidden Treasures

"The promises of the Lord are promises that are pure, silver refined in a furnace on the ground, purified seven times."
                                                   Psalms 12:6

Now that you are a prayer, how do you uncover what God has hidden within you? How do you begin your promising hunt for rare jewels?

You uncover your hidden possibilities by becoming attuned to God's guidelines. He will give you the clues to follow. These are like the rules of a game, the ingredients of a recipe. Leave one out and you may miss the joy of discovery.

First, a prayer trusts and *believes God's word*. The Bible says that you and I as human beings are created just a little lower than the angels. We are created in the image of God and, therefore, are vessels containing vast possibilities. We are unique. One reason many people fail to discover their talents and capabilities is because they compare themselves with someone they feel is a little better than they are. In what areas of your life do you compare yourself to others?

God wants you to be distinctive, not a carbon copy of someone else. When you realize that, you'll be fantastic! Then you've gained the greatest clue in your search for buried treasure.

> **I am a person of tremendous value for God created me and loves me.**

Clue-in to Hidden Treasures

"We thank God constantly for this, that when you received the word of God, you accepted it not as the word of men, but what it really is, the word of God."

1 Thessalonians 2:13

J. C. Agajanian, the prominent race track promoter with the Indianapolis 500 once showed me a fascinating gold nugget on a chain which he wears. He told me how years ago he agreed to advertise a young kid and his motorcycle stunts. The agreement was for every person the young boy brought in, he'd receive one dollar. After the stunt was completed, J. C. called his treasurer and said, "Make the check out for more than the agreement—the kid was great."

When the young stuntman received his check he demanded to see J. C. He stormed in and said, "This is too much. I know because my friends counted the people coming in. I learned a long time ago not to trust promoters like you."

J. C. corrected the boy, "I didn't make a mistake, you earned it all."

Years later J. C. received the gold nugget with the inscription, "To J. C. Agajanian, your word is as good as gold." On the back side it said, "From Evil Knievel."

God's word is as good as gold too! He says there is a tremendous treasure waiting inside you to be discovered. Believe God's word and discover your potential!

God's word is as good as gold—His riches can not be measured!

Clue-in to Hidden Treasures

"And if you look for it as for silver and search for it as for hidden treasure, then you will understand the fear of the Lord and find the knowledge of God."

Proverbs 2:5

The second step in discovering your potentials is to *seek God's will for your life.* First you believe God's word, then you seek His will.

How can you know God's will for you? You remember that the secret of success is to find a need and fill it. Begin to look for a hurt or a problem. Then when you find a hurt, heal it. When you find a legitimate need, bring to it the most creative solution you can.

Meeting needs is what our ministry is all about. We keep alive by knowing what the modern day hurts are. If you find a need and fill it, you will find God's will.

What needs do you see today? List at least five, whether they are in your family, your community, or your world. How can you begin to fill the needs?

       Needs   My Way to Fill Them

1. _____
2. _____
3. _____
4. _____
5. _____

> **When I see a need—I will fill it, for God has filled my needs!**

Clue-in to Hidden Treasures

"For we are God's workmanship, created in Christ Jesus to do good works, which God prepared in advance for us to do."
Ephesians 2:10

As a church and as a ministry, we are a success. And we are putting this success under God's control. Do you know why we wanted to succeed so badly and have the Crystal Cathedral built? Because we wanted to build a creative enterprise that could generate resources to do the good that nobody else is doing today.

Not long ago, we made a commitment to build a medical relief center in Chiapas, Mexico. Two of our elders went through the jungles to check out the situation. They saw a man with two white horns growing out of his leg. The man, Manuel, had broken his leg, and with no way to fix it, the bones protruded, leaving him emaciated and crippled.

I thank God that we are a success, because that gives us power to help people who are really hurting. Let go, and let God take over your success, and you'll find the hidden treasure of meeting others' needs!

Check back at your list of needs you wrote down yesterday. Have you helped to meet those needs yet? You can—today!

I will let go and let God take over my success!

Clue-in to Hidden Treasures

"For the Lord watches over all the plans and paths of Godly people."

Psalms 1:6

As a prayer in search of God's riches, the next clue is to *follow God's way.* What is God's way? It is the way of faith. If you believe His word and seek His will, an idea will come into your mind. It may appear to be an impossible idea, but if you are trusting God, then you will have to stick your neck out and run the possibility of failure. Remember the old slogan: "Even a turtle doesn't get ahead unless he sticks his neck out."

Maybe the impossible idea God has given you concerns the needs you wrote down before. Maybe the idea is a dream of a certain gift or ability you've been waiting to exercise in your life. What is it? If it seems impossible, it's from God. He always gives you an idea so big that He can be a part of it.

Will you follow God's way? What is the idea He's giving you? _____

_____

_____

> **If the road I'm on seems impossible to follow—then I know God's guiding me down his path!**

Clue-in to Hidden Treasures

"No eye has seen, nor ear heard, nor the heart of anyone conceived, what God has prepared for those who love Him."
1 Corinthians 2:9

This treasure hunt is getting more exciting every day. God is directing you. He is pouring out ideas and clues into your mind. As you get closer to God through His word, you desire more to be in His will. As you seek for His will, you will be led in His way.

God has shown you some needs in the lives of those around you. He has also sent you some creative ideas to meet these needs. Are these ideas "impossible"? Great! They're from God.

To truly follow His way, you need to make plans. Set goals. Draw a map to follow and see these dreams materialize.

Today spend time to allow God to direct the possible ways your potential will develop, your idea bloom, and those needs be met. Start with five ways, even if they seem impossible too.

1. _____
2. _____
3. _____
4. _____
5. _____

**God is putting His plan in effect—I know,
because it seems "impossible"!**

Clue-in to Hidden Treasures

"In everything you do, put God first, and He will direct you and crown your efforts with success!"

Proverbs 3:6

When you believe in God's word, seek God's will and follow God's way, you will behold *God's wonder.* If you attempt the impossible for Him, your life will turn out to be an amazing accomplishment. There will be times when you'll want to quit, but that's when God's wonder is shown!

Remember the story of Jesus and the fishermen? Peter and the others had fished all night without catching anything. For Peter, that incomparable fisherman, to catch nothing is like Beverly Sills not hitting a high note. It's like Norman Vincent Peale, that great positive thinker to say, "It won't work!" But even the superstars strike out once in a while.

Jesus turned to Peter and said, "Go into deeper water and cast your net down on the other side." Though he'd toiled all night and caught nothing, Peter did as he was told. Suddenly he felt the glorious weight of the fish in his net. There were so many that the net began to tear as he struggled to lift it into the boat.

When you've toiled all night and caught nothing, what do you do?

Don't cash in, cast into deeper water! God has something special in store for you—a sunken treasure! God will fill your empty net. Jesus Christ will fill your empty life with joy. You will behold God's wonder!

> **I will cast into deeper waters and accept the burden of success—I will behold God's wonder!**

Search for Hidden Treasures

"Teach me your way, O Lord, and I will walk in your truth."
Psalms 86:11

I've found that God hides His treasures in three places. First of all, *God conceals His treasures in our thoughts.* When you begin to search out the treasures God has hidden within you, you will first begin to find them in your thinking.

Just recently I read about an English author named Williams who was plagued by an idea. This idea came to him while he was eating breakfast: What if he were to write a story about a golden rabbit who carried messages between the moon and the sun? And what if in the story he placed clues about a buried treasure? But he said to the idea, "Go away and please don't come back!" But at dinner time the idea came back and brought with it a score of other ideas, so finally he decided to give the idea a try.

Williams wrote a book and included several paintings of this rabbit. He built his story around clues as to where to find hidden treasure. Then he made a rabbit of solid gold, adorned it with rubies and pearls and, in the light of the full moon, he buried it in the English countryside. The golden rabbit has an estimated value of about $30,000. By following the riddles and clues in Williams' story, someone will one day discover the golden rabbit.

And you know what? Today that book is on the bestseller list in England.

What's your idea? Say "yes" to it today.

Yes, Lord.

Search for Hidden Treasures

"If any of you lacks wisdom, ask God, who gives to all generously and without reproaching, and it will be given."
James 1:5

Dr. Paul Harrison, a missionary for our church in Saudi Arabia used to tell of one tremendous problem the Arabs, who lived in bleak, sandy deserts, constantly had to deal with. It was that of keeping their sheep alive. It seemed that the sheep were constantly being poisoned by a black substance which oozed from the ground and swirled through the animal's watering holes. At that time, the Arabs didn't know that the black substance was of far greater value to them than their flocks of sheep. Unknowingly they had discovered oil.

God may have treasures at our fingertips now. But sometimes we suffer from locked-in thinking. We see only our side of the situation and from our perspective of time. We need to break loose and allow God to flow His creative ideas into our minds so we see what He has for us.

Prayer can be the spiritual exercise you need to draw closer to God so that you are attuned to his thoughts. Learn to pray expectantly:

Thank you, Lord, for the exciting ideas you are waiting to send into my mind! I'd explode with enthusiasm if I could think of all the positive thoughts waiting to come out of my God-inspired brain. Amen.

God's ideas are falling greatly into my mind today as I keep in constant prayer.

Search for Hidden Treasures

"Look among the nations and see; wonder and be astounded.
For I am doing a work in your days that you would not believe
if told."

Habakkuk 1:5

I remember riding through a very tough section of Detroit, Michigan. There were many houses boarded up along the streets. Nearly all had cracked windows and a pervading sense of decay. And many were occupied.

Then I saw something that shocked me. In the middle of one desolate block stood one house that lacked the look of decay prevalent in all the others. It stood out because it was in perfect condition—no boards on the windows, no cracked panes of glass, no weeds growing in the front lawn. I was especially touched to see little planter boxes at each side of the doorway in which were growing lovely fresh flowers. On the porch of this little cottage sat the lady of the house—a rather portly, attractive, black woman. As I recall, she looked not only very pretty, but very happy. She had discovered the possibilities in her situation. In the midst of an ugly neighborhood, she made her home pretty. She sat in her chair like a queen. "It is the glory of God to conceal a thing. And it is the glory of kings to reveal it."

God conceals treasures in every situation. Search for them. Seek them out.

What situation seems a mess in your life today?

> **Nothing will happen to me that doesn't hold**
> **God's riches within it!**

Search for Hidden Treasures

"For still the vision awaits its time; it hastens to the end—it will not lie. If it seems slow, wait for it, it will surely come, it will not delay."

Habakkuk 2:3

The second place God hides his treasures is in under the layers of time. "Inch by Inch, Anything's a Cinch!" In time the Grand Canyon has progressed from a tiny stream bed into a place of majestic beauty. In time a tiny acorn becomes a mighty oak, one of nature's works of art.

God conceals his treasures in time. When Bach was writing his music, critics of his own day put him down as a horrible musician. But today his music is adored by millions—and no one can even remember the names of the critics! When Picasso first began to paint in the style cubism, critics thought him mad. Today you could retire on the income from an original Picasso, so highly is his work now valued.

I believe that our Crystal Cathedral's true value is also hidden in time. I don't believe there's a single human being alive today who can begin to guess what God will do for hurting people around the world through the Crystal Cathedral.

Where do you look for hidden treasures? Look in time. Look now at what you are doing today. Someday the treasure will be revealed!

Don't cut tomorrow out of your calendar? Believe in God's time.

> **I believe in God's timing—He holds the master calendar!**

Search for Hidden Treasures

"Count it all joy, my friends, when you meet various trials, for you know that the testing of your faith produces steadfastness."

James 1:2,3

You really have to dare to live and move ahead by faith if you expect to uncover God's hidden rewards. There will be days when you constantly turn up empty handed. Believe in time, never believe in never!

You know the story of my daughter Carol and how she was almost killed in a motorcycle accident. The last picture we have of her with both legs is one taken when she was in her softball uniform.

She said to me a while back, "Dad, I'm going to sign up for softball again this year." "That's great!" I responded, not wanting to discourage her. Carol has an artificial leg which begins just below the knee. However her knee still bends only at a 30° angle so she walks very stiffly. As of yet, she is unable to run.

So I took her to the local school where all the parents were lining up with their girls to sign up for the girls softball team. Carol signed up and then went to check out her uniform. When we returned to the car I asked, "Carol, tell me something. How do you expect to play softball if you can't run?" She looked at me directly and replied, "I've got that figured out, Dad. When you hit home runs, you don't have to run! So I've made my mind up to be the home run king."

Treasures are hidden in time. But it takes work to find them. Don't quit, rather get the grit—God's determination.

God's delays are not God's denials!

Search for Hidden Treasures

"I can do all things through Christ who strengthens me."
Philippians 4:13

God's treasures are concealed in thoughts and in time. *The third place God hides his treasures is in trouble.* I'm convinced that in every troubled experience there are precious treasures waiting for those who keep trusting God.

One of the most beautiful members of this church was Jeanne Van Allen. She has since gone to be with her Lord, but I remember how she found rare treasures in her troubles.

About ten years ago her husband, Ed, a great pilot, volunteered to fly a new plane to a mission outpost in New Guinea. Ed left out of Long Beach and was to refuel in Hawaii. But somewhere between the mainland and the island, Ed sent a distress signal. His plane never reached Honolulu and he was never heard from again.

When the time came for Jeanne to declare Ed legally dead, she said to me, "I have faith in the sovereignty of God. I know that somehow God has a plan and a purpose through all this. So," she continued, "instead of lying down and quitting, I'm gonna prove to the memory of my husband what a success I can be. I'm gonna have the courage to do all the things I always wanted to do! And you know what, Dr. Schuller," she exclaimed. "The gonna's keep me going!"

I challenge you to find some "gonna's." God will furnish the supply of ideas. It's your glory to pursue them!

I'm gonna keep on keeping on!

Search for Hidden Treasures

"Let us know, let us press on to know the Lord; his going forth is sure as the dawn; he will come to us as the showers, as the spring rains that water the earth."

Hosea 6:3

I remember one morning when I took a motor boat ride across the Sea of Galilee. Suddenly, in the middle of the lake the operator of the boat cut the motor and I wondered for a moment if we were out of gas. When I inquired, he said, "No. I thought it would be nice, Dr. Schuller, if you could just listen to the quietness out here."

There must come a time in each of our lives when we cut the motor, stop the boat and just pause to be still and recognize the mighty presence of God.

Take time to feel the stillness, hear the silence and search your soul. Ask yourself, "What do I really want in life? If I get it, will I be satisifed? If I keep living my life the way I have been, will I ever reach that goal?" In a beautifully powerful verse from the Bible, God says, "Be still and know that I am God." That's something we all need to do.

There is a beautiful treasure inside of you, it is this idea: Through your thoughts, through your time, and through your trouble, your life can be a walking inspiration as you worship God. You can make the world a more beautiful place because you are His and He is yours.

> **I hear God's still small voice as I come into His presence.**

Beauty—Your Hidden Treasure

"He reflects the glory of God and bears the very stamp of his nature, upholding the universe by his word of power."
                                                    Hebrews 1:3

As you search for God's treasures, you'll discover the rarest, most valuable gem. It can't be priced—it's worth more than gold or silver. It's the sparkling, twinkling, reflective quality— called BEAUTY.

Beauty is the hidden treasure waiting to shine from your life! Beauty is the rarest, richest gem that anyone can hold! You have it—God has given it! Beauty brings out your dignity. Beauty uplifts, inspires, directs and guides. It keeps developing your inner possibilities so that you can become the whole person God wants you to be. Jesus is that kind of beauty. *Discover Jesus and Discover Beauty!*

"One thing have I desired of the Lord; that will I seek after: that I might *behold the beauty of the Lord."* Beauty is your open door to mental and emotional health. When a person beholds the beauty of the Lord, he becomes a fully integrated, emotionally healthy human being. To behold the beauty of the Lord is more than appreciating flowers, trees, green grass and sunshine. To behold the beauty of the Lord is to Be-Hold the beauty of the Lord and to Be-Come and reflect (or hold) the beauty of the Lord in your heart and life. A beautiful person is someone who can be an inspiration to someone. You can be a beautiful person.

I have discovered Christ—I have discovered beauty!

Beauty—Your Hidden Treasure

"Create in me a clean heart, O God, filled with clean thoughts and right desires."

Psalms 51:10

Have you discovered your hidden treasures, or do you still feel like a diamond in the rough? Then let me show you how the secrets of beauty can polish, shape and facet you with six bright qualities which will reflect the beauty of God in your daily life. I have wonderful news for you: *"Anybody can be a beautiful person."*

One of my favorite Bible verses comes from Psalm 27. The Psalmist expresses his deepest desire, *"One thing have I desired of the Lord; that will I seek after: That I might behold the beauty of the Lord."* The Psalmist is verbalizing what we now know to be a profound psychological need: The need for beauty. Beauty isn't a luxury; it isn't the cherry on the sundae. Beauty is a fundamental necessity for emotional health. Why? Because the person who is sensitive, responsive and appreciative of beauty just naturally becomes joyful and enthusiastic about the world from which such beauty springs. Hence he or she achieves an internal peace and security that attracts people.

Beauty can become your open door. Through that open door, enthusiasm, love and light will march into your life. *Beauty is no luxury; it's a necessity.*

> **Lord, I need to be the beautiful person you intended me to be!**

Beauty—Your Hidden Treasure

"Let no one despise your youth, but set the believers an example in speech and conduct, in love, in faith, in purity."
1 Timothy 4:12

I want to summarize these ideas in a way you will remember them. In the word, BEAUTY, *B stands for boost.* Jesus does that for us—He gives us the boost, the encouragement in life we need. *Beauty is giving people a boost.*

A beautiful person is a Boosting person.

Leslie Hale, my friend in Belfast, Ireland, told me the story of a man who came to him after a large public meeting. The man pushed through the crowd to reach Leslie, then handed him a letter.

When Leslie opened the letter, he recognized the letterhead of the mental hospital. It read: "To whom it may concern: This is to certify that (the name of the man who delivered the letter) has been a patient at the mental hospital in Belfast, North Ireland. It is the judgment of those in authority here that he is now considered sane and sensible."

"That proves I'm sane, doesn't it?" the man demanded. "That's right," Leslie agreed. "They should know. They're experts." "They're experts. They should know," the man repeated, smiling.

That was the only boost he needed. He returned the letter and envelope to his pocket. "I watched him go out of the door and climb on his bicycle," Leslie said. "Just before he pedaled away, he turned, smiled and said, 'Hey, let me see your letter.'"

Do you have a letter? I don't. That's why every human being needs a boost now and then.

It's beautiful to boost!

Beauty—Your Hidden Treasure

"If I speak in the tongues of men and of angels, but have not love, I am a noisy gong or a clanging cymbal."
1 Corinthians 13:1

E—Beautiful people are *Enlightening* people. They enlighten others to the beautiful possibilities within themselves. We live in a world so saturated with negative thinking that every person—even the super successful—struggles with self-confidence and needs that extra boost now and then.

Beauty enlightens us so we can clearly see the beautiful possibilities that lie within. Beauty helps others develop a keen perception of the world around them and helps them appreciate that world.

An enlightening person helps us become sensitive to the wonders around us. He helps us appreciate our own potential and encourages us to become all that we can be. He enables us to worship God in the beauty of holiness by helping us to become whole and complete ourselves.

What person in particular comes to mind when you think of someone who has enlightened your life? _____

_____

Now who can you think of that you can be that same kind of beautiful person to today, or this week? _____

_____

I am enlightened with Christ's love to see the needs of those around me!

Beauty—Your Hidden Treasure

"Blessed are the pure in heart, for they shall see God."
                                                    Matthew 5:8

A—Be an *Amusing person.* Beautiful people can make you laugh. What makes Pope John Paul II so attractive? Part of his beauty is his sense of humor. Good clean comedians are ministers of God. I remember my boss from the only other job I ever had as a young man in Chicago, Illinois. His name was Bill Bruin. Bill had had cancer of the throat which necessitated the removal of his larynx. The only way he was able to communicate was with the aid of a little instrument, three inches long, which looked like a flashlight. He would put the instrument up to his throat, and when he talked, his voice sounded like that of a robot.

But Bill turned his problem into an opportunity through possibility thinking. He developed a marvelous comedy routine. Every time there was a party, Bill became the center of attention. Just as the gathering would get kind of loud, he would make a siren-like sound. Everybody would drop what they were doing and look around for the cops and Bill would have a laugh. He was a beautiful person—the comedian without a voice box.

You are an amusing person when you let your beauty shine through. Be beautiful to someone today. Let someone laugh! Let someone love! Let someone learn that God heals through humor. He really does!

I love to laugh because I love!

Beauty—Your Hidden Treasure

"Let kindly love continue. Do not neglect to show hospitality to strangers, for thereby some have entertained angels unawares."

Hebrews 13:1, 2

U—A beautiful person is an *Uplifting* person. With all the problems, obstacles and tensions people face in today's world, everybody needs an uplift every day. When you inspire someone else, you feel like a beautiful person. That feeling is the key that opens the door to internal self-esteem, enthusiasm and joy.

Jesus was this type of uplift. He put strong wings on weary hearts. He inspires and encourages us to keep striving to be the best we can be and to take advantage of the greatness within ourselves. Jesus always uplifts so that we can see above our own needs and problems to those around us.

How has Jesus been your uplift? _____

_____

How can you uplift those around you? _____

_____

Thank you, Jesus, for your uplift!

Beauty—Your Hidden Treasure

"And I pray that the sharing of your faith may promote the knowledge of all the good that is ours in Christ."

Philemon 1:6

T—Be a *Teaching* person. Take the time to listen to people who need advice and comfort. Everybody needs a counselor at some time in their lives. I know a minister who decided to become a bartender. After years away at college and seminary, he went to school to learn how to mix drinks. He decided that most people who have problems don't talk to ministers, psychiatrists or professional counselors. He discovered that many of the people with hurts often try to escape through alcohol at the neighborhood bar. He decided he'd have to get close to them, so for three years he worked as a bartender. He became a beautiful influence upon the lives of many people. He uplifted, guided and taught the people who came to him for advice. And he led many to Christ and the Church.

Today I will try to teach _____ about the love of Jesus Christ!

Give me patience, Lord, to teach another.

Beauty—Your Hidden Treasure

"Blessed are the peacemakers, for they shall be called children of God."

Matthew 5:9

The last letter in the word beauty is Y—Be a *Yielding* person. If I list some opposite terms, you'll understand the beauty that comes with yielding. An unattractive individual is stubborn, locked into narrow-minded thinking, concretized, inflexible, non-negotiable; everything is black or white. Compromise is an unfamiliar term.

A yielding person knows how to bend when life seems to crumble. He can pick himself up and continue living without being wrapped in bitterness and self-pity. A yielding person is big enough to say, "I'm sorry. I was wrong, please forgive me."

You are a beautiful person, because you are a yielding person! Where can you exercise this ability in your life today? Write it down and pray God will let you be an inspiration to others as you do it! _____

_____

_____

_____

_____

> **As I yield to God's love—I feel beautiful!**

Beauty—Your Hidden Treasure

"For there is one God, and there is one mediator between God and his children, the man Christ Jesus, who gave himself a ransom for all . . ."

1 Timothy 2:5

Recently someone sent me an article from the Chicago *Tribune.*

The headline reads, "Bear Quarterback Finds Religion—Evans' Life Changes Off the Field Too." The story told of how Vince Evans, quarterback for the Chicago Bears, had suddenly developed a tremendous sense of self-confidence and showed remarkable potential. In the last few weeks, he had thrown more than his share of touchdown passes. According to Evans, something happened last Easter that made him more confident. "I was watching Reverend Robert Schuller of Garden Grove, California, on television," said Evans. "He was talking about the resurrection. It was cloudy at that particular time. Just as he said 'Jesus had risen,' the sun came out. I knew Jesus Christ had come into my life and I overflowed with tears. I was always religiously inclined, but I never had a personal relationship with God until then." The rest of the story told how Vince Evans now lets his faith make a difference in his attitude toward daily life—for him that's playing football.

When you open up to a beautiful idea—your attitude will change! Jesus Christ is my idea of a beautiful idea. If you will open up your life to Jesus, you will become a more beautiful person.

> **I will open up to beauty. I will open up to change. I will open up to Jesus!**

Beauty—Your Hidden Treasure

*"As for me, God forbid that I should boast about anything ex-
cept the cross of our Lord Jesus Christ."*

Galatians 6:14

Some of you may have missed discovering the most wonderful treasure of all—a personal relationship with Jesus
Christ.

I was sharing this fact with a man on the plane and he
kept confusing Jesus with the Bible. He said, "I try to be a
good Christian and read my Bible, but I always land up for-
getting to do it."

I explained to him that being a Christian is not just someone who goes to church every Sunday and prays and reads
the Bible every day. I said, "I'm now going to say something
that may sound heretical, but it's true. The truth is, the Bible
is unimportant. *Jesus Christ is the important issue.* You're
saved by the blood, not by the book. The entire purpose of
the Bible is to point us to Jesus Christ.

"Does your wife wear a diamond ring?" I asked. "Yes,"
he replied, "a very big diamond." "What does the rest of the
ring look like?" I queried. "It's a simple gold band," he answered. "Jesus is the diamond in Christianity," I explained.
"The Bible is the gold band whose sole purpose is to hold
forth the diamond in all its sparkling brilliance. You say you
can't understand the Old Testament. Then read the Gospels
over and over again."

Jesus Christ is the greatest gem of all. His blood is priceless. His love is endless, and his beauty is glorious! Discover
the words of Jesus—He's the most beautiful idea ever conceived.

**Thank you, Jesus—You are my living
treasure!**

The Tassel Is Worth the Hassle

Be a Star!

"Except you become as a little child, you shall not enter the Kingdom of God."

Matthew 18:3

Jiminy Cricket said to Pinocchio: "When you wish upon a star, makes no difference who you are!" Wouldn't it be wonderful if we could always keep those child-like qualities? It's so easy for a child to expect the whole world to be beautiful.

When I was a young boy I spent my childhood days in the open country, in the northwestern farm regions of Iowa. I remember looking forward to the evening so I could gaze into the heavens and spot the first bright star that would appear in the vast sky. This past week a good friend of mine shared a similar experience. Born in Louisiana, he used to watch for the first star at night, make a wish on it and then turn a cartwheel. "If you made a wish and turned a perfect cartwheel," he said, "the wish was bound to come true!"

The danger is that as we mature, we become cynical and lose our capacity to wish upon a star and to dream our dreams. We become so interested in facts, that we lose the romance and the mystery of life.

God has given you the capacity to be a child with the ability to wish and to wonder.

I'm always meeting people who have a vibrant faith—they are childlike. Jesus said: "Except you become as a little child, you shall not enter the Kingdom of God." (Matthew 18:3) When I meet someone who has experienced Jesus Christ, I have met a person who is childlike! And God wants us to wish upon a Star—He made us with that potential!

> **Like a little child—I believe in the star of hope in Jesus Christ!**

Be a Star!

"It is God at work in you giving you the will and the power to achieve his purpose!"

Philippians 2:13

Why don't we dream more dreams? Why do we put down that childish act? *Because we're afraid to fail!* We develop a reputation and that makes the fear of failure a terrible thing. In order to get over this fear, you need to learn the simple lesson that changed my life. It was this sentence, *"I'd rather attempt to do something great and fail than attempt to do nothing and succeed!"*

When you realize that failure really is an unacceptable and totally selfish concept, then you can go back to a child-like faith. You'll dare to dream. You'll dream impossible dreams, because when God gives you a dream it's always an impossible dream.

When you were a child you dared to dream because you were secure. Your mother and father encouraged and supported you. But now when you are standing on your own, where do you go for support?

I believe that prayer gives that support. You become a child again when you get on your knees and learn to pray the way a child does. When you do, God will guide you. He will support you. He will give you his seemingly impossible dream. With it He will take away your fear so you will dare to wish upon a Star!

> **I am not afraid to dream: with God by my side I can not fail!**

Be a Star!

"Let your light so shine before men, that they may see your good works and give glory to your Father who is in heaven."
Matthew 5:16

As human beings there is one thing that makes us distinct from other creatures. *We can wish upon a star—and we can wish to be Stars!*

We can dream our dreams, and those include being stars! In that way we are truly worshiping God. Real worship is when you take God's dream that he wants to give you, and become the person he wants you to be. You can be a Shining Star!

What would the nights be without the stars? What would the human race do, with all of its problems and predicaments, if there were no stars among the human family? *The stars in the human family are the people who shine like bright lights in the dark nights offering cheer, comfort and hope.*

Anyone can be a star—a star child, a star mother, a star father, a star manager, or a star employee! Whatever you are, you can be a star!

How can you be a star to those around you today? Write down specific ways to shine where you are.

_____

_____

_____

Thank you, Lord, for making me star quality!

Be a Star!

"Now as you excel in everything—in faith, in utterance, knowledge, in all earnestness, and in your love for us—see that you excel in this gracious work also."

2 Corinthians 8:7

As we mature and lose our childlike faith in God's plans, we need to retrain ourselves. Believe as a child, wish upon a star; decide to dream God's dream. In order to do so, start at the beginning.

First, *decide you want to be a star.* You may be saying, "But I am satisfied with the way I am." I recently had lunch with a man who is very well known. In the course of our conversation he uttered a statement that I think is very revealing. "Dr. Schuller," he said, "a big problem in our country today is that there is such a mediocrity of affection." He's correct in his diagnosis. Mediocre people lack joy in caring and affection. *A star is someone who excels.*

Mediocrity in affection—that's why God makes such a difference. If He really comes into our lives, we care about people. You really want to be a star. You really are not satisfied with mediocrity. At the deepest level people are really happy when they excel at something.

If you could "star" in anything, what would it be?

I want to be a star! I believe!

Be a Star!

"For we aim at what is honorable not only in the Lord's sight but also in the sight of all."

2 Corinthians 8:21

A star is somebody who lifts somebody else's life! And that gives you terrific joy! You want to be a star. *A star is somebody who excels in something.* There are few fulfillments or emotional satisfactions that surpass the sense that in some way I am not mediocre or average or poor; I excel!

My mother excelled in baking apple pies. She loved it and as a result it fed her self-esteem. You might say baking apple pies was my mother's ego trip, but it was a sanctified ego trip because she was always giving the pies away to the sick and needy.

The other day my wife and I went out for breakfast to a little place we'd never been to before. We wanted to be alone so we could talk. The table was outside and it was a pleasant morning. The waitress came up to our table bounding with enthusiasm. "It's a beautiful morning, isn't it?" she exclaimed before she even gave us the menu. I hadn't taken time to notice. "Yes, it's a lovely morning," I said. "Look how the sun is filtering through those trees," she added. "Yes, it's beautiful," I replied. "You're going to have a great breakfast," she enthused, before we even placed our order. I was sold! I want to go back there because she excelled as a waitress.

You can be a star too! When you excel in something you have a tremendous personal fulfillment. That feeling is the very blessing of God. He designed you to be a star. Somehow, someway, someplace, you want to be a star!

Yes—I want to excel!

Be a Star!

"Therefore be imitators of God as beloved children."
Ephesians 5:1

Second, you need to be a *star!* I'll tell you why you need to be a star. Deeper than the want is the need because your deepest need is the need to be needed. It's true!

A very depressed man came to me and said, "Schuller. I don't make any difference. I'm not important." "Yes, you are!" I exclaimed. "You are important to somebody!" But he said, "No, I'm not. Take a bucket of water, put your finger in it then pull it out. How big a hole is left? That's me. I'm nothing. I'm nobody. I don't make any difference."

What a depressing view of life. My answer to him was, "In a world with so many people lonely, confused, hurting and feeling rejected and insecure, there is no excuse for anybody not feeling needed. Somebody needs you! And if you haven't found out who needs you, it means you have been playing it safe. You don't want to get involved. You don't want to make commitments. You don't want to sign any papers. You don't want to put a ring on your finger. You want your freedom so you don't get involved.

"If you choose to make no commitments, then don't feel sorry for yourself if you feel nobody needs you. Don't be surprised if you don't feel important. Put your finger in the bucket, and pull it out—nobody will miss you. But you will be the loser because you need to feel important!"

You need to be a star because it's God's plan for your life. If you become a star, you pay a price for it. It demands involvement. It requires commitment. It involves caring.

I need to be a star—I need to be needed!

Be a Star!

"What does the Lord require of you? But to do justly, love mercifully, and walk humbly with your God."

Micah 6:8

You want to be a star, you need to be a star, and *you can be a star!* It's so simple. It's a matter of deciding.

I have a life to live. I want it to amount to something. I want to excel in love and caring and affection. So how do you get that way? It doesn't come naturally, my friend. I'm very selfish. So are you, by nature. We are all inclined to be greedy. By nature, I don't want to give things away. I want to keep them. By nature, I want to have all I can. I think of myself first and everybody else last. That's human nature. But you know it's possible for human nature to be changed into divine nature. That's why some people speak of being born again. It's what happens when you really accept Jesus Christ into your life.

Anyone can be a star! You start when you let Jesus Christ come into your life. Say, "Jesus, here is my mind, think through it. Jesus, here are my eyes, twinkle through them. Jesus, here is my face, smile through it. Jesus, here are my hands, lift somebody who has a load through them." And that's super living! Be a star, start wherever you are!

Jesus Christ, come into my life, and make me a star to shine Your love!

Price the Prize

"But you are a chosen race, a royal priesthood, a holy nation, God's own people, that you may declare the wonderful deeds of him who called you out of darkness into his marvelous light."
                                                                1 Peter 2:9

We have just celebrated the 25th anniversary of this ministry. When we started 25 years ago, we did so without money, membership or property. We had nothing but a beautiful exciting dream. During these years, I've claimed the promise of God in Proverbs 16:3. "Commit your work to the Lord and it will succeed."

God wants you and me to succeed and be stars for one simple reason: In a world where so many people are hungry, hurting and in need of help, we have to be a part of the solution, not part of the problem. That's why we make no apologies for success. The alternative to success is failure. And by failing, we become a burden to someone else. But life's joy comes to you when you can put strong wings on someone's weary heart.

Let me share with you what I believe is God's formula for our success. As I look back over this ministry, I can say it really works:

ROLE + GOAL + TOLL = SUCCESS

Your role as a star is to shine out to those around you and offer to the emotionally starved person the answer to life in Jesus Christ!

There is one reason more than any other why people fail. They set their goals before they define their roles. We have defined our roles. Now make some goals!

> **When so many people are hurting and hungry
> and afraid, I need to be a star of hope!**

Price the Prize

"Every one to whom God has given wealth and possessions and power to enjoy them, and to accept the lot and find enjoyment in the toil—this is the gift of God."

Ecclesiastes 5:19

Three fundamental principles will help you to set your goals. The first is this: *God has a special prize for every person.* Second, *there is a price for every prize.* And third, *the bigger the prize, the greater the price.*

God has a special prize of infinite value especially for you. As a star, an achiever—there will be a great gain. If you could imagine all life's greatest prizes, honors, gifts or values that could be awarded to you, what would be the greatest of them all? Some would say, "The greatest prize of them all is power." Others would say, "No, not power. The greatest prize is pleasure."

Some with a more Christ-influenced value system might say, "The greatest prize isn't power, pleasure, or promotion. The greatest prize is peace of mind." That is indeed a wonderful feeling.

But I submit that the greatest prize any person can possess is the knowledge and awareness that, teamed up with God in the one life that you have to live, you can do something beautiful for Him.

Only one life—t'will soon be past.
Only what's done for Christ will last.

It's a good feeling to know that your life makes a difference.

Only what's done for Christ will last!

Price the Prize

"Let those who boast boast in the Lord. For it is not the one who commends himself who is approved, but the one whom the Lord commends."

2 Corinthians 10:17,18

No matter who you are, you have a choice as to whether or not you will accept this prize. Will you be a star? Will you be an inspiration to others?

There are basically four kinds of people. First, there are the *cop-outs*. These people set no goals and make no decisions.

Second, there are the *hold-outs*. They have a beautiful dream, but they're afraid to respond to its challenge because they aren't sure they can make it. These people have lost all childlike faith.

Then third, there are the *drop-outs*. They start to make their dream come true. They know their role. They set their goals, but when the going gets tough, they quit. They don't pay the toll.

Finally, there are the ALL-OUTS. They are the people who know their role. They want and need and are going to be stars; Star-students, Star-parents; Star-waitresses. They want to shine out as an inspiration to others. And they set their goals. They ask, "How can I live the one life I have and make it something beautiful for God?" Their goals are God-inspired, a team effort. And the *all-outs* never quit. They keep on keeping on, even when the toll gets heavy. They're dedicated. They're committed.

You can be an *all-out*. It's your choice. Make the commitment to excellence!

> **I'm giving my all-out to the dream God has given me!**

Price the Prize

"For God is not so unjust as to overlook your work and the love which you showed for his sake in serving the saints."
                                                        Hebrews 6:10

When you make a commitment to excel, there will always be a cost. No honor comes cheaply. No reward comes easily. TO EVERY PRIZE IDEA, THERE IS A PRICE TAG.

Maybe you have Christian friends who seem to have incredible powers of faith. They've gone through the personal tragedy of losing a child or mate, and yet they can smile through their tears. Their faces virtually glow. And as you note their calm, peaceful assurance, you say to yourself, "If only I had that kind of faith . . . ." Don't you think they paid a price for that faith?

Everything has its price. You can excel in your dream. You can graduate from your class with honors. You can raise a loving family. You can help those around you. But to do so you need to make the commitment.

How is your relationship with your Lord? Have you made the commitment? Are you living it *all-out?*

Take these moments now to let God speak to you. Reevaluate your commitment to Him. Are you living the role of a dedicated believer? Have you set the goals of faith in action? Will you pay the toll for the power of faith?

> **I will pay the toll—to fulfill my role—I am a servant of God!**

Price the Prize

"For you know the grace of our Lord Jesus Christ, that though he was rich, yet for your sake he became poor, so that by his poverty you might become rich."

2 Corinthians 8:9

Jim Poppen was not exactly an exemplary student. There were people who questioned his intellectual capacity. But Jim was committed!

One Christmas, Jim's father awoke suddenly when he heard a noise in the night. Mr. Poppen stole downstairs and tiptoed into the dark kitchen. There he found Jim tying knots around chair legs as fast as he could. Sure that his son had flipped, Mr. Poppen exclaimed, "Jim, what in the world are you doing?!" "It's okay, Dad." Jim explained. "I've decided I'm going to be a brain surgeon. I've got to teach my fingers to tie knots very fast and accurately where I cannot see anything—just like the surgeon operating on a human skull."

His father laughed that night, but Jim did become a brain surgeon—one of the best in the world.

Once when sought by a close friend, Dr. Poppen was finally tracked down in a remote village 12,000 feet high in the Andes, in Bogota, Colombia. Jim's reason was simple for being there. "They can't afford the high costs of medical care in Boston, so I decided to come here and take care of them."

When Jim Poppen died, people of all colors and class jammed the memorial service to pay tribute to a man who proved that, by giving life all you've got, you can leave a mark behind and do something beautiful.

> **The prize God has for me is unbelievable—it is salvation!**

Price the Prize

"For godly grief produces a repentance that leads to salvation and brings no regret."

2 Corinthians 7:10

First of all there is a prize for every person. Second, there is a price for every prize. *And third,* THE BIGGER THE PRIZE, THE GREATER THE PRICE. The biggest prize ever offered by God to any person was the honor of being called the Savior of men. That honor God bestowed on Jesus Christ. Jesus paid for that privilege with his life—He suffered an agonizing death on the cross. But because of His sacrifice, we have available to us a prize of infinite value and immeasurable worth. What is the greatest prize that you can receive? Salvation!

Is there a price for this wonderful prize? You bet. The price you pay is the total commitment to Christ. No copping out. No holding out. But only all-out!

I invite you to pay the price; accept the glorious prize of God's salvation and eternal love. The prize is infinitely worth the price. One of the best rewards of salvation is the awareness of God's unconditional, undying, imperishable love.

Yesterday my daughter Gretchen and I were out in the garden. Gretchen plucked a flower and said, "Daddy, this flower is for God." As she pulled the first petal, she said, "He loves me." Then she pulled the next: "He loves me." And the next. "He loves me." Until she had but one petal left and smiling brightly, she finished the rhyme: "He loves me."

He loves me.

Price the Prize

"And Jesus said, 'No one who puts his hand to the plow and looks back is fit for the kingdom of God.' "

Luke 9:62

The Crystal Cathedral's Minister of Missions is Paul Hostetter. For some years he lived in the nearly inaccessible jungles at the border of Guatemala and Mexico. One day he flew in to see me.

"Paul," I asked. "What can I do for you?" "What we really need," he explained, "is a medical relief center up in our territory. We serve 40,000 Indians in the area who don't speak Spanish. When Spanish doctors do manage to see them, they can't communicate their needs.

"Just a few weeks ago," he continued, "a young 17-year-old mother gave birth to her child in a small, remote mud shack. She was bleeding uncontrollably, and so her husband carried her to me. The trip took hours by foot path. When she arrived, she was dead."

"What would it cost, Paul?" I asked. "About $1 million," he answered. Before I could think of what to say, I assured him, "We'll assume the leadership role for raising the money to build the medical relief center. Paul, we'll help you. I don't know how, but I know we can do it somehow, some way."

Every prize has its price. The medical relief center in Chiapas, Mexico is a costly project, but we've made the commitment. The bigger the prize—the bigger the price.

Yes God—I will pay the price!

Handle the Hassles

"Better is the end of a thing than its beginning; and the patient in spirit is better than the proud in spirit."

Ecclesiastes 6:8

My son, who got his master's of divinity at Fuller Theological Seminary, graduated from my Alma Mater, Hope College in Holland, Michigan, seven years ago. The moment he received his B.A. degree was one of the proudest moments of my life.

After the ceremony, we met outside. Beaming with delight, we hugged each other and slapped one another on the back. "You made it!" I exclaimed. "Yes," he said, grinning broadly. "I made it. But it was tough." "It was worth it, but at times I wondered. It was quite a hassle." As he spoke those words, my eyes were drawn to the tassel flowing from his cap. Touching it lightly, I said, *"The tassel is worth the hassle."* "You bet!" my son affirmed enthusiastically.

If you make your decisions based upon how comfortable, easy, convenient or painless your choices are, then don't ever expect great rewards. Hassle-free living is tassel-free living. Anytime anybody is marketing anything with integrity, you can be sure that the tassel is in proportion to the hassle. *Pay a big price and you can expect a good return!*

Take these moments to pray expectantly for the plan God has for your life. With his help, you can handle the hassles.

I will handle the hassles and hope for the harvest.

Handle the Hassles

"Therefore, my beloved friends, be steadfast, immovable, always abounding in the work of the Lord, knowing that in the Lord your labor is not in vain."

1 Corinthians 15:58

As human beings, we need the hassles of life. We need the struggles and problems of everyday living to make us strong and capable. We need to pay the price to appreciate the prize.

Hassle-free living is tassel-free living. We need the tensions that hassles produce because tensions loose their own pensions. Many of you may be saying to yourself, "Who wants difficulty, trouble, problems, or hassles? If God is so good, why can't he give us our heart's desires without the hassles?"

I want to share with you three ideas that may change your attitude about hassles. I'll bring you through the process that literally saved me from emotional and spiritual death when I faced my hassles.

But right now, reflect on your dream. God has given you one. He wants you to be a star. You've made the commitment to pay the price. But now the hassles have come, or will be coming soon. What are the hassles you face today?

_____

_____

_____

_____

> **My hassles will be my handles to hold on tight to God's strong hand!**

Handle the Hassles

"Be watchful, stand firm in your faith, be courageous, be strong."

1 Corinthians 15:13

What makes a hassle a hassle? It's the element of uncertainty. Winston Churchill said, "A person can stand up against almost anything. But he cannot stand up against uncertainties or mysteries."

That statement may well be true, but I'm sure Winston Churchill would be quick to agree that life, without the tensions produced by uncertainties, is virtually hell. It is the unpredictable quality of life that leaves room for the spontaneity which allows our lives to be infused with unplanned surprises and unexpected serendipities!

What would life be like without the tension produced by uncertainty? If we remove the tension from steel it becomes brittle iron. If we remove the hassles from our lives, our lives would be uninspired and boring. What would a contest be like if the conclusion were foregone?

Suspense is a fundamental, psychological, emotional need. If there never were any kind of suspense; if we knew beforehand what the outcome of our endeavors would be; then we would not be dependent upon God and could not be driven to the anxiety that can produce authentic, passionate prayer. We need our hassles because they produce suspense.

This hassle has me in suspense—how exciting!

Handle the Hassles

"But thou, O Lord, knowest me; thou seest me, and triest my mind toward thee."

Jeremiah 12:3

First of all, *hassles suspend* us so that we can become dependent upon God. The *second thing they do is show us our growth potential.*

Personal growth comes when we learn through our hassles what our potential capabilities and capacities for learning really are. Hassles show us how we can grow.

Not long ago I heard on television an interview with one of the runners in the Boston Marathon. "Why did you run the race?" the young woman asked. "Was the race a physically pleasurable experience?" "No," the runner answered. "As a matter of fact, it was pretty painful—especially the last few hills."

As a runner myself, I agree, running can be painful. There are many mornings I have to drag myself from my bed and run my daily miles. I often find that pushing myself to the limits of my endurance can really be a hassle.

I listened with anticipation when the reporter pressed the marathon winner why he subjected himself to the grueling 26-mile race. The runner said, "I ran the race because of the glorious impossibility of it."

Until we are faced with a glorious impossibility, we don't know what we are, who we are, or what we can do.

> **I will run the tough road—and I will not quit!**

Handle the Hassles

"For now we see in a mirror dimly, but then face to face. Now I know in part, then I shall understand fully, even as I have been fully understood."

1 Corinthians 13:12

Our hassles become the mirrors through which we can become acquainted with the person each of us refers to as "me." We ask ourselves, "Do I, by the grace of God, have the ability to be a manager or decision maker? Do I have the potential within me to become a saint reflecting God's beauty, love and kindness? Who am I, what can I become?" We will never know the answers to these questions until we tackle our hassles.

There are many Christians who go through life-shattering grief and tragedy. But when they look back at the experience, they affirm that God provided them with extra strength and support. By His grace, they discovered they could withstand the test—they were not the weaklings they thought they were. And because of the experience, they became stronger and more capable.

We all need hassles to help us uncover our greatest potential. And when you commit yourself to God's call for your life, then you know that you are going to have to face the biggest hassle of all. Because when God gives you an idea or a challenge, you can be sure that locked into it will be more problems and more difficulties than you could possibly overcome alone. God's ideas will always be so big that they will be humanly impossible. But let me assure you, the tassel is worth the hassle when you're following God's way, God's will, God's Word and God's wonderful schemes.

The tassel is worth the hassle!

Handle the Hassles

"Because you have been faithful unto death, I will give to you, my friend, a crown of life that never fails."
Revelation 2:10

Finally, *Hassles stimulate you.* God doesn't want His children to vegetate. He wants us to be productive and vitally alive. Hassles keep us from dying of boredom.

Why do super rich, super successful people continue to work? I have some friends and acquaintances who are among the most wealthy people in the world. But they don't take time for extended vacations—they're too busy! They're too involved with people and with life to just lie in the sun.

God's plan for you is not to let you luxuriate and die in your success. He has a plan and a dream for you and He wants your life to be stimulating and exciting.

I have news for you. Your decision to let God take charge of your life will be a hassle. *But the tassel is worth the hassle.* One day your life in this world will come to an end. Sooner than you realize, your immortal soul will stand before God. And if you have trusted your life to Him, then out of the brilliant, pure light will step a Friend. You will recognize Him because His name is Jesus Christ. And He'll place the crown of eternal salvation on your head. As you walk in your spendid commencement to the throne of God, you will know beyond the shadow of a doubt that the tassel was indeed worth the hassle.

I'm excited to see beyond the hassle!

Handle the Hassles

"The one who endures to the end will be saved."
Matthew 10:22

As the hassles in life come—as they will, receive them with joy. Let them work for you. A few days ago you listed the hassles facing you. Are these the same hassles today? Then practice how to turn today's hassles into a positive force.

First list the hassle. Then write down how that hassle has kept you in suspense; third, record what that has shown you about yourself; and finally, think how the hassle has stimulated you.

Today's hassle:	Left me in suspense about:	Showed me this about myself:	Stimulated me to:

Thank you, Lord, for hassles!

Carry the Cross

"In everything you do, put God first, and He will crown your efforts with success."

Proverbs 3:6

This month we have defined our role—to be a star! A star friend, a star businessman, a star athlete. A star is someone who excels—and shines God's love with excellence.

Secondly, we have made goals to shine like stars. Your goal is to make the one life you have plentiful for God.

Finally, you have estimated the toll of this project. You are willing to pay the price. With the toll comes hassles. Hassles work for you to keep you in suspense, to show you more of yourself, and to stimulate you to keep believing in God's "impossibility."

Remember our formula:

ROLE + GOAL + TOLL = SUCCESS.

The final point I want to make to you is this: *God will see you through to ultimate success.* What is ultimate success? It may not be reaching the immediate goal that you're working on today. Because what you want, at a deeper level than the immediate goal, is self-respect when you are alone with your thoughts and your God.

So God gives you a dream. Don't back away from it because you might fail. Win or lose, if you follow God's plan, you will be able to live with yourself with respect, because you will know that you did what you had to do.

> **I need to respect myself—I need to believe in God's dream!**

Carry the Cross

"Do not withhold good from those to whom it is due, when it is in your power to do it."

Proverbs 3:27

How do you succeed in life? The secret of success is to find a need and fill it; to find a hurt and heal it; to find a problem and solve it; to find a barrier and tear it down. The secret of success is to meet a need.

In a free enterprising society, no business is going to be a permanent success unless it honestly seeks to serve the consumer with integrity. Every good businessman knows that ultimately only service succeeds.

Here's another principle. It is impossible to serve without denying yourself. Therefore, *it is impossible to be a servant without bearing a cross.* The profound theological concept is this: *You cannot succeed unless you serve!* You cannot serve unless you deny yourself. You cannot deny yourself without taking up a cross.

How will you serve others today? List specific ways.

_____

_____

_____

I will serve those around me today—I will succeed.

Carry the Cross

"For the moment all discipline seems painful rather than pleasant; later it yields the peaceful fruit of righteousness to those who have been trained by it."

Hebrews 12:11

A sentence in the Bible that Jesus spoke has been hard for me to accept for a long time. He said, "If you want to be my disciple then deny yourself, take up your cross, and follow me." (Luke 14:27) My problem was that I felt I didn't have a cross. So I asked God why I didn't have a cross. And He said, "You do."

Then I started realizing that about three or four years ago, after we had been on TV for quite a while, I was no longer a private person in public. I couldn't do anything without meeting people.

I was in a cafe recently, eating lunch with my wife. We were having a very intense conversation and I was not smiling. In fact, I had a frown on my face. Arvella leaned over and whispered under her breath, "Bob, there's a couple over there and I'm sure they recognize you. You better smile." So I went through my very intense conversation smiling from ear to ear. I expressed to her the frustrations that I was going through at the time—the difficulties, the problems, with a smile on my face.

When you run into people with a smile, you get a lift. If you run into a person and he's got a frown, it pushes you down. I had no right not to deliver to those people, through nonverbal communication. I had an obligation to lift them. That's my cross.

I will take up my cross!

Carry the Cross

"Consider him who endured from sinners such hostility against himself, so that you may not grow weary or fainthearted."
Hebrews 13:3

When you bear the cross of success, you make a sacrifice. Maybe the sacrifice is time or money. It may be privacy or a personal possession. Every success has a cross, and every cross means sacrifice.

But the beauty of our Christian faith is that it is impossible to sacrifice yourself in service to your fellow persons without being personally, abundantly rewarded. Our Lord sought to fill the need of humanity. People needed forgiveness; people needed a sense of self-worth, dignity, and self-respect. Jesus saw the need. To meet the need He sacrificed Himself. But always, after Good Friday there is Easter morning! Blessings always boomerang!

Sacrifice always produces some form of inner or outer success. For what is success? Success is a sense of self-esteem that comes when you know you helped somebody who was in need. And every legitimate businessman knows what I mean. Your greatest joy in being in business is not seeing how much profit you made. The greatest joy is seeing the delighted face of a customer who found a solution to a problem in a product or a service that you honestly offered.

What sacrifice will you make today as you bear your cross? _____

_____

_____

Sacrifice is success!

Carry the Cross

"The one who sows sparingly will also reap sparingly, and the one who sows bountifully will also reap bountifully."
2 Corinthians 9:6

When you serve others, you will truly discover success. It is an impossibility to serve others and not find the inner self-fulfilling esteem you seek. For true success is the self respect you receive when you build up others.

As you give to those around you, you will receive more than you ever imagined. And as you give your life to God, He will give you the inner joy of knowing you've made your life an investment. It is impossible to sow the seeds and not regain the original seed!

I remember when my father, an Iowa farmer, went through a total disaster one year. It was in the '30s when the drought swept in from the Dakotas. The wind was dry and fierce. It became our enemy as it peeled off the rich, black soil and swirled it like drifting dunes in the gullies and canyons. The harvest season came and my father harvested not the one hundred wagon loads we usually harvested, but a meager one-half wagon load. My father looked to the heavens and cried out, "I thank you, God, that I have lost nothing. I have regained the seed I planted in the springtime!"

Be a success—learn to be generous to others, and life will be generous to you.

I will sow my seeds bountifully!

197

Carry the Cross

"Love one another with kindly affection; outdo one another in showing honor. Never flag in zeal, be aglow with the Spirit, serve the Lord."

Romans 12:10,11

When we began this ministry in a drive-in theater 24 years ago, Mrs. Schuller and I were the entire staff.

Finally, after several months, we were able to afford our first professional minister of music. Her name was Lea Ora Mead and she took charge of our first choir composed of an odd number of volunteer singers who met for rehearsals in our home.

For six years we conducted this church in the drive-in theater. Every Sunday morning, I climbed on to the sticky tar paper roof of the snack bar and delivered my messages in the rain, the chilly wind, or the blazing sun. And standing right behind me leading the choir was Lea Ora Mead.

With the building of the Crystal Cathedral an anonymous friend donated a cash gift to the pillar of steel project in honor of this beautiful woman. When informed of this, Lea Ora asked, "Who could possibly remember me—I moved away years ago." "Lea Ora," I assured her, "there's no way you can ever know how much good you did for people in your lifetime."

When you make a sacrifice—it is always rewarded. It may be years before you ever see results, but God who sees all things will reward you! Think back to something you did years ago for someone else. How has God since rewarded you?

Only God can count the apples in one seed!

Carry the Cross

One of the most exciting promises Jesus gave us was, *"Give and you shall receive."*

Luke 6:38

This is so true! My cross may be to smile and always be an uplift, but the rewards are immeasurable. *You can never outgive God!*

I'll never forget the beautiful face of a young Oriental girl who came up to me one day. She said, "Dr. Schuller, I have to meet you because you saved my life!" I asked her, "How did I save your life?" And she told me her story.

"I was a poor student in high school, Dr. Schuller," she began. "I graduated but it was a real struggle. I knew I wasn't smart enough to get through college.

"I wasn't going to give myself another treatment of failure, Dr. Schuller," she explained. "That's when I started tuning into the Hour of Power and you talked about possibility thinking. I saw your smile and heard you say that you thought God wanted you to build a Crystal Cathedral and that it was going to cost millions of dollars. I thought, 'If Dr. Schuller can do that, maybe I can get through college.' I decided then and there that I would try at least one semester of college.

"So I applied and I did get accepted, and I finished the first semester with a B average! You did save my life. You see, I decided I was going to kill myself when I graduated from high school, but now I am alive!"

God always gives more than we can imagine!

Carry the Cross

"And you shall be my people, and I will be your God."
                   Jeremiah 30:22

The success that comes from God will feed your self-esteem but it will lead you through the valley of potential humiliation before the crown of Godly pride is placed upon your head. That's what the cross means.

You say, if God is interested in self-esteem, why would He let Jesus die on a cross? What a shameful death. Was Christ's self-esteem being fulfilled when He hung naked on a cross? Yes!

For there is no self-esteem without sacrifice. There is no sacrifice without being exposed to the possibility of ridicule.

Success always comes with a cross because the cross sanctifies the self-esteem from what would otherwise turn out to be dangerous, ruthless pride.

What's the difference between dangerous egotism and wholesome divine self-esteem? The difference is the cross you are willing to bear to fulfill God's will. And so, before God can give you the crown, the grand and glorious redemptive holy pride, he will purge you and make your self-esteem sanctified and sacred.

Sanctify me, Lord!

Carry the Cross

"And the Word became flesh and dwelt among us, full of grace and truth; we have beheld his glory, glory as of the only Son from the Father."

John 1:14

Jesus Christ lived the greatest success in the world! He knew his role. He was the Son of God. He dared to make the goal. He made the one life he had a beautiful thing for God. He found needs and filled them. He uncovered hurts and healed them. And Jesus Christ paid the toll. He was ridiculed and despised and went as far as to die on the cross.

But Christ knew the success that was to come. On Easter day, he defeated death and came back to life! And Jesus knew his worth, his success fed his self-esteem. He wanted to draw all men to himself. Why? Because he knew the joy of success. He suffered the cross to sanctify his self-esteem. And he bore the cross to sanctify your self-esteem. He wants to draw all men to Him so He can draw all men to God. That's success! That's Jesus Christ!

Jesus Christ—you are my North Star!

How Possibility Thinkers
Become Successful Leaders

Your Leadership Potential

"Do not be conformed to this world, but be ye transformed by the renewing of your mind that you may prove what is the good and acceptable and perfect will of God."

Romans 12:1,2

ANYONE CAN BE A LEADER! A husband, a wife, a father, a parent, an employee—yes, anybody can be a leader. What is a leader? A leader is someone who is discovering God's plan and possibilities. Let me tell you how over the next few days by using five words that rhyme.

First, a leader is someone who *GROWS!* He's a little higher than those around him. Look at a group of trees. There is always one that is just a little higher than those surrounding it. It is leadership in growth! In every little community, colony, and collection of persons there is somebody who stands out! And that person is a leader who is growing!

A leader is someone who allows his thinking to grow big enough for God's idea to fit in. If you think bigger than you've ever thought before, you are growing! Your consciousness is expanding, you're a leader!

As the Scripture verse for today says, do not be conformed to this world! This world thinks small! Be transformed by the renewing of your mind, and when your mind is renewed it will become elastic, it will stretch, and you will grow!

> **With Your help, Lord, I can grow into Your instrument. Teach me.**

Your Leadership Potential

"Blessed is the Lord, for he has shown me that his never-failing love protects me like the walls of a fort."

Psalms 31:21

A leader is somebody who not only grows, but he *KNOWS*. He knows his business. He speaks with confidence. Some people fail because they don't grow in their knowledge. Success is 50 percent preparation and 50 percent inspiration and perspiration.

Some people fail as leaders because they just stop growing. Others fail as leaders because they stop knowing their own business and they don't keep pace. A leader is somebody who knows! He knows that he has a choice either to drift or to decide.

When I was a boy growing up on our Iowa farm, I used to enjoy going to the Floyd River, a narrow and muddy stream. Once I sat there hour after hour and never caught a fish. Then my brother pointed to something floating down the center of the river. It was a dead fish. That's when the concept entered my infant mind. Even a dead fish can float down the stream! Live fish swim against the current.

You and I have the choice, either to drift with the currents of life, surrendering leadership of our life to forces around us over which we have no control. Or we have the choice to be alive and swim against the current and be the vital forces we were meant to be. Anyone can be a leader! You make the decisions that will determine the development of your possibilities!

Today I make the decision to follow you, Jesus. Guide me.

Your Leadership Potential

"Happy are all who perfectly follow the laws of God."
Psalms 119:1

Some people's lives are one crisis intervention after another, while others seem to be achieving one success just a little bigger than the last one. What's the difference? It's a matter of leadership! A leader grows, knows and then SHOWS! She speaks up! He reflects his leadership qualities.

Within your community, your committee, or your group, something is probably imperfect and nobody is doing anything about it. Leadership is growing a little higher than others. It's knowing what can be done and then it's showing others how to do it by example. All it requires is what we call possibility thinking, or a positive mental attitude.

You demonstrate leadership by showing people a dream of what they can be. When a person builds a dream into a human imagination, that's power. And you can do that. A mother to a child, a father to a child, a husband to a wife, a wife to a husband, an employer to an employee, and employee to an employer.

Right now think of a positive suggestion you could make toward change in the right direction. Maybe it's on one of your committees. Maybe it's how you handle your relationship with your children. Or maybe it's a better idea for a church group. Write it here.

Make the time this week to present this idea.

I want to share my God-given ideas with others.

Your Leadership Potential

"And when we obey him, every path he guides us on is fragrant with loving kindness and his truth."

Psalms 25:10

Leaders don't just show how to do it, they do it themselves! They lead the way before success is certain! Nothing is more important than to wipe out the fear of failure.

Failure doesn't mean you're a failure. It means you haven't succeeded yet.

Failure doesn't mean you have accomplished nothing. It means you have learned something.

Failure doesn't mean you are a fool. It means you have a lot of faith.

Failure doesn't mean you've been disgraced. It means you were willing to try.

Failure doesn't mean you don't have it. It means you must do it differently.

Failure doesn't mean you are inferior. It means you are not perfect.

Failure doesn't mean you wasted your life. It means you can start over.

Failure doesn't mean you ought to give up. It means you must try harder.

Failure doesn't mean you never made it. It means it'll take longer.

Failure doesn't mean God has abandoned you. It means He has a better idea.

What would you be leading today if you knew you could not fail? Write it here.

_____

_____

I am centered in Christ! Therefore I am a success!

Your Leadership Potential

"Then the Lord said to Moses, 'Quit praying and get the people moving!'"

Exodus 14:15

A leader BESTOWS! He bestows self-esteem on people and himself in the process. That's the way we have to succeed! *Success is building self-respect in yourself and in others through dedication to great ideas.*

I have had the privilege of meeting what you would call "great people" and I know many of them personally. I want to say something about them. There are no great people, only ordinary people with an extraordinary amount of nerve who committed themselves to extraordinary ideas! That's all! When you get to meet them, they are just very ordinary people who have made extraordinary decisions. And then in the process, they bestow self-respect on themselves and on others.

A leader goes ahead of everybody else. Not only in his thinking, but in doing, and that's why people cop out in leadership. They don't want to make a commitment, because they don't want to pay the price. The price is going forward and that's tough. But that's what leadership is all about!

What price are you hesitating to pay? What would you achieve if there was no price involved?

Think of one small step you could take toward that objective. Would you be willing to do that much today?

> **Today with God's help, I can begin the project I've been putting off.**

Your Leadership Potential

"If then you have been raised with Christ, seek the things that are above, where Christ is."

Colossians 3:1

There are two kinds of birds that fly over the California deserts—the tiny hummingbirds and the great vultures. The vultures, with outstretched wings, make their silent sweeping soar, until they spot the carcass of some dead animal and torpedo down upon it. In all the vast desert, the carcass is all they see. The tiny hummingbird, on the other hand, flies over the same terrain never noticing the carcass. He hovers near a cactus and spies a tiny pink blossom erupting from the thorns and, spearing it with his long thin bill, draws the honey from the bloom.

The vulture sees only the carcass while the hummingbird sees only the blossom. Each creature sees what he looks for. This is a parable of life.

As a human being, you will find what you look for. If you look for the negative in life, you will see it. If you search for the positive, that is what will become evident. We refer to these people as possibility thinkers or impossibility thinkers—leaders or followers, if you will.

Today I want you to know that you have a choice. You can be a leader or a follower. Leaders are people who respect themselves so much that they take charge of their destiny and carve out their futures, often times against seemingly impossible odds. Followers, on the other hand, merely accept the fate that life puts before them.

I choose to be a leader for Christ!

Your Leadership Potential

"Whatever you wish will happen. And the light of heaven will shine upon the road ahead of you."

Job 22:24

People who lead are possessed by dreams, and by dynamic, positive thoughts. If you have a dream, you have a great future. How do you choose a dream? By getting in tune with God. When we listen only to God's ideas as they come into our minds, our dreams oftentimes save our future.

In 1979 we commemorated the 50th anniversary of the Great Depression and the stock market crash on Wall Street. But while some people were committing suicide on one side of Manhattan, a man named J. G. Roscoe made multiplied millions at the height of the market crash. In 1929 just before the onset of the depression, he got a dream. He dreamed of building the tallest skyscraper in the world in New York City. People said it couldn't be done. Others prophesied that it would be a financial catastrophe. But he sold all of his stock at the height of the market and even convinced others to do so to finance his project. Days after he and his supporters had cashed in their stock, the market crashed, bringing poverty upon thousands. If he hadn't had the courage to invest all he had in his dream, he would have lost everything.

One year later, he began building his monument, the Empire State Building. What a triumph!

Do you have a dream? Are you believing God for it? Without regard to how long it will take, outline how you can accomplish this dream step by step.

I face today with a dream! God's dream!

Never Surrender Leadership

"Yes, be bold and strong! Banish fear and doubt! For remember, the Lord your God is with you wherever you go."
                                        Joshua 1:9

Only you, of all creatures, are able to make your own decisions, to guide your own destiny. What does assuming a leadership role actually mean? A leader is someone who establishes goals. A leader must give people a sense of vision of what they can be.

When I first started my ministry, Dr. Rosenberg advised me, "Never surrender leadership to anyone or anything. You alone are ultimately responsible and accountable to God for the work He has assigned to you!"

Unfortunately the truth is, the vast majority of persons constantly surrender leadership in their private lives, family lives, professional lives and in their career pursuits. Over the next week, let me share with you many ways in which people surrender their leadership.

First of all, some people surrender leadership to faces. Many public figures, who are supposed to be leaders, surrender to this kind of pressure. As they walk into an auditorium to speak, they note the raised eyebrows or the skeptical glances. Paraverbally, through body language, they sense a subtle form of rejection or possible disagreement. Intimidated, they back down on their stand. NEVER SURRENDER LEADERSHIP TO FACES!

> God has given me a courageous, all-conquering spirit. He has given me the spirit of Jesus Christ.

Never Surrender Leadership

"The godly are bold as lions!"

Proverbs 28:1

NEVER SURRENDER LEADERSHIP TO FORCES!
As I once said, the shoe doesn't tell the foot how big to grow. The body doesn't surrender growth leadership to the garment. The size of your family is not dictated by the number of bedrooms you have. The size of a congregation is not to be determined by the size of an available structure.

There are many negative forces that attempt to exert control over us. But when faced with problems of any kind, financial, political, personal or professional, never surrender leadership.

NEVER SURRENDER LEADERSHIP TO FARCES!
Farces are lies; masks that distort the truth. There are people in this country who belong to Asian, African, Mexican or Puerto Rican minority groups who have been indoctrinated with the idea that they are genetically and intellectually inferior to other races. That belief is an absolute farce. Racial prejudice is based on a lie.

NEVER SURRENDER LEADERSHIP TO FENCES!
Fences are limiting concepts you allow to infiltrate your brain and smother your thinking. Fences come in the form of thoughts like, "I can never do that. I don't have an education." Or, "It's impossible. I don't have the right connections." You must break out of your fenced-in, locked-in thinking.

**Jesus has freed me from fenced-in thinking.
My mind is renewed and refreshed!**

Never Surrender Leadership

"I am holding you by your right hand—I, the Lord your God—and I say to you, don't be afraid; I am here to help you."

Isaiah 41:13

NEVER SURRENDER LEADERSHIP TO FRIENDS! There is always a temptation to surrender leadership to members of your peer group.

It's amazing how many people allow vital life decisions to be dictated by the fact that they're intimidated by the social circle in which they move. Culture is calling the shots for them. Oftentimes the social structure accepts something that was considered morally wrong only ten or twenty years ago. People dictated by their peers would say, "Okay, let's do it. Everybody is," even though they might know deep inside that their actions are wrong. *Too often people don't hear with their ears; they hear through their peers.*

People of every age must realize the danger of succumbing to peer pressure. But young people are especially susceptible to this kind of influence. Too often society says that our problems can be solved chemically. Many people turn to cocaine, pills, alcohol or other forms of narcotics. Anyone who surrenders control of his or her life to some form of chemistry to get a lift or for relaxation has surrendered leadership to the bottle, the bag, the pill or the spoon. That person is no longer in control of his own life. Your brain is a fantastic instrument. Stimulate it with creative ideas. Don't surrender leadership to friends.

> **Only in you, Lord, do I find total acceptance—for I am your child.**

Never Surrender Leadership

"God loves you very much . . . don't be afraid! Calm yourself; be strong—yes, be strong!"

Daniel 10:19

Never surrender leadership to faces, forces, farces or fences. AND NEVER SURRENDER LEADERSHIP TO NEGATIVE FANTASIES!

God will put a brilliant idea into your brain and your first impulse is to move with it. But then you allow yourself to paint negative pictures in your brain of what would happen if . . . "I might be rejected or my friends might laugh at me," you think. You can be sure that any time you think bigger than the average person, you will arouse criticism.

NEVER SURRENDER LEADERSHIP TO YOUR FEARS! God did not give us the spirit of fear. That means that if you're surrendering to fears, you can be sure the fears did not come from God.

NEVER SURRENDER LEADERSHIP TO FRUS-TRATIONS! You can never move ahead without encountering problems. Every good idea has something wrong with it. The best possibilities contain problems. No matter what great idea you conceive of, someone will find something wrong with it. But problems only call for creative polishing of a dream or goal, not its demolition. There's quite a difference.

> **My fears are slipping away. I can feel courage growing as I reach out to God. He comes to me and knows who I am.**

Never Surrender Leadership

"They that wait upon the Lord shall renew their strength. They shall mount up with wings like eagles; they shall run and not be weary; they shall walk and not faint."

Isaiah 40:31

NEVER SURRENDER LEADERSHIP TO FATIGUE! Everybody has a weary moment. Everyone gets tired once in awhile. That's why it's important to know when you're running tired and then back off for awhile. If you don't you'll make wrong decisions.

Today historians still wonder if President Franklin D. Roosevelt surrendered leadership to fatigue at the Yalta Conference. At the time he was a very sick man. Perhaps if he had been in better health he would never have surrendered the eastern block of nations to Soviet influence.

There are times when you should not see people. I've had to make that discovery myself. Occasionally I find it necessary to cancel an important appointment due to fatigue. There are times I've had to say, "My friend, I truly want to see you, but you deserve me at my best, not at my worst. I'm too tired. It will wait. It will simply have to."

Even Jesus found it necessary to rest. Remember the time the multitudes pressed upon Him at the shores of Lake Galilee? They stood there reaching to Him, calling Him, needing Him, but He stepped into a boat and pulled away. He left them for a little while to go to the mountains to rest and pray.

> **Only in you, Lord, do I find complete rest and peaceful sleep.**

Never Surrender Leadership

"He will make the darkness bright before them and smooth and straighten out the road ahead."

Isaiah 42:16

We've already got a long list of leadership-stealers, but here's another one: NEVER SURRENDER LEADERSHIP TO FRENZIES.

Perhaps you are going through a very, very difficult time. Maybe you've lost a husband, a wife or a child. Maybe you've lost a limb or are seriously ill. Perhaps you've lost a large sum of money or are being consumed by inflation. In any of these circumstances, many people tend to become frantic and make the wrong decisions.

When faced with a catastrophic situation, do nothing until your mind is clear enough to function rationally.

In tragic times that is often the advice I give to people. More than once a widow has come to me after her husband has died and said, "I'm going to move. I think I'm going to sell the house and move back East." Or, "I think I'll move in with the children." I always caution, "Never make a major decision in a time of personal frenzy."

Can you recall a time when you made a decision under stress and it turned out to be a poor decision? Reflect back over that situation. Determine how you can avoid doing it in the future.

You are teaching me, Lord. I am learning
from my mistakes and I am grateful to you.

Never Surrender Leadership

"Your attitude should be the kind that was shown to us by Jesus Christ."

Philippians 2:5

This one may surprise you, but: NEVER SURRENDER LEADERSHIP TO FACTS! We are often bombarded with sad facts. It may be a fact that you're having problems in marriage or in business. It may be a fact that you don't know how you'll get through the hard times that are stretching ahead of you.

Dr. Karl Menninger, a great psychiatrist, made one of the wisest statements I've ever heard. He said, "Attitude is more important than facts." When you refuse to surrender leadership to facts, your attitude continues to remain in control. Your attitude must be positive.

I once counseled a young lady who had many serious problems. She was headed in the wrong direction—a direction that could have eventully led her to moral disaster. As I began to talk to her, she interrupted. "But Dr. Schuller," she said, "You don't understand the problems I have." And then she told me her parents were divorced. They had fought over her and played her against one another. She elaborated on all her many difficulties and then concluded, "That's the reason I am what I am. If you'd had the problems I do, I think you'd be what I am too. And that's a fact."

"It's a fact you have problems," I began. "But it's also true you're turning your problems into an excuse." *When you let the problem become an excuse, you've surrendered leadership of your life.*

My attitude is becoming positive because
Jesus is controlling my thoughts.

Never Surrender Leadership

"When a person falls, he jumps up again!"

Jeremiah 8:4

NEVER SURRENDER LEADERSHIP TO FAULTS! Just the other day I was talking to a friend of mine who is running a very large retail operation. But business wasn't going well. "I don't know what's wrong," he said. "Can you tell me?" I paused a moment and then said, "Do you want me to be honest or kind?" "Be honest," he said. "Well, to be honest," I began, "it seems you hire the worst people for the most important jobs."

"What do you mean?" he demanded. "My vice presidents, controller and sales manager are the very best, most qualified people." "I'm sure that's very true," I replied. "But the most important people are the clerks who talk to your customers. Often I get the impression they simply don't care about the business or the customers."

"Let me put it another way," I continued. "You have a very lovely, very expensive car. It has all the luxuries, but if you have a bad spark plug, you're not going anywhere. The people in your organization who greet the public are your spark plugs. And yet you hire the most inefficient people for the most important jobs."

Don't surrender leadership to faults. Take charge of your own life and be open enough to grow from the mistakes you make.

I am being filled with your wisdom, Father, because I am open to your will!

Never Surrender Leadership

"And so, Lord, my only hope is in you!"

Psalms 39:7

Many people fail because they surrender to the fracturing experiences of life. They suffer a brokenness that leaves them without faith for the future.

A friend of mine, a wonderful young man 22 years of age, recently suffered a hurt which left him deeply embittered. His young wife ran off with another man. "I'm never going to trust another woman," he vowed. "Let your dreams shape your future," I said to him. "Don't believe in the hurts."

NEVER SURRENDER LEADERSHIP TO FRAC-TURES.

Don't let brokenness, disruption or pain determine your future plans. A former secretary of mine once had a lovely, adorable poodle. When the poodle died she was deeply grieved. "When are you going to get another puppy, Betty?" I asked her one day. "I'm never going to get another dog. Never," she responded. "Why not?" I asked. "Because it hurts too much when you lose them." "Betty," I said, "you can't surrender to a hurt." Never let the grief, the aches and the breaking experiences of life make your future decisions.

Don't get depressed and discouraged because you've "missed the boat." Don't surrender leadership of your mood or your future to the fracturing experiences of life. Keep your ideal in command. And if for some reason things don't go right, then refuse to surrender leadership to fractures and frailties. And accept the humility God wants you to include among your human values.

> **I lift my hurts to you, O God! You take them and replace them with hope!**

Never Surrender Leadership

"I will keep on expecting you to help me. I praise you more and more."

Psalms 7:14

There are always cynical people who predict doom for the future.

NEVER SURRENDER LEADERSHIP TO NEGATIVE FORECASTS!

I remember I did pretty well in my undergraduate work at Hope College. But there is one "F" that stands out vividly in my memory. That was the grade I received in English composition. In oratory debate and extemporaneous speaking I received "A" grades. But in written composition, I got an "F."

My English teacher, who knew my reputation on campus, drew me aside one day and gave me what he felt was good advice. He told me to stick to speaking and not try to write.

Well, many years later, when my oldest child was ready for college, my income simply was not enough to meet the expenses. Desperately I prayed, "God, I want my children to have a good education. What do you want me to do?"

God gave me my answer. He inspired me to write a book called *Move Ahead with Possibility Thinking.* That book has put three of my five children through college. But it would never have been written had I believed in the negative forecast of my professor so many years ago.

What negative forecast have you listened to? _____

Look to Jesus for a new future!

Together, Lord, we can do things that seem impossible to the rest of the world!

Leaders Follow God

"And the one who comes to me I will never turn away."
                                              John 6:37

We've been discussing all the areas of life in which we must not surrender leadership. Instead, surrender leadership to one force—the force that started this whole universe in the first place, *God Himself.*

SURRENDER LEADERSHIP TO FAITH IN JESUS CHRIST! Believe you can be somebody beautiful no matter how often you've fallen. You can be saved no matter how often you've stumbled. Just believe that God exists and that He is a rewarder of those who diligently seek Him!

When God created the human being, he created a creature different from all the birds, fish, reptiles, and mammals. *He created a creature capable of love.* Now when the human being is possessed by love, he becomes a natural believer, for faith is the face of love. Any person who truly believes is profoundly motivated and compelled by love at the deepest level. When a person accepts Jesus Christ as Lord and Savior, His Holy Spirit comes in and love possesses that person.

Let faith be in control of every decision that you make and of your every action. When Jesus is the light of your heart, mind and soul, you will be filled with love, the root of a great leader!

> **Thank you, God, that I can surrender leadership to You and that You will never let me down.**

Leaders Follow God

"Come, let's talk this over! says the Lord; no matter how deep the stain of your sins, I can take it out and make you as clean as freshly fallen snow. Even if you are stained as red as crimson, I can make you white as wool."

Isaiah 1:18

Surrender leadership of your destiny only to God Himself Who, through the Holy Spirit, will guide you as you seek His wisdom.

This past week I talked with a lady who unknowingly was drawn into a highly sophisticated prostitution ring. First alcohol and then drugs broke down her moral stamina until finally she became a prostitute.

She told me that she had been deceived and been held under their influence through drugs and alcohol. It was so horrible she wanted to kill herself. Her parents suggested she watch Hour of Power, which she did.

"I listened to your program for only one reason," she said, "to prove that you were a phony and to prove to my folks they were wrong." Her next words came softly as she smiled through her tears. "I was the one who was wrong. The Lord came into my life and now I'm a new person. I'm clean. I'm saved." She was born again, a new person. As I looked at her it was almost impossible to believe what she had experienced.

It's incredible to see how a human life can be totally transformed when God comes into that life.

What transformations have taken place in your life since you have come to know Jesus?

> **How blessed I am that Jesus loves me enough to save me and transform me!**

Leaders Follow God

"Keep your eyes on Jesus, our leader and instructor."
Hebrews 12:2

It's so easy to lose control of your own destiny. It's so easy to surrender leadership of your own life to others. Suddenly someone else is making your decisions for you and you've lost control. To be a responsible person means you must be accountable for your own actions. Make your own decisions.

But making your own decisions takes nerve. That's why it's impossible to live without faith. Faith is an essential element of successful decision making. If you don't have faith, my friend, you won't have the courage to make your own decisions. And if you're not doing the choosing, you're doing the losing. Either you are deciding, or you're sliding.

It's amazing the ideas that come into human minds. And it always seems that when someone gets a great idea, three or four others will list reasons why it can't be done or why it won't work. Nine out of ten negative thinking people are experts in their field! I once said in one of my books, the most dangerous force in the world is a negative thinking expert! It's incredible how far you can take an idea if you'll just have a little faith.

I plan to win! And with God's help, I will reach my goal!

Leaders Follow God

"Let God train you, for he is doing what any loving father does for his children."

Hebrews 12:7

Last year we celebrated the 25th anniversary of this church. Throughout those 25 years we've had a rule on our church board: Any time somebody comes along with a good, inspiring, need-filling idea, nobody is allowed to ask at the onset, "How much will it cost?" Instead we ask these questions: "Will it help hurting people? Will it be a great thing for God? Is anybody else doing it?" After those questions are answered, then we make a decision. And once the decision is made, we don't ask, "How much will it cost?" but rather, "How will we finance it?" There's a difference.

If we began with the question of how much a new idea would ultimately cost, we would never move anywhere. Very few times is the financing of any new idea readily available. We've never had the money for anything when we started. But as I've said before, no business has a money problem. No church has a money problem. No corporation has a money problem. No family has a money problem. It's always an idea problem!

If an idea is loaded with human need-filling potential, the idea will attract support. It's incredibly simple, but true.

Never surrender leadership of your life to anything but faith. Always focus your thoughts and attention on faith in God and He will lead you to the crest of your mountain.

My future is bright! God is my inspiration!

Leaders Follow God

"Blessed is the one who trusts in the Lord, He is like a tree planted by the water, that sends out its root by the stream, and does not fear when heat comes, for its leaves remain green."
Jeremiah 17:7,8

I find it interesting to note that in any group, the majority of people will just listen to what is being said. If a suggestion comes up, most people will merely nod their heads. But usually one or two people will offer a creative option or solution to the situation. These people are the leaders.

One of the tragedies in our society is that too many families lack parental leadership. Too often families follow the lead of society rather than leading their families to create a better society.

Not long ago a father told me he had given his daughter permission to live with her boyfriend. "All the other kids seem to be living with whomever they choose," he said, "so I told my daughter to go ahead and do what she wanted to. I don't care." When I heard this statement I asked the man, "What are you? A parent? Or a parrot?" A parrot will merely repeat what he hears. But a parent is someone who provides guidance.

I think of my home as a kingdom. I am the king. My wife is the queen. And my children are a prince and princesses. Just as the laws differ from one city to another, so the laws of the Schuller kingdom differ from those of surrounding kingdoms. We are parents, not parrots.

Be a leader not a follower. The number one mark of a leader is that he thinks *critically* and *creatively*.

I will lead those around me with a creative, critical spirit!

Leaders Follow God

"Great is our Lord, and abundant in power; his understanding is beyond measure."

Psalms 147:5

A leader talks confidently and enthusiastically. Too often people fail to promote a positive idea simply because they want guarantees. But the only valid guarantees are the promises of God.

Leaders are not easily intimidated. Their talk is confident and rational, not emotional. Eric Berne, the author of *Games People Play,* made some valid statements about winners and losers. These same truths can also apply to leaders and followers. "Life is simple," Dr. Berne said, "all you have to do about problems is make decisions. But people want certainty. Losers spend their lives thinking about what they're going to do. Winners, on the other hand, are not afraid to unpack their bags and get going. Losers say, 'but' and 'if only.' Winners use three words in their vocabulary more than any others. What words are they? 'yes,' 'no,' and 'wow!'

"Wow!" Dr. Berne continues, "expresses the healthy, childlike wonder and capacity for enthusiasm possessed by a true winner which becomes the foundation and tap root for authentic self confidence." With that kind of confidence, anyone can be a great leader.

What idea can you present today, that will let those around you say, "Wow!"

Wow—I am a child of God, yes Lord! I will lead others.

Leaders Follow God

"Then Peter said, 'Lo, we have left everything and followed you . . . .'"

Matthew 19:27

Leaders know that beginning is half done. They don't care how small the first step is, they try.

While I was in college, Dr. Bud Henga, my history teacher, stopped in the middle of a class lecture to ask, "How many of you have started your term papers?" No one, save one or two students, raised their hands. He looked pretty upset by the small response and he began to pace the room.

Finally he stopped and looking through each one of us with his piercing gaze, he bellowed, "You can forget everything you've ever learned in college. You can throw away your degree, but don't you ever forget what I am going to tell you right now. Remember these four little words for the rest of your lives. They will take you farther than a score of college degrees."

You can bet with that kind of pronouncement he had my complete attention. He paused for a moment and then counting the words on four fingers he said, "Beginning is half done." I think everybody went home and started their term papers. I know I did.

Beginning is half done!

Leaders Follow God

"Therefore, my friends, be steadfast, immovable, always abounding in the work of the Lord, knowing that in the Lord your labor is not in vain."

1 Corinthians 15:58

Leaders are not afraid to tackle the obstacles and problems that stand in the way—no matter how impossible—and turn those obstacles into opportunities.

In 1953 a group of young kids in a Midwest high school decided they wanted to do something with their lives. Finally they decided to start a scholarship fund for Camp Courage, a camp for the handicapped. They also wanted to raise money for the buildings and equipment needed by Camp Courage—but how? How could high school students raise that kind of money?

But they didn't let that thought deter them. They said, "Who can tell where this project will ultimately end?" And so, with one small step, they began to tackle their problem. They asked farmers if they could pick up some of the corn lying in the fields that had been dropped by the pickers—gleaning the fields if you will. The farmers gave the kids their permission and so they collected, detasseled and sold the corn in roadside stands.

The grand total of all they've raised has just passed the million-dollar mark. They have built buildings, bought equipment for the handicapped and given scholarships to the blind, amputees, and the deaf.

It's beautiful what you can do with your life if God is in control!

I will tackle the obstacle facing me today!

Leaders Manage to Succeed

"But it is God who establishes us with you in Christ, and has commissioned us; he has put his seal upon us and given us his spirit in our hearts as a guarantee."

2 Corinthians 1:21,22

Ninety percent of the people who face problems must eventually admit that those problems were the result of a decision they either made or failed to make. Often when I've counseled people privately they would say to me, "I have a problem." When I listened to them relate the situation to me, I would have to say, "You don't have a problem to solve. You have a decision to make."

I urge you to take charge of your life and be a decision making person. Learn to control your moods and your reactions in such a way that you will enhance your situation rather than hinder it. I believe with all my heart that a person who really accepts Jesus Christ is changed emotionally. He becomes the kind of person who can control himself. He becomes a winner. Jesus will help you to successfully manage your life.

If you have never decided to come under the management of Jesus Christ, maybe this is the decision you need to make today. Otherwise God may be giving you a dream but you are unsure to commit yourself. To be a leader, you must make decisions. Gideon had trouble deciding to follow God's call. Yet God used even Gideon after he finally made the choice to lead.

What decision do you need to make today?

I will make my decisions—I will control my emotions—I will commit my life to the one who will lead me!

229

Leaders Manage to Succeed

". . . and he has put all things under his feet and has made him (Christ) the head over all things . . . ."

Ephesians 1:22

Leaders succeed because they manage their lives efficiently and effectively. Jesus was just such a manager. Jesus took charge over His life and His destiny!

His death on the cross was not the result of His being tricked or trapped. Nor did He commit suicide. No group of people or institution can be blamed for cornering and executing Jesus. He made a sacrifice whereby He made the greatest contribution to humankind that anyone could ever make. He gave the world a message that no one else could give.

This beautiful, wonderful human being was crucified. But in the public act of crucifixion, he looked upon his executioners and said to God in heaven, "Father, forgive them." And God forgave. If God can forgive people for nailing a man like Jesus to the cross, then God can forgive any sin. That means hope for you and for me. Therefore, the cross is not a negative symbol. It is a positive symbol of God's unconditional forgiveness and salvation. It was Christ's plan.

> **Jesus is the greatest leader—as I follow Him I will learn how to succeed—through sacrifice!**

Leaders Manage to Succeed

"Build upon the foundation of the apostles and prophets, Christ Jesus himself being the cornerstone."

Ephesians 2:20

One of the lectures I often give to heads of corporations deals with "Managing by Objectives." You don't succeed without planning. Leaders take charge of their situation and never surrender leadership. They plan to achieve measurable, manageable goals and objectives that incarnate their value system. Jesus practiced this kind of goal setting.

Some people say that successful people have more money, more time, better connections or more talent, education and training. Now that's not true at all, because the secret of success is not what you have or how you manage what you have, but how you develop and control all the resources at your disposal that could possibly contribute to achievement.

Gideon had only 300 men, yet he knew that he could succeed. God was with him. Yet he also had an effective strategy.

What is your strategy? What measurable, manageable goals and objectives are you making? Leaders manage to succeed. So can you. Start today.

I don't need any more money, time or talents! I only need to manage what I have.

Leaders Manage to Succeed

"Let all bitterness and wrath and anger and clamor and slan-
der be put away from you, with all malice, and be kind to one
another, tender hearted, forgiving one another as God in
Christ forgave you."

Ephesians 5:31,32

What is management? Management is learning how not
to waste anything. Management is being productive, constructive, and creative.

Managers succeed because they manage their time in the
best possible way. That's why they always seem to have time
for so many things. They never program into their calendar
anything that's not basic and essential. What's marginal or
trivial is never scheduled.

Many people wonder why I have such a super happy
marriage in spite of the busy world I live in. The main reason is that I "Manage by Objectives." One of my primary
objectives is to have the greatest marriage and family in the
world. That's why I write on every Monday night in my calendar, "A date with my wife, Arvella." I control my calendar and my calendar controls me. My values determine my
objectives, and my objectives are translated into calendar
commitments. It's a system that works beautifully.

What steps do you need to make to "Manage by Objectives?" Maybe the first step is to stop waste. Learn to be
creative—not wasteful. What have you decided to stop
wasting, now that you are learning to manage construc-
tively?_____

_____

I value life—I will never waste mine!

Leaders Manage to Succeed

"Let your eyes look directly forward, and your gaze be straight before you. Take heed to the path of your feet, then all your ways will be sure."

Proverbs 4:25,26

You must manage money, energy, time and talent. There are people who are incredibly talented, marvelously skilled, beautifully educated, and specially trained, and yet they still don't produce. Why? Because they don't know how to manage their resources. That's one skill they haven't acquired.

Some persons fail because they don't know how to manage people. Here is my four-step formula for getting along with people successfully. First, be friendly. Second, be frank. Third, be fair. And fourth, be firm.

You can learn to manage time, money, opportunities, problems, energy, and people but if you don't know how to manage yourself, then you will still not succeed. How do you manage your moods, your ups and downs? Do you need a drink? Do you need drugs? Do you get depressed and quit? If so, then you need a Manager above yourself. Successful managers don't try to avoid difficult situations by escaping from them. They always look for a good idea. Successful people know how to handle good ideas!

The source of great ideas is the creative intelligence which formed the universe itself—God Almighty. Do you want to succeed? Then take charge and establish your goal. Manage talent, training, time, money, energy, problems and people, but most important of all, manage yourself.

I will manage to succeed as God manages me!

Leaders Manage to Succeed

"There will always be temptations to sin, Jesus said one day to his disciples, 'but woe to the one who does the tempting!'"
Luke 17:1

The other day I went to breakfast with a friend of mine. I took him to a place with a huge menu of omelets. It has such a large selection that one man who went there with me got angry. He said, "I've got enough decisions to make today without having to go through this!"

I took another friend there another time and he said, "Where do I begin?" And as he began trying to decide, he noticed that I did not have a menu. He said, "Don't you want to see a menu?" I said, "No." He asked, "Why?" And I answered, "I made a decision some time ago never to surrender leadership to the menu. If I look at the menu, I'm likely to order something I want, rather than something I know is good for me."

Today our society is surrendering leadership to the menu. We look at life with its menu so big and with no moral restraints. If we're in the mood for fornication, that's on the menu. Adultery? That's on the menu. Stealing, lying, cheating? There they are. And just as soon as we begin looking at all those choices, we've surrendered leadership to the menu.

Surrender only to Jesus. Let Him manage your life. We need someone smarter than we are to tell us where to draw the line. We need to recognize that we have alternatives! And Jesus Christ is the best One!

Jesus Christ—I surrender to you!

Change Your Life Through Prayer

The Purpose of Prayer

"And whatever you ask in prayer, you will receive it if you have faith."

Matthew 21:22

Does God give everybody anything he asks for when he asks for it? No, He does not! Our Bible verse says that God answers all *prayer*. Jesus did not say that God answers all selfish begging, childish crying and pitiful pleading. Jesus does say that God answers all *prayer!*

I have heard people pray for what I considered to be nothing more than an utterly materialistic, selfish request. When they received no miraculous answer to their selfish request to a deity, they in doubt and cynicism said, "See, prayer does not work!" They called it prayer but God did not call it a prayer.

Prayer is not a scheme whereby we can move God to our lives, rather it is a spiritual exercise where we draw ourselves to God until we are a part of His plan and His purpose. When we are in harmony with God's universal plan and purpose then we have peace. When we are out of harmony with God and his universal plan and purpose, there will be inner frustration, tension and conflict.

A great deal of crying, begging and complaining which goes under the label of prayer is not prayer at all in the mind of God! With that understanding and definition of prayer, I would like to give you one of the most positive statements you could ever grasp:

"TRUE PRAYER IS ALWAYS ANSWERED BY OUR LIVING GOD! ALWAYS!"

> **Today, Lord, I will draw from you the power to begin a new kind of prayer life.**

The Purpose of Prayer

"And when you draw close to God, God will draw close to you."

James 4:8

What is *true prayer?* Let me illustrate:

You are in a boat
You approach the shore.
You throw the anchor out until it digs into the sand.
You take hold of the anchor rope and pull on it until
    your boat slides onto the sandy beach.

What have you done? You have *not* moved the shore to the boat. You have moved the boat to the shore.
The whole purpose of prayer is
        not to give you what you want when you want
        it; but to turn you into the kind of person
        God wanted you to be when He put you on
        Planet Earth.

Where is your life in relationship to God today? Do you need to move the boat closer to the shore? You can through prayer. Why not spend these moments now to draw close to Him.

> **My heart is tuned to the spirit of God. I can
> feel His values becoming my values.**

The Purpose of Prayer

"I love the Lord because He hears my prayers and answers them. Because He bends and listens, I will pray as long as I breathe."

Psalms 116:1,2

The most effective prayer ever prayed was by Jesus of Nazareth. The Lord's Prayer handles effectively, repetitiously, day after day, the six most destructive, negative emotions that would rob us of joy and vitality—the inferiority complex, discouragement, anxiety, guilt, resentment and fear.

> Our Father, Who art in heaven, hallowed be Thy name (inferiority complex)
>
> Thy kingdom come, Thy will be done on earth as it is in heaven. (discouragement)
>
> Give us this day our daily bread, (anxiety)
>
> And forgive us our debts (guilt)
>
> As we forgive our debtors. (resentment)
>
> Lead us not into temptation, but deliver us from evil, (fear)
>
> For Thine is the kingdom and the power and the glory forever.

Because Jesus told us to pray in "like manner," we will be analyzing each part of the Lord's Prayer to determine the many, many insights which can bring new depths to your prayer life.

Now reread the prayer and release your negative emotions to Jesus. Feel His presence deep in your spirit. Feel forgiveness. Feel His love.

> **I love today with faith and confidence, for God knows me and is with me.**

The Purpose of Prayer

"Search me, O God, and know my heart; test my thoughts. Point out anything you find in me that makes you sad, and lead me along the path of everlasting life."

Psalms 139:23,24

The ultimate human value is self-respect and self-esteem. We are all God's children. As soon as you offer the prayer, *"Our Father Who art in heaven,"* you are saying that you accept every other human being on planet earth as your potential brother and sister. If that is not what you are saying then you cannot repeat the Lord's Prayer because it is not *my* Father, but *our* Father Who art in heaven. And that means you are obligated to treat every other human being with respect!

All people are created in the image of God and that means the most despicable person should still be treated with respect. You do not respect his abnormal, ungodly behavior, but you make a distinction between the behavior and the person. Jesus did that! He did not approve sinful behavior, but He didn't call the person a sinner.

Read each of the following stories. How did Jesus treat each of these people? Did they deserve it?

Luke 19:1-10 _____

John 8:3-11 _____

Luke 10:30-37 _____

> **Thank you Father, for the love You give to all Your children. I am so happy to be a member of Your family.**

The Purpose of Prayer

"For His Holy Spirit speaks to us deep in our hearts and tells us that we really are God's children."

Romans 8:16

"Our Father who art in heaven." Stop right there! Every human being is a child of God for whom Jesus Christ died on the cross and rose on Easter morning and sent His Holy Spirit in Pentecost. The Lord's Prayer begins by saying, "all human beings are brothers and sisters of each other, and because we are created in the image of God, we are to be treated with respect and dignity!"

I shall never forget Colonel King. He was a black man who was born and raised in the South. We met when I was in Okinawa on a mission with the Air Force. The minute I stepped off the airplane he was at my side offering to be my escort and guide. What a tremendous help he was! When my visit was up I said, "How can I thank you for all you've done for me? You really treated me first class!" He paused for a second and then said, "I gave you first class treatment during your visit, not because you're Dr. Schuller, but because you're a human being. Every human being deserves to be treated first class."

Think about your actions over the past week. Did you give someone less than first class treatment? Write down the incident and suggest ways in which you could have improved your treatment of that person.

> **Today I will treat all my brothers and sisters in Christ with the respect and love each deserves as a child of God.**

The Purpose of Prayer

"... for your promises are backed by all the honor of your name."

Psalms 138:2

Our Father, Who art in Heaven, hallowed be Thy name.

If God is your Father and you are His child, you're somebody terrific! The Lord's Prayer settles your sense of inferiority once and for all!

Jesus begins by giving us a complete healing from an inferiority complex. A human being's obvious tendency is to put himself down. The Lord's Prayer deals with this at the outset. God is our Father! We are His children! We are members of His family! We have His honorable name!

Do you feel close enough to God to call Him your Father? Do you feel close enough to go to Him anytime?

Write your Heavenly Father a letter telling Him why you are proud to be a member of His family.

_____

_____

_____

_____

_____

My heavenly Father is present. He is close to me. I nestle in His deep love for me.

The Purpose of Prayer

"For God is at work within you, helping you want to obey him, and then helping you do what He wants."

Philippians 2:13

"Thy kingdom come, Thy will be done."

The second negative emotion that the Lord's Prayer destroys is discouragement. God has a plan and a dream for your life, and He's not planning to fail; you can be sure of that. God has a will for your life and He doesn't expect you to be a loser either. As Ethel Waters said, "God don't sponsor no flops." Therefore, you don't have to be discouraged if you're walking with Him.

What recent discouragement have you faced?

_____

_____

_____

Pray the prayer, "Thy Kingdom come, Thy will be done." Now literally cross out the discouragement.

GOD DON'T SPONSOR NO FLOPS!

God's will is surging within me. I want to please Him.

The Peace of Prayer

"Remember, your Father knows exactly what you need even before you ask him!"

Matthew 6:8

The third negative emotion, anxiety, can be a paralyzing, depressing, stifling, ultimately defeating negative emotion. Anxiety is dealt with by *"Give us this day our daily bread."* Why be anxious when God will supply your needs?

I remember those trying months of 1978 when Mrs. Schuller and I were spending many hours with our daughter Carol when her leg was amputated below the knee. We struggled with uncertainty, not knowing whether or not the doctors would be able to save her knee or her thigh. And I remember how much comfort we received when Carol looked at us and said, "I'll tell you one thing, Dad, if they take my knee and if they take my thigh, it won't change God's plan for my life one bit."

God knows what you need. There was a time when Carol really thought she needed a knee and a thigh, but then she came to realize God's plan doesn't hinge on a knee, or a thigh, or an eye, or whether you can speak or hear. Only God knows what you need, and that's what He will supply.

The word bread deals with life's *necessities.* We must, therefore, *trust God for the crust.* What you need, He will provide. That is exciting!

Examine your most recent petitions to God in light of your *needs* and your *wants.*

Lord, I trust You to determine my needs and to fulfill them. Thank you, Father, for loving me that much.

The Peace of Prayer

"Jesus replied, 'I am the Bread of Life . . .'"

John 6:35

Now here's exciting news! When God gives us what we need, it may not seem like a noteworthy thing. The most important things in life aren't too flashy, flamboyant, or dramatic. What's showy about a crust of bread? Yet it is this very thing that sustains our life. And so Jesus came quietly into the world without fanfare, without trumpets, without a grand parade. A baby born in a manger amid the cattle. And yet he said, "I am the Bread of Life . . . ." The crust didn't seem to have much class.

What is the crust that God gives to you? We call it possibility thinking. That's what you need. And when God gives us something, He never gives us a thing, it's always a *thought!* Things wear out, rust, go out of style, but *thoughts are eternal!* What you need are thoughts—positive thoughts—possibility thinking.

"Give us this day our daily bread." God will give you what you need: creative, inspiring, possibility-pregnant ideas! You need those God-inspired thoughts when you face problems. At such a time, the crust of bread will be the thought from God that says, "Do not quit," or "Try it this way." He helps you see the possibility of victory in the toughest times.

Christ is my crust of bread. He gives me the ideas, and so instead of being overwhelmed when I'm faced with a problem, the problem turns into an opportunity!

O Christ, bread of my life, sustain me with Your great love and understanding. Let Your thoughts become my thoughts.

The Peace of Prayer

"So there is now no condemnation awaiting those who belong to Christ Jesus."

Romans 8:1

Guilt is the fourth negative emotion Jesus deals with in the Lord's Prayer, *"Forgive us our debts."*

Fred Smith said it: "You know what hell would be for me? It would be that when I stand before God, He would tell me all the things I could have done in my life, if only I'd had more faith." Hell would be if God ever told me all of the diamond ideas that I allowed to flow wastefully through my brain. Hell would be if God ever told me all of the beautiful relationships I could have had if only I'd been more patient. Hell would be if God told me all of the accomplishments I could have achieved in life if I had been willing to pay the price.

And that's guilt. Deep down in us, there is the gnawing feeling that we're not doing what we ought. And my guilt can assault me and destroy my happiness in a moment. So how do we handle guilt? First, we must define areas in which we are experiencing guilt. Make a list below of the things you feel guilty about.

_____

Second, we need to ask God's forgiveness for all our wasted opportunities. Do that now.

> **Thank you, Lord, for Your total forgiveness.**
> **My guilt is being replaced by Your peace.**

The Peace of Prayer

"When you are praying, first forgive anyone you are holding a grudge against, so that your Father in heaven will forgive you your sins too."

Mark 11:25

Nothing will slaughter your self-esteem faster than treating people with resentment. But the Lord's Prayer rids us of this negative emotion when we sincerely say, *"as we forgive our debtors."*

During the first World War, the German armies swept over Belgium, destroying many of the cities. One day after the war was over, a Catholic nun with a group of her little students paused at a small Catholic shrine at the edge of the village. They knelt in prayer and began to repeat the Lord's Prayer. But they couldn't utter one phrase.

Around them was the rubble and the ruin, the resentment and the hurt of the war years. The small group started again, "Forgive us our trespasses as we . . . ." They could go no further—until from behind them came a strong man's voice—"As we forgive those who trespass against us." They looked around and saw King Albert! With his great spirit of forgiveness, he led the way!

Christ, our King, shows us how to conquer resentment and hurt. It was our King who cried from the cross, "Father, forgive them, for they know not what they do."

Perhaps you need to forgive someone. Ask your King—Jesus Christ—to give you the ability. God can help you be a forgiving person. And He will flood your being with love, peace and joy!

> **You, Lord, are helping me now to forgive others as You have forgiven me.**

The Peace of Prayer

"God at work in you will give you the will and the power to achieve his purpose."

Philippians 1:6

"And lead us not into temptation . . . ."

God knows how tempted you are, but when you're tempted to sin, it's because you don't know how worthy you are. Worthy people will not stoop to the shame of sin!

> *Self-esteem, rooted in God's call, generates enthusiasm for God's work, which positively eliminates temptation from your life.*

God's way to lead you clear of temptation is to get you so enthusiastically involved in His work that you'll have no time to be tempted.

You are a child of God! The tragedy is that too many people have not discovered their divine heritage so they live like animals. Somebody recently said to me, "The biggest problem in America today is crime." Why are people criminals? If people had a sense of pride and self-esteem that comes through their relationship with God the Heavenly Father, they wouldn't stoop to crime. It would be beneath their dignity.

There are some things our family just will not do. It's the same way with God's family. When you have a consciousness that you belong to the family of God, you develop the most healing, helpful and divine sense of righteous pride. It will not be a sinful pride, it will be a redemptive pride.

> **I am being filled with enthusiasm for God's ideas, plans and work.**

The Peace of Prayer

"Now change your mind and attitude to God and turn to Him so He can cleanse away your sins and send you wonderful times of refreshment from the presence of the Lord."

Acts 3:19

The Lord's Prayer has been the single most significant prayer ever prayed in any religion throughout the centuries because it deals with the deepest negative human emotions that could and would restrict or constrict the spirit of *enthusiasm!*

I believe that if the Lord were to restate that prayer He would say three things: First, *I need you.* Second, *I'll lead you.* And third, *I'll feed you.*

God needs you—that is the basis of authentic self-esteem. Whether you are an entertainer, a truck driver, a school teacher, a lawyer, a mechanic, or whatever you do, God needs you. That's powerful!

God leads you—God really does need you to accomplish His plan, and He'll lead you to do something special and significant where you are.

God feeds you—God feeds only when we agree to follow where He leads. If you wait to follow His leading until you can be sure of His feeding, He'll never show you.

When God gives you a dream it will be so big that you'll have to remain dependent on Him. It's His way of keeping you humble. How does possibility thinking deal with the problem of humility? Simple! You possibilitize until you get an idea from God that is big enough for God to fit in—so big that if you don't remain totally dependent upon Him, there's no way you can ever succeed!

Thank you, Lord, for the security of knowing that you are my partner in life. My success is then assured!

The Peace of Prayer

"God turned into good what was meant for evil."
Genesis 50:20

I think the most beautiful phrase in the Lord's Prayer is *"Deliver us from evil."* That power-packed little sentence is one of the reasons that the Lord's Prayer gives such tremendous, eternal, profoundly deep peace of mind to those who pray it and realize the significance of what they are saying.

Interestingly enough, Jesus did not say, "Deliver us from pain." He knew there would be pain. He did not say, "Deliver us from problems." He knew there would be problems in anyone who is growing and developing. Great success always generates great challenges. He did not say, "Deliver us from tears." He knew there would be tears. Jesus wept.

Jesus did not teach us to pray for deliverance from tears, pain, struggle, difficulty or even apprehension. But He did teach us to pray, "Deliver us from evil."

St. Paul says, "You are not your own, you are bought with a price." God doesn't rent you; He buys you. He holds title to you. You become His son, His daughter, His child, when you give Him lordship over your life. And when God adopts you as His child, He does so with a purpose. God has a plan for you. You're saved *from* evil; you're saved *for* service; and you're saved *into* significance. Your life has real worth and importance. Jesus said, "I know my sheep. And nobody, and nothing can pluck them out of my hand."

Jesus is changing my life. My heart is overflowing with confidence and enthusiasm!

The Peace of Prayer

"Don't let evil get the upper hand, but conquer evil by doing good."

Romans 12:21

God promises us that any human being who wants salvation can have it. That means He will come into your life and make a permanent alteration which shall irreversibly, divinely transform your deepest character so that you shall never, never live a life that shall be a shame or a reproach to you or to anyone else. He'll help you to develop your innermost potential for good in such a way that, through your pursuit of God's possibilities for your life, you will become the person He wants you to be. When you are so busy doing what He wants you to do, you are protected from being distracted and destroyed by the evil potential which surrounds you. *"Deliver us from evil."*

Salvation is a free gift of God. When God makes a gift, that's different from a loan! If you receive a loan from someone, it might be pulled back; but a gift is yours forever. Once God gives you His commitment to save you from the potential of evil, nothing can cause Him to break His promise to watch over you.

When God delivers us from evil, He turns us into beautiful people. Remember, any fool can count the seeds in an apple, but only God can count the apples in a seed. If you ask God to save you, He'll save you for eternity. And He'll use you in ways you won't even know about. Believe me, God will do something wonderful with the life you give to Him!

> **Move through me. Work through me. Love through me, Lord. I relinquish myself to you.**

The Power of Prayer

"So don't be afraid little flock. For it gives your Father great happiness to give you the Kingdom."

Luke 12:32

The Lord's Prayer closes with that sublime sentence, *"For Thine is the kingdom, and the power, and the glory, forever."*

What is God trying to accomplish? He wants to build a kingdom—a society of human beings where mutual self-respect; self-esteem and the dignity of every person is at the core of the entire human movement. He wants to create a kingdom where people no longer hurl insults at one another, where we would never try to shame or embarrass a fellow human being.

We all live three lives. The first of these lives is nine months long. As an unborn infant, we cannot comprehend the fact that soon our comfortable, secure surroundings will be violated by a virtual bombardment of sights, sounds and sensations. Are we really born, or do we die? Both. It is in this second life that the soul evolves in preparation for eternity. In those few brief years we spend on earth, we are to learn how to relate to people cordially and respectfully, because that's the way we glorify God. And when this life is finished, if we've learned our lessons well and are prepared by redemption, we enter the Kingdom of Heaven. What is God building? He is building a kingdom on earth headed for an eternal heaven.

Today I will glorify my Lord by how I handle my relationships with others.

The Power of Prayer

"May God who gives patience, steadiness, and encouragement help you to live in complete harmony with each other—each with the attitude of Christ toward the other."

Romans 15:5

If God wants to build a kingdom where we don't insult each other, He must begin by dealing with this problem of our insecurities. God's power to overcome our hidden insecurities is demonstrated in three ways: *through the power of salvation, the power of inspiration, and the power of example.* The power of salvation is found in the power of the cross.

God understands our nature. The failings of human nature can be summed up in two simple sentences: Imperfections observed become insecurities harbored; insecurities harbored become insults that are hurled.

When you become aware that you are not perfect, that produces internal insecurities that you attempt to conceal. You become afraid that should your shortcomings or faults be exposed, you might fall under some sort of judgment. Imperfections covered up become insults which you hurl at those around you.

Think back to a time when you insulted someone. What was the insecurity you were feeling? Write it here. _____

_____

Now, talk to Jesus about those feelings. Ask Him to reveal to you the root of the insecurity. Then release it to His Almighty care.

I am free! Jesus bears my insecurities and burdens! I am free to do His will!

The Power of Prayer

"For everything comes from God alone. Everything lives by his power, and everything is for his glory. To him be glory evermore."

Romans 11:36

If someone is insulting, embarrassing, or offending another person's dignity, you can be sure he has a problem of insecurity. Insults produced by hidden insecurities can be expressed in three ways: *verbally,* through the spoken word; *nonverbally* through body language; and *paraverbally* through sighs and grunts. No matter how they are expressed, insults hurled only reveal insecurities harbored.

How does God deal with this problem? *"For thine is the power . . ."* God sent His Son into this world. When you go to Jesus in prayer, it's as if He calls you into His office and closes the door. There, as you stand alone in His presence, He pulls out the record. "I know you," He says. "I know everything there is to know about your life." As you kneel before Him waiting for condemnation, you notice the scars on His hands and you see the shadow of the cross falling over Him.

And He comes to you and embraces you, and with tears in His eyes He whispers, "It doesn't matter. I love you, anyway."

You have experienced exposure, forgiveness, acceptance and affirmation! You walk away with your dignity recovered. Paradise lost becomes paradise regained.

> **By Your power I have been redeemed! Praise the Lord!**

The Power of Prayer

"So warmly welcome each other into the church, just as Christ has warmly welcomed you; then God will be glorified."
Romans 15:7

Why does God bother with a race of people who treat Him with arrogance, haughtiness, and pride? The answer is simple. God created the human race, and He will not be a loser. He will pay the price to reconcile us to Himself because He wants the glory of success. God's desire is to build a new culture within human society—a kingdom that will extend into eternity. *"For Thine is the glory, forever."*

In psychology there is an old saying, "Emotional maturity is measured by a person's ability to deprive himself of immediate gratification in order to achieve a long-range, more valued objective." If you are a person who can sacrifice immediate pleasure or enjoyment for a long-term goal of a higher value, that's a mark of maturity.

God takes the long look at things and sees the final picture. Someday the final curtain will fall. If you accept salvation, you will be a part of His kingdom forever.

The core of God's character is honor. He has promised you the spirit of Christ so that you can be secure enough to treat your fellow human beings with dignity. As you pray the words, *"For Thine is the kingdom and the power and the glory, forever,"* remember how much He loves you. He will never turn you away.

> **You are my ultimate security, Lord. Because of you, I am eternal!**

The Power of Prayer

"He is close to all who call on him sincerely."

Psalms 145:18

There are two levels of prayer. The first level is communication; verbal, paraverbal, and nonverbal. Prayers that are offered only on the verbal level frequently perform no miracles. The great miracles happen when prayer moves from verbalization to the second level, *visualization.* Here, prayer enters the realm of the imagination and mind! A mental picture takes place of what you've been praying about. You enter the realm of the spiritual universe and within that realm you discover positive and negative spiritual forces.

The power of visualization has never been fully tapped. It is incredibly, immeasurably potent! When prayer enters the realm of visualization/imagination, it can perform miracles of physical healing. In fact, just to pray for a healing without experiencing it at the transcended visualization level will always lead to frustration and failure. Prayer has to get into the level of dramatic metaphorical visualization we call "scenic imagination."

In your mind now, create a mental picture of a place you enjoy. Visualize all the reasons why you love to be there. "See" every aspect of it. "Smell" the familiar scents. "Touch" the special things. "Feel" the joy of being there. Through your mind, you can "experience" the joy of being there and be refreshed by it. The amazing thing is that you can accomplish it from your living room chair!

> **God, you are opening doors in my mind
> to draw me even closer to You.**

The Power of Prayer

"... And because you answer prayer, all people will come to you with their requests."

Psalms 65:2

The power of a scenic imagination! It can change your personality! It can strengthen your faith! It can put a twinkle in your eye. If you have a problem with somebody, only you can turn that relationship into a possibility by mentally visualizing them not as a problem but as a possibility.

As long as you visualize them in your mind as an enemy, an obstacle, or a problem, they *will* be a problem because our experiences with persons are always reflections. So you can change the worst people into the best people when you begin to imagine them as beautiful people.

Scenic imagination has that power—to heal relationships! It's where relationships are restored, restructured and re-created! It has incredible miracle-working power. It has the power to take your impossible dreams and make them realities!

Is there a breakdown in your relationship with someone? Visualize that person as a beautiful child of God. Release your hurts and fill your heart with good thoughts about that person. In prayer, visualize a repaired, improved relationship, and then expect a miracle!

The power of prayer is enhancing my life and the lives of others!

The Power of Prayer

"Continue steadfast in prayer, being watchful in it with thanksgiving."

Colossians 4:2

Your imagination can heal you! It is the level where healings take place—of the body, of the mind, of the memory, and of the soul. Your imagination can change your life! Scenic imagination is the level where miracles happen! And it can lift your whole achievement level.

The scientific reality is that we have *six* senses, not five. Touch, taste, sight, smell, hearing and *the sixth sense, imagination!* It's a sense that transcends time and space. The other five senses are locked into a time and space frame, but the sixth sense is eternal. You can use your imagination in the farthest corner of the world. On a cold day you can imagine it being hot and you can literally perspire! That is a fact!

In your mind, clearly picture Jesus with His arms outstretched. Watch His hands coming toward you, His strong arms enfolding you, His shoulder comforting you. Imagine yourself feeling secure as you snuggle in His arms and relax. Stay there as long as you like and "experience" His deep love for you.

I am totally immersed in God's healing power.

The Possibilities of Prayer

"If with all your heart you truly seek Me, you shall surely find Me."

Jeremiah 29:13

Prayer will give you the *wisdom to know.*

When I was attending Hope College in Michigan, one weekend I came home to preach on Sunday in a little country church. I saw the organist and felt as if I had been hit by lightning. Immediately I liked her and asked her out for a date the next night.

The following morning, I wrote to my fraternity brother that I had met the girl I was going to marry. And I did marry her! We've been married for over 30 years and I know of no one who has had a happier, more successful marriage.

How could such a thing happen? I'd been praying for years that I would find the right girl to marry. "Please, God," I prayed many times, "don't let me make a mistake." I know how easily such mistakes are made. But I can say that I knew without a doubt that Arvella DeHaan was the girl for me. There wasn't a moment of hesitation or an ounce of reservation—I knew!

PRAYER GIVES THE WISDOM TO KNOW!

I can act with confidence for I am in God's capable hands!

The Possibilities of Prayer

"... your strength must come from the Lord's mighty power within you."

Ephesians 6:10

Through prayer God gives you the wisdom to know, then He gives you *the courage to go!*

Even though I knew that Arvella was the girl for me, it still required courage to go through with our plans. One week before our wedding date, invitations had been mailed, Arvella had finished her wedding gown, and I confided to my mother, "I don't think I can go through with it. I don't think I can surrender my freedom. I'll never get used to it." But God bless my mother in heaven today, she gave me the courage to go ahead. "Harold," she said, calling me by my middle name, "you're going into the ministry, right?" "Yes," I answered. "Then that means you're going to be urging people to make decisions based on faith. Now's the time you have to make the right decision. You know Arvella's the girl for you." "Yes, I do know that," I answered, faith and courage renewed. God gave me the wisdom to know and then in that final moment of hesitation, He gave me the *courage to go.*

Why does anyone need the courage to go even though he already has the wisdom to know? One simple reason: God always gives you an opportunity that's loaded with unsolved problems. He never calls you into an activity that's risk-free—nothing could be more dangerous. When you've got the *wisdom to know,* you need the *courage to go.*

> **I face today with courage—God's courage! I feel His power running through me!**

The Possibilities of Prayer

"Each morning I will look at you in heaven and lay my requests before you, praying earnestly."

Psalms 5:3

Prayer is actually practiced on four levels. First there is the prayer of *petition*. At that level you are asking God for some material answer to your prayer. For instance, "God save my life," is a prayer of petition. Petition is recognized in the Bible as a legitimate form of prayer.

Make a list of your petitions.

_____   _____

_____   _____

_____   _____

The second level of prayer is *intercession,* which places one on a slightly higher level and it, too, is very scriptural. In intercession, I'm not praying for myself, but for another. It allows us to practice being compassionate and unselfish.

Make a list of those you want to intercede for in prayer.

_____   _____

_____   _____

_____   _____

**You hear and answer my prayers, Lord.
I am grateful!**

The Possibilities of Prayer

"Now all praise to God for His wonderful kindness to us and his favor that he has poured out upon us, because we belong to his dearly loved Son."

Ephesians 1:6

At the third level of prayer, *praise,* one does not ask anything of God, but thanks Him for who He is, what He's done and what He's going to do. Perhaps you've been to a prayer meeting that was actually a praise meeting. There is a time for thanksgiving.

One day while sitting in my office, I received a call from Lois Wendall, my first executive secretary who served so faithfully for 12 years in the early days of this ministry. When she told me she had cancer I went to her home to be with her and comfort her.

About seven years later she asked me if I remembered what I had prayed for the day I went to her home. When I told her I did not, she said, "I'll never forget it. The whole time we prayed you did nothing but thank God. You said, 'Thank you, God, that we've discovered the cancer. Thank you, God, that we're living in a country where there's surgery. Thank You that we have chemotherapy available. Thank You that Lois is not without the comfort of a husband. Thank You that we have medical insurance that can take care of the bills. Thank you, God, that she has faith so that she will not have to go through this without spiritual resources.' I was in shock when you came, but by the time you were finished, I had courage to handle my therapy."

> **I just want to praise you, Father, Son and Holy Spirit!**

The Possibilities of Prayer

"I will pray morning, noon, and night, pleading aloud with God; and he will hear and answer."

Psalms 55:17

Then there is the highest level of prayer—a level which, unfortunately, many people never learn. *That is the prayer of dialogue.*

In a dialogue with God, you ask Him questions and then you wait and listen for the "still, small voice" inside your head to give you His answer.

Many of you know that when we launched the Crystal Cathedral, we didn't have the money to begin. We couldn't even secure a reasonable bank loan. But we broke ground and dug a hole because God was saying, "Go." He gave us the courage to follow Him.

Practice dialogue prayer now. Have a conversation with God. Talk to Him. Ask Him questions. Then listen, and He will answer you.

Now write down His answers.

_____

_____

_____

_____

Heavenly Father, I commit myself totally to You. I will listen for Your direction.

The Possibilities of Prayer

"O rest in the Lord, wait patiently for Him and He shall give thee thy heart's desire."

Psalms 37:7

How does God answer prayer? Always God answers prayer in one of four ways!

When the conditions are not right God says, "No!" Actually, He is even then giving you what you really want which is what is best for you. What you really want is to be the greatest person you can be! So when God says "no" to your prayer, it is because He has a better way for turning you into a greater person!

When the time is not right God says, "Slow." God's timing is perfect!

Patience is what we need in prayer. I know of people who really don't suffer from doubt as much as they suffer from impatience. Reread Psalms 37:7:

O rest in the Lord,
  wait patiently,
    wait patiently,
      wait patiently for Him.

A genuine, honest, sincere prayer that is offered to God never dies. God doesn't forget about it. It is like a seed planted and at the right time it will sprout and it will grow.

> I am God's creation. He knows what is best for me! I trust him when He says, "No," or "Slow."

The Possibilities of Prayer

"You are close beside me, guarding, guiding all the way."
Psalms 23:4

When YOU are not right, God answers *"Grow!"* God never answers the prayers of people until they are ready for it.

If you have prayers that are not being answered, maybe you have to grow! If you face an unsolved problem, perhaps you have to do something yourself.

The self-centered person must grow in unselfishness.

The cautious person must grow in courage.

The reckless person must grow in carefulness.

The timid person must grow in confidence.

The self-belittling person must grow in self-love.

The dominating person must grow in sensitivity.

The critical person must grow in tolerance.

The negative person must grow in positive attitudes.

The power-hungry person must grow in kindness and gentleness.

The pleasure-seeking person must grow in compassion.

The God-ignoring soul must become a God-adoring soul.

Recommit your life to Jesus right now. Ask Him to touch your heart at its deepest level. Give Him permission to change you in the ways He feels would be best for your growth.

> **I am yours, Lord. I give you my permission to use me as your instrument. To change me as you see fit.**

The Possibilities of Prayer

"It is God himself who has made us what we are and given us new lives from Christ Jesus."

Ephesians 2:10

When everything is right, God says, "Go!" Then miracles happen!

A hopeless alcoholic is set free!
A drug addict is released!
A doubter becomes as a child in his belief!
A church rises out of an orange grove!
Diseased tissue responds to treatment, and healing begins!

The door to your dream suddenly swings open ... and there stands God saying, *"GO!"*

What prayer has God said "Go!" to today?

_____

_____

_____

Watch miracles happen!

Jesus makes both me and my life beautiful!

The Possibilities of Prayer

"The prayer of the righteous is powerful and effective."
                                                        James 5:16

Dear Heavenly Father, we thank You for Your presence within us on this, another beautiful day when we can lift our eyes toward You in song and praise.

O God, in so many ways, through so many influences You reach out to us until we respond and have a relationship with you that is wonderful.

In this world where there is so much hurt, You have come, O God, to offer salvation from life's aimlessness through Your son, Jesus Christ. How we thank You!

> You adopt us into your family.
> You give us sanctified pride.
> You give us exciting dreams.

We ask now that you lift our thoughts to higher levels, expand our faith, clarify our thinking and renew our strength.

Through Your Son, Jesus Christ, we pray,
Amen.

                                        by Robert A. Schuller

---

Prayer is a progress!

If You've Got the Grit,
You'll Never Quit!

Mountain-Moving Faith

"What is faith? It is the confident assurance that something we want is going to happen. It is the certainty that what we hope for is waiting for us, even though we cannot see it up ahead."
Hebrews 11:1

Faith is the ability to trust in God. It means believing in Him. Depending on Him. Obeying Him. Faith is keeping your eyes on Jesus Christ.

The first step toward developing a strong faith is to begin a personal, intimate relationship with Jesus.

Think of your very best friend in the world. How did the two of you develop your close relationship? If you're like most people, you talked a lot. You found out everything about each other, likes, dislikes, hurts, disappointments, failures, happy times, successes and triumphs.

Well, get to know Jesus the same way. Tell Him all about you! And find out as much as you can about Him. Begin through His Word, the Bible.

Look up the following Scriptures. What do they tell you about Jesus?

Luke 2:41-52   _____

Matthew 4:1-11   _____

John 2:1-12   _____

John 10:22-30   _____

Mark 2:1-12   _____

John 14:6-11   _____

> **My thoughts are focused on Jesus. I
> feel His spirit within me.**

Mountain-Moving Faith

"Obey me and I will be your God and you shall be my people; only do as I say and all shall be well."

Jeremiah 7:23

The Bible is God's outline for all people. It is the "living" Word of God. Through His Word, God reveals Himself and His plan for all His children.

Let's look at the lives of some of the people in the Bible, and examine how their faith affected their lives.

Noah is a good example. Noah trusted God. When he heard God's warning about the flood, Noah believed Him even though there was yet no sign of rain. Can you imagine how his neighbors must have scoffed at him? Why they must have thought him downright stupid for building an enormous ark on dry land miles away from any body of water.

But Noah believed *anyway,* in direct contrast to the sin and disbelief of the rest of the world. He obeyed when everyone else disobeyed! And because of his faith, God honored him.

What can we learn about faith from Noah? Noah was obedient to God's Word.

Do you know when God wants you to be obedient? Read the commandments given to Moses in Exodus 20:1-17. Write them in your own words.

_____

_____

_____

_____

> As I understand what you expect from me,
> Lord, I can move toward you in a close,
> loving relationship.

Mountain-Moving Faith

"Children of God in the old days were famous for their faith."
Hebrews 11:2

Read the following Scriptures to see how God uses ordinary people for extraordinary challenges!

The many miracles God performed through Exodus, Chapters 1-14, using Moses, whose faith needed to be strengthened for the job of leading God's children out of bondage.

The faith that saved Rahab, the prostitute; and Joshua's obedience to God in Joshua, Chapter 6.

Daniel's faith was tested when he was thrown into the lions' den. Read Daniel, Chapter 6.

Paul's faith did not falter in prison or in chains, but he kept his eyes on Jesus. Read Ephesians 6:10-20.

Which of these faithful ordinary people do you most relate to?

_____

Why?

_____

_____

> **I can feel Christ's power in my life filling me with a strong faith.**

Mountain-Moving Faith

"Obedience is far better than sacrifice."

1 Samuel 15:22

The story of Abraham and Sarah shows how trust and obedience are intertwined with faith.

Sarah *trusted* the Lord to keep His promise to her of giving her a baby. Because of her faith, as an old woman past her child-bearing years, she conceived and gave birth to a son. And God further blessed her faith that a whole nation came from this union.

Abraham was further tested by God. He offered up Isaac, the miracle child that Sarah had borne him, and was ready to slay him as God had commanded. Imagine how much pain Abraham felt as he was torn between his fatherly love for this son he had wanted for so many long years; and the deep love he had for his powerful God Who demanded obedience.

Is there an area of your life that you need to bring under obedience to God? Make a note of it below. Now tell God about it right now.

_____

_____

_____

_____

> **Forgive me Lord, for my disobedience.**
> **Already I can feel confidence within me as I**
> **recognize you are working in my life.**

Mountain-Moving Faith

"If you have faith even as small as a tiny mustard seed, you can say to your mountain, 'Move' and it will go far away. Nothing will be impossible to you!"

Matthew 17:20

Now you have seen how faith has worked for some of the people in the Bible. Do you think faith can work for you?

Some of you have written to me saying, "Dr. Schuller, you talk about possibility thinking. You say that faith moves mountains. Yet I am in anguish because my mountain has not moved. Was Jesus wrong? Did He make a mistake?"

My immediate reply is, "We all have a lot to learn, especially about faith and possibility thinking."

For example, a child builds a language base from one-syllable sounds until his vocabulary increases and his communication becomes more clear. As his education progresses, the dictionary opens up an almost unlimited resource of words; and his communication can be even more precise.

So it is with faith. Begin with a base of understanding God's Word. Increase to an immovable belief in Christ's power and promises. And your mountain will move!

> **With Christ's help, I can build a mountain-moving faith!**

Mountain-Moving Faith

". . . as God has dealt to every one the measure of faith."
                                        Romans 12:3

First, realize that God has already given you the measure of faith you need now! You have enough faith *right now* to begin His purpose for your life!

Faith is like a muscle. As you exercise it, it increases, strengthens and matures. Just like a seed in the ground must be cared for and requires water, sun and good earth to flourish; so does our faith require the knowledge of God's Word and the courage to practice what it says.

Most of the time, solutions to problems come through the creative ideas that God sends us. Do you believe in your creative ability? Do you believe in your own brilliance?

Since our Almighty God made you, and since we know that He cannot make a mistake, then we can conclude that we have within us the resources to solve our problems. God has given them to us!

What problem do you have that seems insurmountable? Give it to God today. Begin to exercise your faith muscle by believing that God will help you find a solution.

Believe that Jesus has taken control of your problem. Believe that a solution is coming in the form of a creative, positive idea. Now write Him a thank you note right now.

_____

_____

> **I have my measure of faith, the greatest miracle-working power. I will begin to exercise it.**

Mountain-Moving Faith

"Yet faith comes from listening to this Good News—the Good News about Christ!"

Romans 10:17

There's a story of a man from the Orient who traveled around the world in search of the smartest guru. He was told that the wise old man lived in a cave high up in the Himalayas, so that was his final destination.

After months of traveling, he came to the foot of the Himalayas. He led his horse up a narrow path until he came to a cave. "Are you the guru who is known for his wisdom around the world?" he called out. He waited and waited until finally the old man walked out into the light, so that he could be seen. "Old man, how can I become brilliant? Where can I find wisdom?" the weary traveler asked. The wise old guru raised his head and looked into the anxious man's eyes. "Where can you find your horse?" And with that he turned and walked back into the dark cave.

His horse was with him all the time! Brilliance and the capacity for wisdom were with him all the time.

I don't care who you are. I don't care how poor you are. I don't care how illiterate you are. You have the same basic brain as any other human being! Believe in yourself!

God is here within you now, through ideas coming into your brain! Believe it!

> **I believe in my God-given brilliance and wisdom.**

Know Your Faith

"For we walk by faith, not by sight."

2 Corinthians 5:7

Faith starts when you begin to believe in the ideas that God sends you! The head of a well-known company decided to test the creativity of average people, so he selected ten uneducated men from one of his factories. The president led them into the executive headquarters, and told them to sit in the big leather chairs around the huge board table. He said, "I have observed you people for some time now and have noticed that you all have remarkable gifts of creativity, which is why I have called you together today. Our company is facing a problem and I believe that you ten men can come up with a solution." He explained all of the details and then left the room for a few hours, a little cynical of the whole idea. When he returned, he discovered they had found a solution!

A great breakthrough was made! They found an answer to the problem that his top corporate research and development personnel had overlooked! The average "bottom of the ladder person" is potentially as creatively brilliant as the top executive who sits in the big office.

Many times, the only difference is that the person on the bottom doesn't realize he is brilliant and doesn't believe in his own ideas.

Each person is brilliant! That's a fact. Each person has incredibly creative potential! And all creative ideas come from God.

> **Common people are brilliant if they'll only believe in their ideas.**

Know Your Faith

"Then, knowing what lies ahead for you, you won't become bored with being a Christian, nor become spiritually dull and indifferent, but you will be anxious to follow the example of those who receive all that God has promised them because of their strong faith and patience."

Hebrews 6:12

I have discovered there are five phases of faith; and if you cut out in any one phase and don't stay with it, you will be disappointed with the results.

Faith is like a seed. If a seed is not planted, it won't bear fruit. You must first plant the seed. But that is just the first phase. Unless the seed is watered, it won't sprout, which is the second phase. Once the seed is planted and watered, growth may begin; but unless it is nourished, the seed won't reach full maturity. It won't blossom! That's the third phase. If it doesn't have proper climate just when the buds are beginning to form, all you'll have is the stock and no fruit, which is the fourth phase. Then when the fruit is ripe, it must be harvested or the winds and rain may drive it down causing the fruit to be unproductive, the fifth phase.

So there are five phases to fruit-bearing from seed time to harvest, and there are five phases to the full cycle of faith! I call them the *nesting, testing, investing, arresting,* and *cresting* phases of faith.

We'll be talking about each phase in depth for the next few days.

My mind is alive with ideas and dreams. God is opening up new vistas before me!

Know Your Faith

"Be still and know that I am God!"

Psalms 46:10

The first phase of faith is the NESTING PHASE. An egg is dropped, an idea is born, a thought comes into the nest of the mind. Now for some people that's the only phase of faith they ever experience. The egg is never hatched! It never goes beyond the nesting phase. These people won't do anything about it. The idea comes and they let it go. It dies in the nest.

God sends us many ideas! Ways to repair broken relationships. How to be financially successful. Where to begin your own personal growth.

What ideas are nesting in your mind today? What beautiful possibilities is God seeking to bring to your attention? For a few minutes be very still and know that God is directing you. Write down the ideas He is placing in your nest. Include them all, even the ones that may first seem impossible!

_____

_____

_____

_____

_____

Remember, the nesting phase is only the beginning!

> **My spirit is still. I am receptive to the ideas God is sending to my nest.**

Know Your Faith

"Blessed are those who trust in the Lord and have made the Lord their hope and confidence. They are like trees planted along a riverbank, with their roots reaching deep into the water."

Jeremiah 17:7,8

After the idea drops into the nest, we begin the TESTING PHASE of faith. This is the time to ask questions. And your questions will arise out of our value system. I have lectured on this to students and leaders in schools and industry. And I always emphasize that decision-making is easy if your value system is clear and unclouded.

When you know the right question, you can know immediately if you have a good idea or a bad idea. Here are the questions I use: Is it really necessary? Is it needed? Is it a beautiful idea? Can I ask God to be my partner in this venture? Faith builds strong muscles when it gets a "yes" to these all-important questions. *When the idea comes, test it!*

_____

_____

_____

_____

God is guiding me through ideas that will
bring solutions to my problems.

Know Your Faith

"The one who trusts in me shall possess the land and inherit my Holy Mountain."

Isaiah 57:13

The reason some people become super achievers is because they learn how to handle the positive ideas God puts into their minds. The truth is, an idea that leads to success is shared with a multitude of people but only the rare person picks it up and makes anything out of it. That's why so many people have read about somebody who accomplished something and said, "I thought of that, but I didn't do anything about it." How do you handle an idea?

The idea is formed in your mind. At that point you can either throw it out or you can accept it. The real tragedy in life that I believe is the single cause of human sorrow is this: We tend to be positive toward negative thoughts and negative toward positive thoughts.

How do you know when to say no? How do you know when to say yes? To know whether it's God's will or the devil's will, ask the question, "God, is this right?"

It's impossible to make a wrong decision if you truly surrender your life totally as you know how to the lordship of Jesus Christ.

> **When I know an idea is God's will, I will say yes!**

Know Your Faith

"Commit everything you do to the Lord. Trust him to help you do it and he will."

Psalms 37:5

No idea is perfect! No idea is without its problems. God sets it up that way in order for us to be humble enough to seek His help all along the way. There is a Bible verse that says, "If you wait until the conditions are perfect, you'll never get anything done."

Remember Steinbeck's famous story, "The Pearl"? A man found a beautiful pearl, but it had one tiny flaw. He thought if he could just remove that little imperfection the pearl would be the biggest and the most priceless one in the world. So he peeled off the first layer, but the flaw was still there. Then he took off the next layer, thinking it would disappear, but the flaw remained. He continued to take off each layer until finally he had no pearl. The flaw was gone now but so was the beautiful prize.

Faith is daring to risk imperfection. The tragic truth is that much of our efforts would be overwhelmingly successful if we dared to run the risk of mediocrity. What we judge to be mediocre may be judged by others to be excellent! Write down the one thing you would do if you could do it perfectly! Remember beginning is half done!

_____

_____

_____

It is better to do something imperfectly, than to do nothing perfectly.

Know Your Faith

"You can get anything—anything you ask for in prayer—if you believe."

Matthew 21:22

Faith begins with an idea or dream, but must deepen before success is realized. It must become a desire! You must want something so badly that someday, somehow, somewhere, sometime, you know you shall have it. More faith is shattered by lack of desire than by real doubt.

To begin with, you must know what you want. Some people fail because they have neglected to visualize in detail what they were trying to achieve. If you have a confused and muddled picture of what you are going after, do not be surprised if you fail. Therefore, an early step in mountain-moving faith is forming a detailed mental picture of your dream.

Which of your ideas that passed the testing phase do you desire most? Write it here in detail. Can you clearly visualize it?

_____

_____

_____

_____

> **I can see my dream clearly and with God's help will achieve it!**

Grow Your Faith

"The apostles said to the Lord, 'We need more faith; tell us how to get it.'"

Luke 17:5

The next step of faith is the INVESTING PHASE!

When faith moves to the investing phase, you make a commitment and move forward! You commit time, money, energy and possibly the most valuable product—your prestige—to the project. But when you have to invest your money, energy or prestige, your faith may begin to falter.

If it does, remember faith doesn't fail you, you fail faith when you don't want to make the investment. When you have to back up your ideas with cash, it is easy for you to get cold feet. The going gets tough when you have to put your money where your mouth is, especially if it's what we call "risk capital." You may lose it all. Some people fail because they don't want to invest cash. Others, because they don't want to risk investing their time or reputation. Even a turtle doesn't get ahead unless he sticks his neck out.

Study the idea that you clearly visualized yesterday. It has reached this third phase of faith. Now what do you have to put on the line—time, energy, pride, money? What is God asking you to do? Dare to believe that your idea is from God, and commit yourself to it. What will your idea cost? Make as accurate a list as possible.

_____   _____

_____   _____

My idea will be successful because God is in it!

Grow Your Faith

"I can do all things through Christ who strengthens me."
Philippians 4:13

Faith is affirming success *before* it comes. Faith is making claims to victory before it is achieved. This is very difficult to do, but most important.

Our instinctive sense of modesty and honesty tends to restrain us from making public statements of our anticipated success. We sense that any announcement of success before it is within our grasp is a sin of presumption and proud boasting. So we have a natural compulsion to say nothing, keep quiet, hope for the best, and when we have won we will make our joyous announcement.

Was St. Paul modest when he said, "I can do all things through Christ who strengthens me"? Was he exaggerating a bit? Was he literally truthful in this affirmation? Or was this an extreme exercise of mountain-moving faith talking?

The truth is that mountain-movers are people who boldly predict success. They know that nothing succeeds like success. So their bold prediction, their brash announcement, is not immodesty—nor is it dishonesty—nor is it cocky pride—it is *faith in depth!*

Is your faith deep enough to predict success before it is within your grasp? Exercise your faith muscle again right now and make your faith claim.

I can feel courage within me undergirding my faith as I make a public announcement of my goal.

Grow Your Faith

*". . . for I know the one in whom I trust, and I am sure that he
is able to safely guard all that I have given him until the day of
his return."*

2 Timothy 1:12

At the fourth phase of faith, the ARRESTING PHASE,
problems seem to surround you. You wonder if you've made
a mistake with your investment. The arresting phase is
God's way of testing us before the final harvest. Will we
really be grateful? Are we ready for Him to give us the big
one? You've invested capital. You've put your name on the
line. You have finally attempted it. Now you run into unexpected problems of unimaginable immensity and it looks
like you're going to sink.

My personal testimony is that every idea that ever came
from God to me took a lot of faith for me to invest my time,
energy and reputation. And after I did, I inevitably ran into
a problem where the whole momentum of the project was
arrested just before success came.

But God is just testing our reliability and our humility. So
be patient when trouble comes and be thankful God is doing
something. Difficulties do occur, but I believe God gives you
ideas that will run into an arresting phase, for this is the time
when God is testing *you!*

God's delays are not God's denials.

Grow Your Faith

"Those who trust in the Lord are steady as Mount Zion, un-moved by any circumstance."

Psalms 125:1

To help get you through the arresting phase of faith, you need a *Source, Course,* and *Force!* You need Jesus Christ. He is the *Source* of inspiration. He also sets the *Course* of inspiration and directs the energy so that something con-structive happens to it, and it doesn't get off on wild tan-gents. And He is the *Force* that keeps the streams of inspira-tion and energy moving so that faith doesn't die in the arresting phase.

Let's say you are going to climb Mt. Everest. You've got everything lined up and by now you've crossed the ocean to India. You've gone through Katmandu airport and you're out there in the foothills. You're at an elevation of 22,000 feet! It's freezing cold and the winds are blowing. You can see the peak, but where will you get the strength to see the climb through to the crest? From the nesting through the ar-resting phases, Jesus is the source! Jesus sets the course! Jesus is the force that is within you! He keeps you going to the cresting phase of faith.

Jesus is the force within me.

Grow Your Faith

"I have a plan for your life, it is a plan for good, not evil. It is a plan to give you a future with hope!"

Jeremiah 29:11

Faith works if you don't give up on it! If you keep on keeping on!

I remember sending a telegram with the above Scripture verse to my friend Hubert Humphrey just before he had major surgery. And he called to tell me of the strength he was drawing from that message.

Everyone needs that inner strengthening that can only come from God who is bigger than you or I. Now when heartache hits, difficulties block your path or progress seems retarded, and you wonder if you should pack up or quit—hang on! Never imagine the trumpet sounding for you until God declares it! We will never know how many people failed because they gave up on faith. Don't ever quit!

I wrote the following Possibility Thinker's Creed to remind myself and others that we must develop the grit, so we don't quit.

POSSIBILITY THINKER'S CREED
When faced with a mountain, I will not quit.
I will keep on striving until I climb over,
find a pass through, tunnel underneath, or simply
stay and turn the mountain into a goldmine with God's help!

Through the ideas that come into my mind,
God is working out His plan for my life.

Grow Your Faith

"Anything is possible if you have faith."

Mark 9:23

DON'T QUIT

"When things go wrong as they sometimes will,
When the road you're trudging seems all uphill,
When the funds are low and the debts are high,
And you want to smile, but you have to sigh,
When cares are pressing you down a bit,
Rest if you must, but don't you quit!

Life is strange with its twists and turns,
As everyone of us sometimes learns.
And many a failure turns about,
When he might have won if he stuck it out.
Don't give up though the pace seems slow,
You may succeed with another blow.

Success is failure turned inside out,
The silver tint of the clouds of doubt.
And you never can tell how close you are,
It may be near when it seems so far.
So, stick to the fight when you're hardest hit,
It's when things get worse that you must not quit!"

> **Today's impossibilities are tomorrow's possibilities!**

Grow Your Faith

"For the Scriptures declare that rivers of living water shall flow from the inmost being of anyone who believes in me."
John 7:37

The final stage of faith is the CRESTING PHASE. The crest comes when we reach the mountaintop and achieve success. All the problems are solved. Salvation comes. The habit is broken. The money is here. The project is accomplished. The chains are broken and deliverance has come.

Look how these five phases of faith worked in Christ's life. His idea of His ministry started to come together when He was 12 years old. He knew that God wanted Him to do something. The *nesting phase* occurred when He realized He must be about His Father's business.

The *testing phase* came when he spent 40 days in the wilderness being tempted by Satan. The *investing phase* came as He spent several years stalking the plains and deserts, preaching, teaching and touching lives. He experienced great popularity with the crowds.

But then came the *arresting phase* as people turned away from Him. The agony in the Garden of Gethsemane and the tremendous shame of the cross led to Jesus crying out, "My God, why have you forsaken me?" It looked like His dream was finished.

But then came the *cresting phase*. He arose on the third day! Easter morning was the crest! And He is alive today! Be patient. God is at work. As you keep on believing, you *will* reach the crest!

> **Almost there, Lord. I can see the top! I can feel your spirit driving me onward and upward. Thank you.**

Grow Your Faith

"Great is your faith! Be it done for you as you desire."
                                            Matthew 15:28

What's the biggest problem facing you today and what are you doing about it?

For instance, let's say you are an executive in a large corporation and you usually wait until the afternoon to face your biggest problems. You give your worst hours to your most difficult problems instead of your best time to your biggest challenge.

If I have a very important decision-making meeting to schedule, I always plan it for 9 o'clock in the morning. Give your biggest problems your best hours and your best time! You will be amazed at how quickly your biggest problem becomes your biggest opportunity!

When you put off facing your biggest problem, subconsciously you become fatigued or depressed because working at the back of your mind is the gnawing awareness that there is something you have to tackle when you get around to it. And just knowing that is enough to make you tired!

With a strong faith, you can face up to a big problem and chip away its complexities a little every day until it becomes easy to resolve. Then you'll probably wonder why it seemed like a big problem at all. Remember: *Inch by inch, anything's a cinch!* And *ounce by ounce, everything counts!*

What's your biggest challenge? What are you going to do about it today?

God and I are an unbeatable team!

Grow Your Faith

"The Kingdom of God is within you."

Luke 71:21

Deep within you lies the power of God. And God waits to give you what you need to make your dreams come true.

BELIEVE IN A BIG GOD! Then make your goals and plans big enough for God to fit into them. Simply ask yourself and God, what would be a great thing for you to do with the rest of your life? Do it now and write down your answer:

_____

_____

_____

_____

Decide now to do it. If you need more education, get it. If it's money you need, find it! If it's talent you need, learn the skills or find someone to share your dream with who has the skills. The important thing is to begin—today!

God gives me dominion over every limitation!

Glow Your Faith

"In everything you do, put God first, and he will direct you and crown your efforts with success."

Proverbs 3:6

Mary Crowley, president of Home Interiors, a very prosperous business, was in Nassau, in the Bahamas, with her husband some years ago. It was a Sunday morning so they decided to go to church. They found a local church filled with nearby citizens. They were all black—she and her husband were the only white people in the congregation. She tells the story about how the huge, silver-haired preacher, with a thundering voice and a rusty, gravelly tone, kept pounding home one theme to his people all morning. He bellowed, "Be somebody! God never takes time to build a nobody! Everybody God creates is created to be somebody!"

That black preacher never knew what an inspiration he was to Mary Crowley, and through her to you and me.

Who is one person you can inspire in the same way today?

_____

Glow your faith!

I can be a somebody! God never takes time to create a nobody!

Glow Your Faith

"God did not give us the spirit of fear but of love and faith and a sound mind."

2 Timothy 1:7

If you listen to God, He will build you up. He'll never tear you down. He'll lift you; He won't condemn you. The gospel means *good news,* not bad news! *God is positive.*

I was in Washington recently and I talked to a father who had two daughters with high positions on Capitol Hill. I said to the father, "How did you ever manage to have two daughters in such powerful positions on Capitol Hill?" And his answer was, "I used to take them to the capitol when they were little girls so they could see the seat of power. My one daughter graduated from high school and I wanted her to go to college. But she said she was going to get a job and become a secretary to a great senator." The father continued, "I didn't want to let her go. I didn't dare let my two daughters leave home and go out to that city without having chaperones or protection."

I asked him who gave in and this is what he told me. "I'm a football fan, and I was watching a game and saw my favorite team get a red penalty flag. They were penalized for defensive holding. It was like a message from God saying, Father, don't be penalized for defensive holding. Don't hold your daughters back! Let them go! Let them fly like a bird! Let them be what they were designed to be!"

Some of you are being penalized for defensive holding. God has a plan for your life. God has a dream for you.

> **God's will is surging with me. I want to please Him.**

Glow Your Faith

"Because of his kindness you have been saved through trusting Christ. And even trusting is not of yourselves; it too is a gift from God."

Ephesians 2:8

Every human being God puts on planet earth has the responsibility of being an inspiration to those around him. *Anybody can be an inspiration to somebody!*

Many of you might think you're not important, but that's because you don't see life in its whole perspective. We have a furnace in our home that has a little pilot light. That small flame has to be faithful in order for the big furnace to work. The pilot ignites the bigger furnace which heats the entire house.

Nobody compliments the pilot light, yet in every successful institution and enterprise, there is at least one person who is the pilot light. He or she throws on the big furnace to make it happen!

Every person can be a pilot light, but first we must recognize the positive qualities about ourselves which we can project to others. Maybe you're a good listener or have a good sense of humor. List at least five positive qualities you have that would give others a lift to be around you.

_____

_____

_____

_____

> **When my faith seems weak, I trust that God is using me as an inspiration to someone!**

Glow Your Faith

"Except a grain of wheat fall in the ground and die, there is no fruit."

John 12:24

There is a calling for you! There is a plan and a dream for you. Every life has a purpose; and every life can be a light.

You may say, "I can't be a light. I've got too much darkness inside. I need to have somebody lighten me up." You know how to get a light on if you are in darkness? The trick is find someone who needs help more than you do! Forget yourself, and let Christ flow through you and it will happen!

Today or tomorrow, you will touch somebody's life for good or ill. You can lift them or you can lower them. You can bring them joy or you can bring despair. Be a glistening personality. People who "glisten" know how to "listen." They know how to hear. They are sensitive. They are receptive so they have a basic, healthy relationship with their family, friends, working companions and with God Himself.

You see, the person who "glistens" is reflecting that he has a deep inner harmony. Choose now to be a glistening personality.

Begin today to practice "listening" to people. During the next 24-hour period, consciously keep from talking and listen to others. You will be amazed how much you will learn . . . *about yourself!*

> **I am beautiful because God made me. I will listen to Him!**

Glow Your Faith

"Ask, and it shall be given you; seek, and you shall find; knock, and it shall be opened unto you."

Matthew 7:7, 8

How can I light up someone else's life when I've got such dark problems deep within? Is that the question you're asking yourself? Then call upon God and *pretend!* Does that sound hypocritical? Let me tell you the story of Henry Fawcett, one of the great distinguished members of Parliament in England.

Henry Fawcett was blind! One day when he was 20 years old, he and his father were out hunting and the father accidentally discharged the gun and shot his son in the face. The boy lived, but he was sightless the rest of his life. The father wanted to kill himself. And young Henry wanted to die, too. He had no hope for he would not be able to read again. He would not be able to study or go back to school.

Then one day he overheard his father crying and condemning himself for ruining his son's life. This was when Henry decided to build his father's hopes. He would pretend! "It's okay, Dad," he said. "Don't worry, I'll soon learn to read. Others can read to me." But in his heart it was a lie. To keep his father from self-destruction, young Henry lived a life of laughter; and optimism; and enthusiasm.

But then something happened. There came a moment when the lie became a reality! The act became the real thing! He had hope! And his hope produced results! And results produced progress! He began, you see, to listen to his own positive statements even when he didn't mean them. He harnessed deep, psychological laws of self-hypnosis.

> **With God's help, today I will bring joy to those around me.**

Glow Your Faith

"For now we are all children of God through faith in Jesus Christ."

Galatians 3:26

We all interrelate on planet earth. Everything we do provokes an action or reaction from someone. You and I are either part of the problem or part of the solution. We are creatures of planet earth—an organismic unity, mutually interdependent. We have to learn to communicate. And in the process we have to understand that each of us has inherited with our birth a responsibility to communicate in such a way that we become an uplifting force to those around us.

Do you know anyone who is hurting? Think of at least five people you know are hurting and write their names below. Then think of how you could be an uplifting contact to them. What could you say to each person to lift his or her spirits?

PERSON'S NAME   UPLIFTING THOUGHT

_____   _____

_____   _____

_____   _____

_____   _____

_____   _____

My task is to turn lights on in the faces of people with whom I relate.

Glow Your Faith

"Be shining lights in a dark world!"

Philippians 2:15

It's a dark world we are living in. Almost every person is walking around with a hidden wound in his heart. They may be smiling, confident, strong or radiant on the outside, but God knows there's a hurt deep inside.

Wow! What a challenge to bring a ray of light to someone who is in darkness. What an inspiration! What purpose for living. And in a world where so many people are hurting, there's no excuse for anybody feeling unimportant or unneeded.

Edward Rosenow, one of the great doctors at the Mayo Clinic for many years, was inspired to begin his career when he was a little boy living in Minnesota. His brother was critically ill so his parents called for the doctor. He said, "My father's and my mother's faces were strained with fear and worry. When the doctor came out of my brother's room, he looked at each of us for a moment and his face broke into a smile. 'You can relax, folks, he's going to be all right!' Then I saw a light come into my mom and dad's faces, and I decided then and there I was going to be a doctor when I grew up because I wanted to put light in people's faces."

Look at the list you made yesterday of people you know are hurting. Select one of the names, and give that person a call or visit. With God's help, you can put a light in someone's face today!

**Through Christ, I can become a shining light
in a dark world.**

God's Gift—The Open Door!

The Open Door to Prosperity

"Those who go out weeping, carrying seeds to sow, will return with songs of joy, carrying sheaves with them."

Psalms 126:6

The top of the news these days seems to be the economic conditions of our country and the world. Everybody is talking about recession and inflation. I heard a story about a man who came home the other day, kissed his wife and asked, "Honey, what are we having for dinner?" "Charles steak," she replied. "What in the world is 'Charles Steak?'" he asked incredulously. "Well," she responded, "at the current price, chuck steak sounds too undignified."

In all seriousness, the economy is no joking matter. How do you go about handling difficult times? Let me share with you a principle of vital importance.

THE RHYMES ARE MORE IMPORTANT THAN THE TIMES.

Whether or not you are mentally in rhyme or harmony with the dynamic, possibility thinking, success producing, God-oriented ideas you encounter is far more important than the state of the economy!

In any era of history, someone is losing money; somebody is making money. So the most important thing to remember at any time, is to be careful of the ideas that you allow to enter your mind—especially when the economy is in an unstable condition.

What are the *times* in your life?

God fill my mind with your ideas as I wait patiently and expectantly for Your guidance.

The Open Door to Prosperity

"Fear thou not; for I am with thee: be not dismayed, for I am thy God; I will strengthen thee; yea, I will help thee; yea, I will uphold thee with the right hand of my righteousness."
Isaiah 41:10

God cares about us, and so He addresses Himself to our economic needs. I want to share with you a Biblical principle that has become a very personal foundation in my own life. I know the reason for my own personal success and the success of this ministry—it's because of this God-given idea: In Malachi 3:10 God says, *"Bring the full tithes into the storehouse that there may be food in my house; and thereby put Me to the test says the Lord of hosts, if I will not open the windows of heaven for you and pour down for you an overflowing blessing."*

This is called tithing—giving a tenth of what God gives us back to Him. *Tithing is not a debt we owe; it is a seed we sow.*

It was many years ago that I first read of this promise of God. I found it all through the Bible—even in the New Testament. This concept is God's answer to the economic problems in an individual's life. "I will bless you," He promises, "if you will have faith in me. I will bless you if you really love Me and are thankful for the gifts I give you." God wants us to learn that he will test our generosity, faith and gratitude by asking us to give back a tenth of what He gives us to His ministry. If we are faithful, He will entrust us with even more. And so the giving and receiving multiply. This is God's lesson in "Economics 100."

> **Praise God! The seeds I sow in faith will be multiplied ten fold!**

The Open Door to Prosperity

"Freely ye have received, freely give . . . ."

Matthew 10:8

When my mother died a few years ago, she was living on a total annual gross income of a little under $3,000. Yet every year she gave $300 to the ministry. I would get a check for that amount each year around Thanksgiving. She lived on the balance of $2,700 during the remainder of the year. But somehow she always managed to have a little something to send the grandchildren each year at Christmas. And every year on their birthdays, they would always receive a card with a dollar bill inside from Grandma. Somehow she managed to maintain her two story house.

When my mother passed away, she left an inheritance that surprised all the children, including myself. Truly, nobody has a money problem—it's always a management problem.

If you have a limited income today, start multiplying it by giving a tenth of it back to God in gratitude. Watch how God will bless you. Sometimes blessings come in the most amazing ways!

What I give is what I get!

The Open Door to Change

"A new heart also will I give you, and a new spirit will I put within you ..."

Ezekiel 11:19

Have you ever felt chained to a bad habit or a negative thought process? Perhaps you're bound by a problem or by unending frustration, and you long to be set free. Listen to the beautiful words of Jesus:

"You shall know the truth and the truth shall make you free!"   John 8:32

Chains? or Change? You make the choice! It's incredible what freedom there can be for you from whatever may be binding you today. But first you must understand "the truth" that allows change to break the chains. Know this: *No problem is too big for God's power and no person is too small for God's love.* Don't ever say, "It's impossible!"

Chains? They can be broken. There can be a great change! Remember, the attitude is *"I CAN."* And the words are *"I WILL."* Your deepest desire is to love yourself. If you love yourself you will believe in God and you will think it's possible. Your only salvation is Jesus Christ who alone can heal and save and redeem. He wants to, He really does!

He is alive! Reach out for Him! He can touch you in His own way! He can save you right now!

I NEED TO BELIEVE IT IS POSSIBLE!

The Open Door to Change

*"I will go before you and make the crooked places straight
. . . ."*

Isaiah 45:2

Not long ago I went to Beverly Hills to marry a good
friend of mine, Glenn Ford. After the ceremony, as I stood
there with some of the Hollywood celebrities, one of them
casually lit up a cigarette. Just as he took his first puff,
Jimmy Stewart turned to John Wayne and said, "Duke,
when did you quit smoking and how did you quit?" John
replied, "I quit when I decided that it was more fun breathing than smoking!"

I think that's great! The lungs are indispensable. You can
get by without hands, arms, legs, eyes, ears, even a portion
of your brain. But you can't get by without at least one lung,
one kidney, a liver and a heart! Take care of your body.
Guard your health and enjoy healthy, abundant living!

Chained? If the desire to break your chains is strong
enough, they can be snapped. You are not bound by anything unless, at a deep level, you want to have that bondage.
It is possible for the chains to be changed. Your greatest
need is to believe that it is possible!

What chain do you believe needs to be broken in your life
today? _____

_____

It is possible: Believe it!

Everything can change!

The Open Door to Change

". . . and every branch that bears fruit, He prunes it, that it might bring forth more fruit."

John 15:2

Since infancy, I have been addicted to something far stronger than cigarettes, heroin or alcohol—bad eating habits! Over-indulging in pies, cakes, pastries, cookies and ice cream has always been a weakness of mine. I knew that such indulgent eating was sinful for me, so I went into a time of relaxation, meditation and two-way prayer.

From the depths of my heart I cried, "Jesus Christ, I believe in you! I think you are the Son of God. But I've never touched you. If you are there, you know about this problem I have. Can you help me?"

And in an instant, I had a vision. I saw in my mind a still, calm, full to overflowing river—so safe that a baby could wade in it. The water was so serene, so calm—as safe as an ice cream cone on a Saturday afternoon. But then the water started moving downstream. Suddenly I saw white caps roaring out of control and at the heart of the flood waters was a gigantic tree that had uprooted. My body was that dead tree!

Then I heard these powerful words: *"I have snatched you from destruction."* And I knew I had been healed of my addiction.

Take this time to relax, meditate and go into two-way prayer concerning your chains.

Today I choose to break my chains and embark upon a glorious freedom in Jesus.

The Open Door to Change

"I will lift up mine eyes unto the hills, from whence comes my help."

Psalms 121:1

"This is the day that the Lord hath made, let us rejoice and be glad in it!" Are you rejoicing today or are you bound by worry and frustration? *Don't make chains for yourself— CHANGE! Jesus said, "I have come to set the captives free."*

There was a time in ancient days when insecure rulers of Constantinople, today known as Istanbul, wanted to make sure they could keep the enemy out of their city so they performed a remarkable feat. They created the largest and heaviest chain ever built by human beings. The links were about a foot and a half long and about two inches thick. This monstrous chain was draped across the harbor to keep foreign ships out of their territory. People still wonder how something that heavy could be maneuvered. We don't really know, but remnants of the chain can still be found today.

Have you drawn a chain across the harbor of your mind? Most of us have a pretty good idea of what we believe, but the thought of new concepts coming in is rather threatening. To have a chain across your mind could prevent new thoughts from streaming in that would bring a cargo of abundance and prosperity to you. Then why do you do it? Because you made the chains! The entrance to your mind is blocked just as the harbor of Constantinople was chained. You are given opportunities, yet you allow yourself to be bound. But you can break the chains and change!

> **Today I will break the chains of fear and negativity to allow the glorious stream of God's great ideas to flow into my mind.**

The Open Door to Change

"O give thanks unto the Lord, for He is good, for His mercy endureth forever."

Psalms 107:1

How do people become bound by chains? By allowing themselves to believe negative thoughts that are put into their minds. Some people willingly *take* the chains and allow themselves to be bound. Others *make* their own chains, and still others *break* free of chains which would restrain them from realizing their full potential.

The Bible says, *"God has not given us a spirit of fear, but of faith, and love and a sound mind."* God does not give us a spirit of doubt, anxiety or worry. God does not give us negative thoughts. You want to make a change? You have to snap the chains of negative thinking. Just as one link leads to another, so does one negative thought pave the way for further negative thinking. Fear produces anxiety, anxiety produces insecurity and soon you have a negative cycle going. You've built a chain that binds you. It's tragic!

But you have a choice! Chains or change? God is love and He wants to snap the chain and bring a wonderful change into your life. Max Scheller said, "Love is becoming aware of the highest possibilities in someone." But who can love that way? Can you or I? No. Only God can love like that! He is love. Love is becoming aware of the highest possibilities in you. And you are set free in His love!

> **I can face the future courageously because I know that in Jesus I have true freedom!**

The Open Door to Change

"For God is not the author of confusion, but of peace . . . ."
1 Corinthians 14:33

Today you face the possibility of confronting the most dynamic, possibility-laden ideas that God has ever placed in your mind. Throughout today many thoughts will come to your mind. Some will be negative. Some will be positive. Some will come from God Himself. But one thing is abundantly clear. God wants you to succeed! He wants you to win! And, if you are to be the tremendous success that He wants you to be, then you must develop the possibilities that He has created within you. Winning begins with positive thinking. *Your thoughts have to soar before you can score and be the winner.*

Naturally, you will have to deal with problems, pressures and difficulties. Whoever said winning would be easy? *But when you find yourself in a bind, you must work with your mind.* You must allow your creative, God-inspired thoughts to soar beyond the obstacles that you may encounter in your way before you can score in life. Soar, then score!

This thought, from God, will let me soar: _____

_____

_____

I will soar—then score!

The Open Door to Change

"Be still and know that I am God . . . ."
                                        Psalms 46:10

Twenty-five years ago, when we held services in a drive-in theatre, God began to unfold in our minds dreams of a church incredibly impossible and utterly fantastic. In those days we had virtually no financial or emotional support from human beings. Many of the people with whom I shared what I knew were God's great ideas thought I was either crazy or on some horrible ego trip!

Today the pieces of that dream are falling into place—a church, a tower, a Crystal Cathedral, a world-wide television ministry, a radio ministry affiliated with the National Broadcasting Company, and a ministry to the military over the Armed Forces Network. We know that as we continue in faith, our dream for God will be a reality!

But along the way, it hasn't been easy. Many times those beautiful dreams seemed totally impossible. *Great dreams always give birth to great difficulties.* When your dream seems impossible and you don't know how you can go on, remember the words of the Psalmist: *"Fret not thyself because of troubles. Trust in the Lord and do good."* God is with you every step of the way.

> **I know God will solve the problem if I have the faith to make the right decision!**

The Open Door to Freedom

"Be not conformed to this world; but be transformed by the renewing of your mind, that you may prove what is good, and acceptable, and perfect will of God."

Romans 12:2

In order to change into a happy, joyful, abundant person, you must snap the negative thinking habit. Glen Cole, a graduate of our Institute for Successful Church Leadership, and a pastor in Washington, told me a story the other day that illustrates this. He boarded an airplane and sat next to a professional basketball player whom he recognized right away. Glen turned to the athlete and said, "When you are guarding a player, what do you look for? What do you really watch? His hands? His eyes? Or his feet?" The young man replied, "I only keep my eye on his bellybutton, because until it moves he isn't going any place!"

I have met many people all over the world who can put on a good show, but until they change their thinking, they aren't going any place.

Let's start practicing positive thoughts right now. In the space below, make a list of some of the many things in your life for which you can give thanks to God.

1. _____   2. _____

3. _____   4. _____

I am praising God for the beautiful things in my life. And as I give thanks, I open my mind to His fabulous joy!

The Open Door to Freedom

"You shall know the truth and the truth shall set you free."
John 8:32

SOME PEOPLE TAKE CHAINS, and because of their style of thinking, allow themselves to be bound. I was born into a poor family. We had no electricity—we couldn't afford it. We had kerosene lamps! I don't remember getting gifts at Christmas time. We went to church and I got some candy in Sunday School. I know what poverty is and my heart goes out to those persons who have known nothing but poverty in their lifetime. But today I want to tell you that you can change! Whether you inherit poverty, oppression or prejudice, you don't have to take it! I'll tell you why: *You are a child of God! He can break those chains!*

What chain do you feel you inherited? _____

_____

Which inheritance is ultimately greater—your earthly families, or that from your heavenly Father? You are a child of God—and all God's children are free!

> **With every step I take today, I leave the broken chains of yesterday further behind.**

311

The Open Door to Freedom

"Jesus said, 'if you can believe, all things are possible.'"
Mark 9:23

One of the greatest men in Judea today is Musa Alami. As he stood one day on the top of a mountain and gazed on the hills of Moab, he saw only one trickle of blue flowing in the vast wasteland—the Jordan river. "If only there was more water," Musa thought. Then he came up with an incredible and impossible idea. "Why not dig for sub-surface water?" So Musa talked to his friends about digging for water but their response was far from favorable. "That's impossible! There is no sub-surface water." But Musa didn't listen to his friends. With almost no money, he began to dig a hollow in the sand. In spite of the constant criticism and mocking from his friends, Musa and a few companions dug for one, two, six months. Then the sand began to change color and finally become moist. With one more shovel full, water began to seep in covering the dry soil. They struck an underground river that had been there tens of thousands of years!

For years the Palestinians believed the negative-thinking experts. They were bound by negative-thinking chains. Don't just accept the chains someone may try to lay upon you. Don't take it—you don't have to! You are a decision-making creature—choose freedom in Jesus!

Abundant life is mine because I am free in Jesus!

The Open Door to Freedom

"For the tree is known by his fruit."

Matthew 12:33

SOME PEOPLE MAKE CHAINS. These people are their own worst enemies. During the national league play-offs this year, the Los Angeles Dodgers played Philadelphia. My friend Burt Hooten was pitching. There were two outs and two strikes against the batter when he pitched the next ball. Burt was so sure that it was a strike, but the umpire called it a ball. That made Burt furious and, of course, the Philadelphia crowd loved it! The fans went crazy! Showing your feelings at an away game is like dropping blood in shark infested waters. Burt was really rattled. He walked the next four batters. But do you know what he told the press? "Some pitchers are knocked out by batters; some pitchers are taken out by an umpire; but the crowd didn't knock me off that mound, and the lineup didn't knock me out. Only one guy knocked me out: Hooten booted Hooten out! I learned a lesson that every professional has to learn again and again. Only we can knock ourselves out."

Don't make your own chains. If you've got a problem, if things are going badly, you are the only one who can decide what it will do to you!

SOME PEOPLE MAKE CHAINS.

> **God is in control of my life and I will choose the winning attitude!**

The Open Door to Freedom

*". . . Let us run with patience the race that is set before us,
looking unto Jesus, the author and finisher of our faith."*
Hebrews 12:1,2

By nature the masses of humanity think negatively. And
so, by nature, the vast majority will put you down. Jesus'
voice is very different. He doesn't run with the herd. Jesus
stands on the hill and He voices a lonely call. He says to you:
You may put yourself down; other people may put you
down; but I believe in you! You are a plan waiting to unfold.
You are a dream waiting to materialize. You are a brilliant
idea waiting to become incarnate. You are an exciting concept of God waiting to be born again. Follow Him and your
productivity will astound you! Listen to His voice and He
will call and choose you to great service.

He is the AUTHOR of your dreams, he places His creative, freeing ideas into your mind.

-and-

He is the FINISHER of your faith. He won't leave you
with a half-finished goal or partially fulfilled dream. LOOK
TO JESUS—HE WON'T LET YOU DOWN!

**Through the power of Jesus, I am changing
into a more beautiful person!**

The Open Door to Freedom

*"But glory, honor, and peace, to every one that works good
. . . ."*

Romans 2:10

SOME PEOPLE BREAK CHAINS! Don't take chains!
Don't make chains! *BREAK Chains!* How do you break
them? You break them by beginning to believe in what you
can become. And how do you do that? By meeting Jesus
Christ. *Love is becoming aware of the highest possibility in-
herent in someone.* That is what Jesus Christ does for you
and that's what He did for me.

I was just a little boy on an Iowa farm when I began to
believe that I could make the world a better place. What a
ridiculous and impossible idea—that if I became a follower
of Jesus Christ and a minister that the world would be a
better and more beautiful place? I'm succeeding now and so
will you if you let Jesus Christ and His spirit permeate every
area of your life.

As you look to Jesus, you can break your chains. You can
choose to change for the better. For when you consciously
and subconsciously commit yourself deeply to Jesus Christ,
He brings out your highest potential. He gives you what I
call a new ego state—the "Christ ego state." And then you
really see change!

**I AM NOT THE SAME PERSON
I WAS YESTERDAY!**

The Open Door to Freedom

"If any of you lack wisdom, let him ask God, that gives to all liberally . . . ."

James 1:5

Do you know where Arabian horses come from. Legend says that the prophet Mohammed decided that he wanted to breed the finest horses on the planet earth, so he searched the world over for one hundred striking mares. After he collected one hundred beautiful animals he led them to the top of a mountain where he corralled them. Directly below them was a cool mountain stream which they could only see and smell. He deprived them of water until they were all wild with thirst. Only then, did he lift the gate allowing all one hundred beasts to take off madly for the water.

All you could see were thundering, stampeding horses with tails flying in the wind, necks arched, nostrils flaring and mouths foaming, pulling themselves through clouds of spraying sand. Just before the stampeding herd reached the water, Mohammed put a bugle to his lips and blew with all his might. All of the horses kept on running except for four mares who dug their hoofs into the sand and stopped. With mouths foaming and necks trembling, they froze, waiting for the next command. "Those four mares will be the seeds of my new breed of horse," Mohammed cried out. "And I will call them Arabians!"

A common person becomes exceptional simply because he hears a different bugle call! Listen to Christ's trumpet and He will call you to greatness.

> **As I listen to God's voice, I am transformed into a new creature.**

The Open Door to Success

"And be ye kind one to another, tender hearted, forgiving one another, even as God for Christ's sake hath forgiven you."
Ephesians 4:32

In my experience, I've discovered there are four ways persons react when they encounter problems. First of all, some people are *STEWERS*—all they do when they face trouble is stew about it. So often stewers are given freedom and opportunity to improve themselves and their lives in college or in their careers. But they don't take advantage of these opportunities. They would rather just sit back and stew about their problems.

Second, some people are *BOOERS*. When they encounter a great idea filled with tremendous possibilities, they laugh. Because they know those ideas are impossible, they "boo" them down. They are the cynics who say, "It can't be done!"

Third, some people are *CHEWERS*. They are the people who, when facing a God-inspired, impossible idea, chew on it. They actively pursue their dream and when they run into a difficulty, they chew up those problems. They literally thrive on the energy produced by facing the challenge at the core of the problem. They know how to chew up problems and draw nourishment from their difficulties. Their frustrations become fruitful because they invigorate and energize them.

Finally, some people are great *DOERS* for God and their community. Doers trust in the Lord and don't fret about their problems—they just go about doing good.

What kind of person are you?

> **Today I'm making a move. I'm yielding to the positive impulse I've resisted long enough!**

The Open Door to Success

"If God be for us, who can be against us?"

Romans 8:31

Joe Jacobs, founder of Jacobs' Engineering Group, one of the world's largest engineering building firms, is a former pulpit guest and a very dear friend of mine. A tremendously brilliant, successful and vivacious man, he has undergone a series of major operations—any one of which could have killed him.

At lunch one day Joe said, "One of the most important statements anyone has ever made to me came after one of my operations. I was in the intensive care unit, right out of the operating room, and I was in such pain and distress that I literally cried. The agony was so intense that tears rolled down my cheeks. As I lay there feeling sorry for myself a nurse came over and looked down at me. 'Mr. Jacobs,' she began matter-of-factly, 'if you'll stop complaining a minute, you'll find out you're still breathing!'"

If you're a stewer, think about that statement. Anyone can find something to stew about. If you feel you're a failure, you can stew about your unrealized dreams. If you're successful, you can stew about the problems that success brings. But remember, no one ever said life would be easy. *There is no gain without pain.* If you're hurting, you're making progress by allowing yourself to grow into the person God wants you to be.

Thank you, God, for troubles that are really blessings in disguise!

The Open Door to Success

"Not that we are competent of ourselves to claim anything as coming from us; our competence is from God."
2 Corinthians 3:5

If you're a booer, then you're one of those people who constantly says to yourself and to others, "You can't do it. Be realistic. It's not practical." But the super achievers who really glorify God by discovering His calling and developing their potential are people who resist the negative cynics who keep booing and putting them down.

I recently had the honor of delivering the baccalaureate address at the Air Force Academy in Colorado Springs for the senior class of 1000 cadets. As I passed through the crowd shaking hands with friends, parents and relatives I was especially quick to notice one lady as she approached me. She had tubes coming out of her nose. They went around her face, joined at the back of her neck and were connected to a tank her husband carried on his shoulders as he followed three feet behind. As I took her hand, she greeted me with teary eyes and said, "Dr. Schuller, I've got you to thank. You see, we live a long way from here and I'm dying of cancer. They all said I could never make the trip, but you inspired me to believe it was possible even though I need oxygen all the time now. At first everyone was so discouraging. But then one possibility thinker spoke up and suggested the tank. And so here I am! I've seen my son graduate and it's the happiest day of my life."

I love Christ too much to ever doubt God!

The Open Door to Success

"Therefore, having this ministry by the mercy of God, we do not lose heart."

2 Corinthians 4:1

There are stewers, there are booers and then there are chewers. They see problems and seemingly impossible situations as challenges that drive them on. Of course they go through pain and periods of internalized turmoil, but they don't give in to these feelings because they know that negative emotions and impulses don't come from God. They face their challenges with a positive attitude and literally believe, *"I can do all things through Christ who strengthens me."*

When you encounter trouble and pain, remember that without trying times, you would be like an overprotected hot house flower—too tender to ever live in the real world. Be a chewer—chew up problems and draw nourishment from them as you grow stronger and more capable with each passing day.

What challenge are you facing today? _____

_____

How can you chew on it and draw energy to thrive? ____

_____

_____

> **Trying times are times to try more faith! I'm
> trying and God is helping.**

The Open Door to Success

"Let your light so shine before all, that they may see your good works, and glorify your Father which is in heaven."
Matthew 5:16

While in Indiana a few months ago, I spoke at a rally for nearly 12,000 persons. The coordinator of the rally is a dynamic Christian and a very successful professional lobbyist. "How did you get into your work?" I asked.

"Well, it all started like this," he began. "I owned my own electronics business and all my capital was tied up in merchandise. One morning I came into the store to find that sometime in the night I had been totally cleaned out! In one night I had lost a total of $170,000. I had to sell my home, the business, everything. Friends and neighbors came to offer their condolences. Everyone was very sympathetic, but sympathy didn't help.

"Then some friends and acquaintances who were actively involved in the politics of the two major parties came to visit and instead of offering me comfort, they asked me a question. 'What are you going to do now?' That's what helped me," my friend confided. "That question took me out of the past and helped me start looking toward the future."

What are you going to do now? That's the key question! So you've suffered a loss or rejection. That's too bad. But you can't look back. Look forward.

It takes two to make a miracle!

The Open Door to Success

*"Behold, God is my salvation; I will trust and not be afraid
. . . ."*

Isaiah 12:2

The center to the solution of every problem is finding out
what God wants you to do and then doing it. We must come
to the point where we can say, "God, I will not stew over my
problems any more. But I will not grab at just any suggested
solution to my problem simply because it seems like a way
out of my situation. I will chew on those suggestions. And if
I feel the solution is Your solution, I will do it." It takes
courage to pray such a prayer.

Put this prayer in your own words, for your particular situation:

_____

_____

_____

_____

_____

_____

**I'd rather attempt to do something great and
fail than attempt to do nothing and succeed!**

The Open Door to Success

"... I am with you always, even unto the end of the world."
Matthew 28:20

Not long ago, I addressed my entire message to a prostitute in New York City who tried to proposition me. But when she saw my face, she recognized me, blushed and ran away before I could share my faith with her and try to help her out of her predicament. In the message I told her that "It takes guts to get out of the ruts." I encouraged her to be brave and think big, beautiful thoughts about what Jesus Christ could do for her.

That sermon aired at 12:00 noon in New York City. That same afternoon, NEW HOPE, our 24-hour counseling-crisis prevention center, received a telephone call from a girl in New York City. "I'm not the girl that Dr. Schuller talked to," she began, "but there are five of us here—all of us prostitutes. Today we sat together and listened to his sermon. Tell Dr. Schuller that five minutes after his program was over, we quickly grabbed the things that we wanted to keep and ran away so our pimp couldn't find us. We've left the business and we're going to find jobs as waitresses."

They are going to be winners because they are doers. And you can be a winner, too. Do you have problems? Stop looking backward and look toward the future that you can have when you commit your entire life to Christ. Ask yourself, "What am I going to do now?"

With God, all things are possible!

The Open Door to Abundant Living

"Behold the fowls of the air; for they sow not, neither do they reap, nor gather into barns; yet your heavenly Father feeds them. Are you not much better than they?"

Matthew 6:26

"The final exam." Or, "The last day on the job." Or, "The funeral is tomorrow." Or, "I got my diploma." Wow! How do you handle life's endings? By remembering *every ending is a new beginning.*

There is a beautiful story in the Gospel of St. Luke about the disciples. They had been out fishing all night and had caught nothing. Finally, after hours had passed, the night came to an end. In discouragement, they looked at the shore and saw someone who called out to them, "How did you do?" "Not good," they yelled back. "We toiled all night and we've caught nothing." The man on the shore called back, "Try throwing your net on the other side." They did and they felt the weight of a big haul. They pulled in the net filled with fish. Just when they thought there were no more possibilities; when they thought the thing was all ended, there was a new beginning! The night stopped; the day began.

How do you handle life's endings? Be positive and listen for the voice of God. He may tell you to throw your net in another spot and you will be surprised what you get. Keep a positive attitude toward life's endings that are out of your control. *Keep a positive attitude!*

Failure is never final!

The Open Door to Abundant Living

"I have come that they might have life and that they might have it more abundantly."

John 10:10

I read a story in the paper the other day about somebody who's out of work because of the recession. He lives in Detroit. In an interview, he said, "I worked 22 years here and all I have now is a bag of tools." They asked him what he did every day. "Oh," he replied, "I just clean my tools and wait for the factory to open. It better open because factory work is all I know. It's all I can do." So all he does is clean his tools and wait for the factory to open.

I want to say three things to that man. First, that factory may never open! Second, stop polishing those tools! Third, learn a new trade! Of course, you can! You could open a business. But you say, "I don't have any money to open a business, and it takes lots of money." I know businesses you can start on a shoestring—on a welfare or unemployment check. *It is possible!*

You can handle life's endings positively or negatively. You have a choice to either look upon every ending as a threat, or you can look at endings as an opportunity!

I won't hold on to what ties me down!

The Open Door to Abundant Living

"Thou wilt show me the path of life; in Thy presence is the fullness of joy; at Thy right hand are pleasures for evermore."
Psalms 16:11

I remember a dear friend of mine who lost her husband many years ago. She was having a difficult time and then suddenly she really pulled herself together. I asked her how she was doing it. And she said, "Well, I enjoyed the 28 years I had with him, but I'm remembering something that you said, Dr. Schuller—to look at what I have left, not at what I've lost. You know what I have left? I have freedom I really didn't have before. When John was alive he never wanted me to work. Now I can go to work and I enjoy it. Also I'm going back to evening school to take some courses. John always wanted me to stay home with him and watch television at night. I enjoyed that, but now I can go back to school. And you know what? I know I'm 60 years old, but I'm going to learn to drive. John never wanted me to drive a car. He didn't trust me on these freeways here in California. I'm free now to do things I couldn't do before."

Every ending *is* a new beginning—absolutely, if we have a positive attitude toward it.

> **I am a child of God and I know He's planned the best for me!**

The Open Door to Abundant Living

". . . Be strong and of a good courage; be not afraid, neither be dismayed: for the Lord your God is with you wherever you go."
Joshua 1:9

A few months ago, I gave the convocation address to open the fall term at Hope College. I had a wonderful time meeting the students. One very bright, attractive young man told me how much the television ministry helped to change his life. He said, "Dr. Schuller, my mother never misses your television program. Then when she was sick with cancer, every week she found strength with you. She died when I was only fifteen years old. After she died, I got in trouble. I made a mess of my life. One day I remembered that mom used to watch your program every Sunday morning. So even while I was still messed up, I turned the television set on one Sunday morning and there you were! I started watching every week. And you know what? I'm now a Christian and you've changed my life! Here I am, a freshman at Hope College!"

That young man found a beautiful new beginning to his life with Christ. And you can too. Each and every day can be a new beginning when you're walking with Him.

> **Before I can do something, I must be somebody —a beautiful person!**

The Open Door to Abundant Living

"Trust in the Lord with all your heart; and lean not unto your own understanding. In all your ways acknowledge Him, and He will direct your paths."

Proverbs 3:5,6

People have said to me, Dr. Schuller, now that the Cathedral is built, are you going to start a college? And I say, "No way." We've got many great Christian colleges in this country. We don't need another one. The ones we have need to be strengthened. I went to one of these great schools, Hope College in Holland, Michigan, one of the top accredited co-educational institutions in the United States. I took many of my courses there in a great old ivy-covered brick building called Van Raalte Hall. And last year I heard a fire had burned it down. So when I went back there, I was kind of anxious to see what the hole in the ground looked like, especially since our class had helped to raise the roof while I attended there. Now it had burned down.

Expecting to see a hole in the ground, what did I find? The ending of an era had turned into a beautiful beginning! They haven't built another building, and they aren't going to. Instead the area is a big green lawn, with trees leading up to the street. The street is closed and is now a mall and a park, and it's beautiful!

You don't like changes? I like improvements! Every ending is an excuse for a new beginning and every new beginning can be better! That's possibility thinking. If you keep a positive attitude, it's so simple!

Thank you, God, for unexpected mountains that turn into miracles!

The Open Door to Abundant Living

"He only is my rock and my salvation . . . ."

Psalms 6:26

Every ending is a new beginning. Either a great beginning or a lonely beginning. And that depends on you! That is your choice. You can either adjust or you can decide. Think about that.

Rene DuBois states that the human being has an infinite capacity to adjust downward. To which I reply, all adjustment is a downward movement. The upward movement is never an adjustment, it is a decision! A commitment! Every ending is a new beginning.

That's really what the gospel is saying to us! At the end of this life, there will be a new beginning for me, and I trust for most of you. It will be the beginning of an eternity with our Friend we love most, and His name is Jesus Christ.

If you feel like you are adjusting downward, decide now to make a commitment to move upward. Commit your life to Jesus Christ. That's the ultimate upward movement. Write a prayer of upward commitment now: _____

_____

_____

_____

> I am at peace knowing that my most profound ending is also my greatest beginning!

The Open Door to Abundant Living

". . . Love one another as I have loved you . . . By this shall all people know that you are My disciples . . . ."

John 13:34,35

I remember an exceptional man who was also a charter member of our church—Norm Rasmussen. What a tall, strong, handsome athlete he was, and dedicated volunteer worker. Norm and his wife had four sons and then a daughter who was a mongoloid. Turning the problem into a project, they bought a home in Northern California. Then they went to the County and asked if there were any unwanted children with brain damage or Downs Syndrome. And they began to take care of these children. They adopted 30 of them! What a great man!

Last summer Norm was water-skiing, when suddenly he was blinded by the sun shining off the water. He slammed, at full speed, into the concrete supporting pillar of the bridge he was skiing under and was killed instantly. I received a note from his wife, Sara, updating me on the children. And she reported that Kent, one of the boys, has completely taken over better than they ever thought he could! "I thank God for him daily," she said. Truly, every ending is a new beginning.

When I first heard of Norm's death, I called Sara and told her, "I know where he is because I know what he was and Who he knew." He knew Jesus Christ. Who goes to heaven and who doesn't? It's a matter of who you know. No friend of Jesus is ever turned away. Every ending is a new beginning.

> **I am living with joyful anticipation because Jesus is my best Friend.**

Move Ahead With Possibility Thinking

The Power Behind Possibility Thinking

". . . You shall not live by bread alone, but by every word that proceeds out of the mouth of God."

Matthew 4:4

What is the power behind possibility thinking?

1) It is the power of a *positive mental attitude.*
2) It is the *reproductive power* that starts with one small decision that blossoms into something beautiful.
3) It's the ultimate *power of the promises of God Himself.*

Either there is a God or there isn't. If God does exist, then either He has spoken or He is silent. As Christians, we believe that God is real and that He has spoken to us through His word, the Bible.

And the exciting thing is, as Christians, God wants to give us power! And He does it through possibility thinking. As we tap into his power, we then have

—the power of a positive mental attitude

—the reproductive power to turn a small decision into something beautiful

—the power of God's promises himself.

God's promises are awesome! He says that *"all things* are possible with God." That's Power!

I have the promises of God. I have power!

The Power Behind Possibility Thinking

"Stir up the gift of God that is within you."

2 Timothy 1:6

Where does the power, the energy, the thrust and the drive behind possibility thinking come from? *First of all from the POWER OF A POSITIVE MENTAL ATTITUDE.*

I am reminded of a story of the little boy overheard talking to himself as he strutted through the backyard, baseball cap sitting jauntily on his head, toting ball and bat. "I'm the greatest baseball player in the world," he said proudly. Then he tossed the ball into the air, swung at it and missed. Undaunted, he picked up the ball, threw it into the air and, as he said to himself, "I'm the greatest ball player ever!" he swung at the ball again. And again he missed. He paused a moment to carefully examine his bat and ball. Then once again he threw the ball into the air. "I'm the greatest baseball player who ever lived!" he said. He swung the bat hard and again he missed the ball. "Wow!" he exclaimed, "what a pitcher!"

There is nothing in the world like a positive mental attitude. God wants you to have this powerful tool. As you begin to realize the power in a positive mental attitude, you'll have made the first step in receiving his glorious gift. In prayer now, why not let God begin to filter out your negative thoughts, and fill you up with positive, exciting expectations!

> With a positive mental attitude, I can transform every time, situation and experience in my life into great possibilities.

The Power Behind Possibility Thinking

"Do not judge by appearances, but judge with right judgment."

John 7:24

A natural law states that whenever a person begins to practice a positive mental attitude, there is a power released—a very natural, human power. God designed human beings so that we produce constructive energy when we think positively and begin to sense the unlimited possibilities in little ideas.

Every situation and every idea can be seen as a potential menace or as a potential masterpiece. Every situation and every idea that is potentially valuable is also risky. When you eliminate the risk factor, you eliminate the opportunity as well. If there is no element of risk, then you are merely doing something that everyone else is doing, which implies the opportune time for pursuing that idea has passed. Opportunities always fall into the hands of leaders who make the decisions to pursue activity where there is still risk involved. They are able to muster the courage for such decisions because of their positive mental attitude.

God's great people are great because of their commitment to a beautiful, risky, God-inspired dream. I invite you to become one of God's great possibility thinkers. Make a commitment today to begin practicing a positive mental attitude.

My problems are possibilities, my obstacles are opportunities because I am committed to God and to greatness!

The Power Behind Possibility Thinking

"I am the bread of life, all who come to me shall not hunger and all who believe in me shall never thirst."

John 6:25

A positive mental attitude is the foundation of the power behind possibility thinking. However, there is a second power which comes into play. I call it the POWER OF RE-PRODUCTIVE POTENTIAL. *When you approach a dynamic possibility with a positive attitude and dare to make risky decisions, no matter how small that first step might be, you begin to see that each idea has within itself an enormous reproductive capacity.*

Each and every hour of every day new thoughts and inspirations are bombarding our minds. But new ideas, like tender young children, must be treated gently and with care or they may fade and die without ever being given a chance to achieve their potential greatness. What new ideas are in your mind today? Write them down no matter how impossible they may seem. Remember, there are infinite possibilities in little beginnings if God is behind the whole idea!

1. _____

2. _____

3. _____

I know I will succeed because I am relying not on my own ability, but on God's ability!

The Power Behind Possibility Thinking

"The righteous shall flourish like the palm tree and shall grow like a cedar in Lebanon."

Psalms 92:12

One man receives an apple. He sees it as a healthy snack, eats it and throws the core away. Another man is given an apple. He sees in it an apple tree. He eats it and plants the seed. In a few years, he has an apple tree. A third man, a true possibility thinker, takes an apple and envisions an orchard. He plants the first tree and when it bears fruit, he says to himself, "There is a market for these apples." He looks for empty ground and plants more trees. Soon his orchard is a reality. But he doesn't stop there. Soon he is making apple pies, apple tarts and apple cider and selling his product at roadside stands. He may even choose to open a restaurant specializing in delicious apple fritters or apple bread.

Any man can count the seeds in an apple, but only God can count the apples in one seed. Don't let negative thinking limit your potential. Remember, possibilitizing holds the power of reproductive potential! Look back at the ideas you wrote down yesterday. You know that without God's help, they are impossible, but through God's power, they will reproduce into scores of newborn dreams. Tap into God's power now by drawing close to Him. Pray for each one of those ideas that God's power might make the impossibility a reality!

God has no wastebaskets!

The Power Behind Possibility Thinking

". . . He is my refuge and my fortress; my God, in Him will I trust."

Psalms 91:2

Twenty-five years ago my wife and I wanted a church that would bring a positive faith to people around the world. Although no one really knew us, within six months there was a group of people who believed in us enough to say, "We'll join you." I said to them, "We have no money. And if we are going to accomplish all that God wants us to do, we are going to need a lot of it." And I presented to them a challenge to stand on the promise of God. In Malachi 3:10 God says, "Bring a tenth of your income to me and prove me. See if I will not open the windows of heaven and pour out such a blessing there will not be room enough to contain it."

I believe every one of those 25 original charter members made a decision to do something they couldn't afford to do—begin taking a tenth of their paychecks and depositing it in the offering. At that time I made a promise to them. I promised that God would keep *His* promise.

Today I want to make that promise to you. *Trust God and He will surely keep His promise to you.* For the greatest power of all is the POWER OF GOD'S PROMISES!

Spend some time researching three promises in scripture that mean a lot to you. Write them down.

1.) ——————— 2.) ——————— 3.) ———————

Now claim these promises as true. Claim Power!

I am looking for miracles because I believe in the promises of God!

337

The Power Behind Possibility Thinking

". . . whatever you do, do all to the glory of God."
1 Corinthians 10:31

Mary Goforth's father, a world renowned missionary, told a very interesting story in one of his books. It seems there was a young woodpecker who was given training on how to properly go about drilling holes in trees.

As a new graduate, he was given his first assignment and his instructors pointed him to an appropriate tree. With extreme confidence, this cocky young woodpecker stretched his wings and flew to the assigned tree. Grabbing hold of the bark with his sturdy feet, he threw back his head and took his first whack. A chip of bark flew from the tree and the eyes of the woodpecker sparkled with pride. Again he threw back his head and took another whack. This time an even larger piece of wood flew from the tree. He was doing great. Then, just as he took his third whack at the tree, lightning struck, splintering the trunk into fragments and sending the woodpecker tumbling to the ground.

Dazed, but not seriously hurt, the young woodpecker looked at the splintered tree and said incredulously, "Wow! To think I did it with only three little whacks!"

Most likely our difficult situations will not be solved with "three little whacks" of our own. But if we're really in tune with God and His will, He intervenes in our lives. Only He can know what great things we can accomplish with Him.

> **With God on my side, impossible problems
> can become exciting possibilities!**

Become a Possibility Thinker Now

"and what is the immeasurable greatness of his power in us who believe . . . ."

Ephesians 1:19

Possibility thinking is a universal principle for successful and dynamic living. There is no power quite like it. It helps you incorporate into your thought process the three basic qualities which will help you to become a successful manager. (Remember, if you're not a manager, you are managed. In order to be happy, fulfilled and successful, you must manage your own life—manage your own future.)

To be a successful manager you need:

1.) The power to make the right decisions.
2.) The power to set effective goals.
3.) The power to creatively solve impossible problems.

In these three power producing areas, possibility thinking works its magic and its miracles.

When you begin to use the awesome power of possibility thinking, then you *are* a possibility thinker! You *can* turn your obstacles into opportunities!

> **I'll keep the faith. God will supply the power.
> And, together we'll win.**

Become a Possibility Thinker Now

"For he has made known to us in all wisdom and insight the mystery of His will . . . ."

Ephesians 1:9

First of all, *Possibility Thinkers use God's power to make the right decisions.*

In psychology we have terms such as intentional inattention and avoidance reaction response to describe the reaction of people to certain stimuli or situations. There are people who are so insecure and feel so inferior that they don't want to face up to a potential life-changing, risk holding decision. This kind of innate reaction is one we must all deal with, for if we avoid dealing with it, it can pose a potential danger to our possible success.

But, if you can escape your rut, if you can make a major decision to believe in God; and follow His will faithfully, then you will be opening up a spiritual lifeline between time and eternity, heaven and earth, God and yourself.

There is a decision that you need to make today. Maybe you've put it off because you're afraid that you'll make the wrong choice. No way! God wants to direct your decisions. Possibility Thinkers face decisions with confidence.

What right decision will you make today?

_____

_____

Have faith! God will solve the problems!

It takes guts to leave the ruts.

Become a Possibility Thinker Now

"Now to him who by the power at work within us is able to do far more abundantly than all we ask or think, to him be glory . . . ."

Ephesians 3:20

How can you achieve a sense of joyful prosperity in your private living? How can you manage to succeed? Possibility Thinkers have learned the secret to success. They are managers of their own lives—not managed by someone or something else. Success is not necessarily fame or fortune. Real success is a sense of inner fulfillment—the ability to enjoy what you have where you are! Possibility thinking managers refuse to allow themselves to be manipulated. First, they make the right decisions; and, second, they set their own goals.

Examine your life goals. Are you a good manager? In looking at the creative ideas God is giving you right now, what goals do you need to make?

> **With God's help, I will make the goals to move forward in the right direction.**

Become a Possibility Thinker Now

"Abide in Me, and I in you. As the branch cannot bear fruit of itself, unless it abides in the vine, neither can you, unless you abide in Me."

John 15:4

One of my hobbies is raising Koi fish. These fish are really amazing creatures. Some of the larger ones will actually suck my fingers (they have no teeth), and let me stroke them on the back.

Some people have asked, "Why are there some big fish and some little ones? How big can they get?" That's a fascinating question. The size of the fish depends on the size of the pond. A Koi fish can live in a small tank, but it will never grow longer than two or three inches. In ponds the size of mine, they will grow up to a foot and a half in length. But if they live in a huge lake where they can swim and stretch, they will grow up to three feet long. It's the stretching that lends itself to greater growth. The size of the fish is in direct relation to the size of the pond.

This observation leads to an interesting principle. Little ideas which fall into little thinking minds produce little achievements. But, when those same little ideas drop into big thinking minds, they become enormous achievements! *The size of your thinking determines the growth of your idea in its ultimate development!*

Possibility Thinkers think big. Their ideas grow big. Their results are big! Become a Possibility Thinker now!

I WILL BUILD A BIG BELIEF!

Become a Possibility Thinker Now

"Every good gift and every perfect gift is from above . . . ."
James 1:17

Not too many months ago America warned the world that Sky Lab was going to fall to earth. A friend of mine who was in Australia during that time shared with me some very interesting observations. "Everywhere I went in Australia," he said, "people were talking about the probability of Sky Lab falling into their country. Inevitably they reacted in two totally different ways. Some people reacted fearfully. 'Oh,' they exclaimed, 'what if it hits our property?' They saw Sky Lab's eminent descent to earth as a potential menace. Others reacted not with a negative, but with a positive mental attitude. 'What if it lands on our place?' they said. 'Won't it be a valuable souvenir?' "

When Sky Lab did fall to earth, it did in fact fall in Australia. Some of the people on whose property it fell never touched it for fear of contracting radio active poisoning. But one young man believed what he had been told about the pieces of Sky Lab being absolutely safe to touch. He flew to San Francisco with his piece of Sky Lab and collected $10,-000 in cash. Because he used possibility thinking, Sky Lab was no menace to him; it was a masterpiece!

Possibility Thinkers see every problem as a possibility, every obstacle a challenge, every hurt a halo.

Today you will face problems. With whose power can you turn them into a glorious possibility?

> **Thank you, Father, for giving me the positive inspiration to see every situation as a potential masterpiece.**

Become a Possibility Thinker Now

". . . this day is a day of good tidings . . . ."

2 Kings 7:9

In 1848 an engineer by the name of Theodore Elliot solved a problem that had hindered commerce for decades. For years farmers and businessmen alike had thought how wonderful it would be to have a railroad that could cross from New York to Canada. But in order to build such a railroad, a bridge was needed to span the Niagara River. Traditional bridge building schemes simply would not work. But Theodore Elliot conceived of a brilliant solution. He proposed the first suspension bridge.

But, he had one problem. How could he suspend a cable across the river which was capable of supporting the weight of two workmen? Again, Elliot got an idea. He announced a kite flying contest and offered a prize of $10 to the first boy who could fly a kite across the gorge and tie the line down on the other side.

Many contestants tried and failed until Homer Walsh, an 11-year-old boy took advantage of a good south wind. And Elliot, by tying the kite string to a series of successively heavier ropes and pulling them across the gorge, was able to string his cable and begin the construction of the world's first suspension bridge.

Possibility Thinkers use their power to creatively solve impossible problems.

> Some things are impossible, Lord! It is impossible for me to see the immeasurable, unlimited possibilities in one fertile idea.

Become a Possibility Thinker Now

"Draw near to God and He will draw near to you . . . ."
James 4:8

I remember when my son was first learning to button his shirts. "I want to do it all by myself," he firmly asserted. And I remember watching his first attempt, as he took the first button and worked it through the second buttonhole. "Wait a minute, Bob," I began. But he brushed me aside and put the second button in the third hole. "Bob," I warned, "this isn't going to work." "It will too," he persisted, "I can do it all by myself." And he put the third button in the fourth hole. When he got to the top, he looked at me with bewilderment. He had one button left with no buttonhole to put it through.

No matter what endeavor you undertake, you're not going to end up right if you don't start out right. Start right! *Commit your life and your goals to God.* Put your faith in Him and you will be surprised how beautifully you will be able to manage your life with the skills He provides.

Use these moments to commit or recommit your goals, your thoughts, your desires, your purpose to the one who knows and cares for you. When you get under the guidance of Jesus Christ, you get under the influence of the greatest Possibility Thinker in the world!

Dear Lord, today I commit to you:

_____

_____

I am starting right with you, Lord!

345

Practice Possibilitizing

"I will sing unto the Lord because He has dealt bountifully with me."

Psalms 13:6

When I think of all the Possibility Thinkers who have given so generously to so many wonderful causes, I think about how these people have learned one of the most important lessons of life. Jesus taught it when He said, *"If you give, you will receive. Your gift will return to you in full and overflowing measure, pressed down, shaken together to make room for more and running over. Whatever measure you give, large or small, it will be used to measure what will be given back to you."* An incredible truth!

Give a little and a little will come back to you. Give a lot and a lot will come back. Every farmer knows that. If you want to keep seed, you have to plant it in the ground to get a bigger harvest in the fall. This is the law of prosperity—the law of possibilitizing—the law of abundance, taught by Jesus.

What opportunity did you have this week to give?

How did you respond? Claim the power of possibility thinking and learn the law of possibilitizing.

If this opportunity comes again, how can you follow Christ's example?

Possibilitizing is multiplying the result.

346

Practice Possibilitizing!

"If anyone serves me, he must follow me; and where I am, there shall my servant be also; if anyone serves me, the Father will honor him."

John 12:26

Possibilitizing is impossible without the giving of yourself in a vulnerable way! When my daughter Carol was 13 years old, she learned this valuable lesson. She heard at that time that the Crystal Cathedral construction would stop unless we had a million-dollar offering. She decided to give what she could. She made a decision to sell her horse, Lady. When she announced that her horse was for sale, a member of the church read the ad and decided he would like to buy it. I took Carol over to the man's house and he gave her a check for $450.00.

Then, the man asked Carol some questions about Lady. "Is she a good horse?" he asked. "Oh, yes," Carol enthused, smiling. "Well," he continued, "I really don't want a horse. I would like to give it to someone who would like a good horse. Do you really like horses?" "Oh, yes," Carol exclaimed. "Well," he said, "I really don't have time to feed Lady so let me tell you what I'll do. I'll give the horse back to you; but, I want you to give her a new name—Crystal Lady!"

Carol was so thrilled! She immediately called a local bank and asked for 450 brand new, unwrinkled one-dollar bills to put into the wheelbarrow the next Sunday morning. Carol learned the lesson we all must learn at one time or another. There are enormous problems that we can conquer—only with the help of God. But, for God, nothing is impossible!

Possibilitizing is anticipating the good!

Practice Possibilitizing!

"I have come as light into the world, that whoever believes in me may not remain in darkness."

John 12:46

Every problem is the same. At the outset they don't look the same; but, when you peel away the outer layers, you will expose the same core. I call the root of every problem *uncertainty*. A German scientist uttered this principle some years ago. There is throughout science, a principle of uncertainty; it is the uncertainty that produces what our minds call problems.

I've learned that the only solution to the problem of uncertainty is faith. Faith is facing up to an uncertainty with a possibility thinking attitude. Believe the best, move forward and you make the best happen. Believe the worst and you do not move forward and the worst has an opportunity to occur.

What, then, is the secret to banishing problems? The secret is to actively practice faith. No problem rooted in uncertainty can withstand the powerful force of faith in God.

When you practice faith, you are possibilitizing.

What problem are you facing today?

_____

_____

_____

Possibilitize! Practice faith. List three ways God can dissolve this problem:

_____

_____

Possibilitizing is overcoming!

Practice Possibilitizing!

"Let not your hearts be troubled; believe in God, believe also in me."

John 13:1

One thing we all must learn is that in order to possibilitize, you must put yourself in a position where you are vulnerable. *If you move into a position where you are not vulnerable, you are not taking a chance. When you are running no risks, you are not operating by faith.*

As I study human life, I look at a person's life as a balance sheet. Some balance sheets are in the black, while others are running in the red. Some are positive, while others are negative. Some are profitable—some are bankrupt. The difference between the positive and the negative life; the black or the red ink; the profitable or the bankrupt life is possibilitizing!

Faith and possibilitizing solve problems! Problem solving becomes added successful living. There is no faith without giving! The person whose life is bankrupt and in the red is basically a selfish person. The person whose life is in the black is a person who is unselfish. He always gets back more than he gives. He took a chance. He gave a huge gift and it's already come back. It's incredible! "Give and it shall be given to you, full measure, shaken, pressed down, overflowing!"

Today I will practice possibilitizing.
I will give _____
to these people _____

Possibilitizing is risky!

Practice Possibilitizing!

"And there is salvation in no one else, for there is no other name under heaven given among us by which we must be saved."

Acts 4:12

Any idea that comes from God is humanly impossible. It is a lesson of success that you have to move out and begin *before* you solve the problem, or else you are not living by faith. Every problem is the same. It's only an uncertainty. The call from God is to put yourself on the line, your life, your gifts, your soul, your all. Then God takes over and turns what you've given Him into a miracle.

Yesterday we learned that faith, or possibilitizing means becoming vulnerable, taking a risk. If you receive an idea that is from God, it's going to be risky.

POSSIBILITIZE!—for with God all things are possible! Practice faith. Complete the following sentence:

I believe in God. I believe He will help me as I put myself out on a limb. Today I'll be vulnerable as I . . . _____

_____

_____

Possibilitizing is visualizing!

Practice Possibilitizing!

"I have a plan for your life. It is a plan for good and not evil. It is a plan to give you a future with hope."

Jeremiah 29:11

Not long ago I met with a young couple who came to visit our church campus from a city far away. They were a beautiful couple—a happy husband and wife; and, in her arms the young woman held a beautiful little baby boy. As we stood together outside the Tower of Hope, they said to me, "Dr. Schuller, this ministry has given us real faith—faith that can turn our scars into stars. It's made us strong for our little boy." And I looked at the darling little three-month-old baby boy, sleeping in the blanket. "May I hold him?" I asked. As I held the warm, sleeping bundle, I wondered what they could have meant—what scars could this small child have put upon their lives?

But without my asking, they explained. "You see, Dr. Schuller, we just got word that both of our child's little legs must be amputated below the knee. He was born without bones between the knee and ankle. God really used Carol's accident to help us see a bright future for him. You gave us faith. We know he's going to be an exceptional child with an exceptional future." And we held hands and prayed together and claimed God's promise to Jeremiah 29:11.

God's greatest gifts are never things, they are always ideas and attitudes. The joy I receive from seeing what God can do with what I give Him really makes my life sizzle with excitement and joy. Trust God, and He will do the same for you.

Possibilitizing is toughening!

Practice Possibilitizing!

"In everything by prayer and supplication with thanksgiving let your requests be made known unto God."

Philippians 4:6

A couple of years ago, I was invited to go up to Vancouver, Canada to lecture to about 200 ministers. At the opening of the conference, I recall meeting the treasurer. He was seated at the registration desk where he collected about $6,000 in cash, which he put in a little metal box. When the conference was about to open, he put the money in the safest place he could think of—the trunk of his car. That afternoon, after the last lecture, he went to the garage to get his car and found it was gone. It had been stolen!

Five or six days later, the police found the car abandoned. It had been completely stripped. An officer called the man and informed him that they had found his car. But amazingly, when he opened the trunk, there was the little metal box still holding the entire $6,000! The thief had never bothered to look for anything of value in the trunk.

The truth is that we oftentimes overlook the greatest potential and value because we simply can't envison such a productive concept coming from such an unlikely source. Some of the greatest concepts come from putting faith in the most unlikely ideas. *When you are possibilitizing, God will come into your mind and give you ideas that will enable you to develop your possibilities to their fullest potential.*

Possibilitizing is Praying!

Produce with Possibilitizing

"The heavens declare the glory of God, and the firmament shows His handiwork."

Psalms 19:1

Not long ago, I sat next to a man on a plane and he asked me what I did. I told him I was a minister. "What do you do?" I asked. "I'm a gambler," he replied, tossing a silver dollar carelessly into the air. "Do you have a faith?" I inquired. "Yes," he replied, "I believe there is a purpose to everything on planet earth." "I agree with that philosophy," I responded. Then, as if he were testing me, he challenged. "What's the purpose of a mouse?" Frankly, he caught me speechless. I hadn't the foggiest idea what the purpose of a mouse could be. But he had an answer on the tip of his tongue. "The purpose of a mouse," he explained, "is to generate job opportunities." He went on to tell me exactly how many jobs in our economy exist to deal with the problem of mice.

Ecology has taught us that there is a purpose to everything under the sun. And if there's a purpose to the wind, water, plants, animals and even mice, then you can be sure there is a purpose for human beings. The Bible tells us that our purpose on planet earth is to develop our God-given creative potential that we might truly glorify our heavenly Father. When we do that, we make God's creation more beautiful and we leave the world a better place because we lived in it.

> **Because I am made in the image of God and share his creative power, I am filled with possibilities for today!**

Produce with Possibilitizing

*"Heaven and earth shall pass away, but My words shall not
pass away."*

Matthew 24:35

In one single, sweeping sentence God gives you a key to
help you unlock your possibilities: "Cast your bread on the
waters and it shall return to you." (Ecclesiastes 11:1) If you
throw something out with dedication, it will come back to
you bringing with it multiplied blessings.

When I first began studying this verse, I came to the conclusion that it honestly didn't make much sense. If you
throw seeds on the water, they will float back to the shore, if
the current flows in the right direction. But if you throw
bread on the water, it will dissolve; it will get soggy. If it
does come back, I don't think either of us would care to eat
it. The text doesn't make much sense until you realize that
the phrase was originally spoken in a culture where fish
provided the basis for economic survival. If you throw bread
on the water, the bread itself will not be edible, but it will
attract the fish to the surface so you can net them.

That's what the writer of Ecclesiastes has in mind. If
you're hungry, take your bread and throw it into the water.
You'll lose your bread, but you'll come back with a meal for
the whole family!

Likewise, a seemingly insignificant, even "dumb" idea according to some minds, rightly handled, can give forth enormous potential. When you give to God, your gift will return
to you multiplied.

> **I realize that the most incredible, impossible
> idea can be something, if God is in it.**

Produce with Possibilitizing

"Those that are of God hear God's words."

John 8:47

For many months after the accident that necessitated the amputation of her leg, my daughter Carol used a wheelchair. Until then, I never realized what a hassle handling a wheelchair could be. Then one day I received a letter postmarked Waterville, Ohio. It was from a man who got an idea about six years ago for a special little device you could attach to your car and use very easily to hang a wheelchair. But everybody he spoke to about it said, "What a dumb idea. Who needs that!" He got no encouragement from his family, his banker, or his friends. "But every Sunday," he wrote, "I got encouragement from one person—Dr. Robert Schuller—who said, 'Believe you can do it and you will do it.' Dr. Schuller," he continued, "the wheelchair carrier is now in production. This device will help a lot of people but I never would have attempted to succeed without you."

What idea do you believe is a possibility, even though others have knocked it down before?

_____

_____

_____

_____

Today I'm willing, waiting and wanting to move ahead with possibility thinking!

Produce with Possibilitizing

". . . By love serve one another."

Galatians 5:13

"Cast your bread on the water and it will come back to you." That sentence contains three vital messages. First of all this sentence is a *warning that what you put out will come back to you.* It is designed to protect you from potential danger. One of life's most fundamental basic truths states, *if you throw out a negative thought, it will produce a negative result.* A negative idea may manifest itself in a moment of self-pity, jealousy, resentment or anger—even a simple, seemingly innocent moment of unkind thought harbored, nurtured and acted upon can be very destructive in its ultimate consequence.

Always remember, if you respond to a negative thought, it will come back to you. What negative thought did you respond to this week? Confession leads to forgiveness, forgiveness brings reconciliation. Reconciliation restores relationships—and a relationship with God produces *Power!*

Oh, Lord, today I confess to responding to this negative thought: _____

_____

_____

> Forgive me, Father, for negative thoughts. Let my mind reflect only upon the beautiful truths you have made known to me.

Produce with Possibilitizing

". . . if only I may accomplish my course and my ministry which I received from the Lord Jesus."

Acts 20:24

"Cast your bread on the water and it shall return to you." This verse is also a *promise that if you respond to positive thoughts, their effects will multiply rapidly.*

This past week I lectured at a convention headed by Jim Jackson, from Kansas. "Seven years ago, Dr. Schuller," Jim began, "I was 55 years of age and flat broke. Many said I could not get a job. So, if you're 55, have no money, and are unemployed, what do you do? You have a card printed and call yourself a consultant." So, that's what he did. He called on an operation called United Farm Agencies and served them for awhile. He saw that they had a principle which involved tying together real estate companies in different parts of America for the purpose of selling farms. "That'd be a great idea, if I could apply that to homes," he thought. So he contacted about 20 different real estate brokerages in America and proceeded to tie them together through a computer and coordinated their multiple listings. That's how his company began seven years ago.

All great projects begin with simple ideas. Cast it to God and support will come from resources you never knew existed.

Even though there may be times I may stand alone, I know You are with me. And, together we will succeed!

357

Produce with Possibilitizing

"And let us not be weary in well doing: for in due season we shall reap if we faint not."

Galatians 6:9

"Cast your bread on the water and it shall return to you." This sentence is also an *invitation to faith. It is an invitation to be a bigger believer because what God asks you to do will not appear to be sensible."* "Throw bread on the water?" you may ask. "But bread is the last thing I have left to eat! Giving up dessert isn't too bad, but the most basic stuff of life is bread and water."

When God asks you to "cast out your bread," *that's an invitation to dynamic belief!* When a big idea comes from God, it is always of such a dimension that in order to act upon it, we have to have so much faith that we place ourselves in a position where the possibility of failure is overwhelming.

What projects do you have in your mind or on your desk today that you have not attempted because you fear failure? Make a "do" list. And then make a list of first steps to be taken. "Cast your bread on the water . . ."—it's an invitation to a bigger faith than you've ever had before.

My Project	My First Step
1. _____	_____
2. _____	_____
3. _____	_____

Thank you, Lord, for the courage that comes from trusting in you. I know that beginning is half done!

Produce with Possibilitizing

"Cast your burden on the Lord, and He will sustain you. He will never suffer the righteous to be moved."

Psalms 55:22

As I told you earlier, when we needed a one-million-dollar offering, to keep construction of the Crystal Cathedral going a couple of years ago, my daughter Carol decided she was going to take her one horse and sell it for $450.00 and drop the money into the offering plate. She sold the horse for $450.00 and somebody gave it right back to her.

Not long after that incident, I got a telephone call that a Flying Tiger cargo plane had left New York and would be landing in a few hours in Los Angeles, California. On the plane was a seven-month-old registered Arabian colt—a gift to Carol Schuller. It was quite a sight to watch the cargo plane land, the lift lower, and this proud, princely creature emerge from the cargo hold—one of the prize colts to be dropped in the stables of Imperial Farms owned by Doug Griffith. Today this beautiful creature is prancing like a regal prince on our property!

God truly multiplies blessings. When we give to Him the very best of ourselves, He multiplies and returns to us a hundredfold. Sometimes when we feel we've failed at something important, we may think of ourselves as worthless. But remember, God sees you and loves you not only for what you are, but for what you can become. When you put your faith in Him, you can become a conductor for a God-inspired idea that will accomplish something good for your family, your church, your community, your company and for yourself.

> **Only God knows the infinite beautiful possibilities waiting to come alive in me!**

Produce with Possibilitizing

"In all things I have shown you that by so toiling one must help the weak, remembering the words of Jesus, how he said, 'It is more blessed to give than to receive.'"

Acts 20:35

Success is a noble word. And I want to share with you how you can produce success. What is the principle of success? I'm going to sum it up in one sentence: CHOOSE THE WINNING ATTITUDE—POSSIBILITIZE!

God wants you to succeed. He made you and He's got a beautiful plan for your life. Affirmation of your belief in personal success is the first step toward a winning attitude. Say to yourself, "I want to succeed. I will succeed."

In a paper first published in 1915, Freud very wisely and correctly pointed out that there are people who actually are "fear-seekers." Just when it looks like they will reach the pinnacle of success, they blow it. They make a wrong decision. They plant their feet firmly and refuse to move forward, to sign the contract or take the challenge. The psychological explanation for this phenomenon would fill volumes, so the best I can do is give you a swift, therapeutic, healing technique to help you overcome this fear of success. That technique is the positive affirmation of your desire and will to succeed. Affirm to yourself that you dare to succeed. You desire to succeed, because you deserve to succeed. Practice possibilitizing. It works!

Thank you, Father for loving me. I will succeed for you.

I am a child of God and therefore I deserve success! I place my faith in God and I will succeed!

Produce with Possibilitizing

"In all these things we are more than conquerors through Him that loved us."

Romans 8:37

When I was in London, England a couple of years ago, I visited a hall where a man named Mallory was honored with a banquet years ago. In the 1920s Mallory led an expedition to try to conquer Mount Everest. The first expedition failed, as did the second. Then, with a team of the best quality and ability, Mallory made a third assault. But in spite of careful planning and extensive safety precautions, disaster struck. An avalanche hit and Mallory and most of his party were killed.

When the few who did survive returned to England, they held a glorious banquet saluting the great people of Mallory's final expedition. As the leader of the survivors stood to acknowledge the applause, he looked around the hall at the framed pictures of Mallory and his comrades who had died.

With tears streaming down his face, he addressed the mountain on behalf of Mallory and his dead friends. "I speak to you, Mount Everest, in the name of all brave men living and those yet unborn," he began. "Mount Everest, you defeated us once; you defeated us twice; you defeated us three times. *But Mount Everest, we shall someday defeat you, because you can't get any bigger and we can!"*

When you run into problems, you will have the calm assurance that they can't get any bigger—but you can! Possibilitize!

> **Thank you, God, for mountains that turn into miracles!**

The Christmas Promise

The Promise of Christmas—Peace

"My Peace I leave with you, my peace I give unto you."
John 14:27

The dark winter sky suddenly blazed with glory as the choir of angels sang, "Peace on earth, goodwill to men." This was the promise that the heavenly host proclaimed to all the world. Yet, for many of us, Christmas heralds not peace, but stress, tension and fear.

Perhaps you get overwhelmed by the hustle and bustle of Christmas shopping. Can there be peace for you? You may be having difficulty in your marriage. You fear that this may be your last Christmas together. Can there be peace for you? You may be suffering from a terminal illness. For you this may be your last Christmas. Can there be peace for you?

Yes! The angels were right when they cried out, "Peace on earth, goodwill to men!"

What situation do you need to find peace in today?

_____

_____

No matter what situation I find myself in today, I can have peace!

The Promise of Christmas—Peace

"Therefore, we have peace with God through our Lord Jesus Christ. More than that we rejoice in our suffering, for suffering produces endurance, and endurance produces character."
                                                    Romans 5:1,3

What is peace? Is it the absence of stress? Is it the absence of tension? Is it the absence of fear?

No. And this is not what the angels promised, nor is it what we'd want. A violin string is useless if it lies limp against the most beautiful instrument. Yet, when it is tuned to its proper tension, it will sing out throughout the largest concert hall.

So it is with us. Tensions can be turned into tuning forces in our lives by helping us to make the most of our gifts and talents.

This, then is the angels' promise. That we can find peace in the midst of tensions and stress—peace that will tune us and turn us into all we're meant to be.

How can the situation you wrote about yesterday tune you—and turn you into the person you are meant to be?

_____

_____

Tune into Jesus and turn your stress into serenity!

365

The Promise of Christmas—Peace

"I have said this to you, that in me you may have peace. In the world you have tribulation; but be of good cheer, I have overcome the world."

John 16:33

If, then, you accept the gift of peace, I am not saying that you will never experience problems. Not at all! It does mean, however, that problems will not depress you and they will not repress you, *but they will impress you with the possibilities of growth.* It's not the problems that get you, but what you let them do to you that is important in life.

The biggest problem I face today is _____

_____

_____

_____

With the help of God, what I plan to do about it is ____

_____

_____

_____

> **I can choose how I will let my problems
> affect me. I will choose peace today!**

The Promise of Christmas—Peace

"And let the peace of Christ rule in your hearts."
Colossians 3:15

One of the most tension-producing times of the year are the 24 days prior to Christmas. We are suddenly faced with an overwhelming deadline of presents to buy, cookies to bake and gifts to make. As the pressure-cooker of time builds, the crowds in the stores grow, and the parking lots overflow, we gradually begin to feel like our tops are ready to blow.

The pressure is inevitable.

We cannot escape it. But we can accept it and work with it if we:
1.) ITEMIZE OUR PRIORITIES.
2.) RECOGNIZE THE REALITIES, and thereby
3.) MINIMIZE OUR HOSTILITIES.

There are only so many hours in a day. We can find peace in the midst of Christmas rush if we stop and look at what's really important, and at those things in life that we really value.

What really are your priorities and values? Think of these peace-producing guidelines now.

> **I will find peace by remembering my priorities and what's really important!**

The Promise of Christmas—Peace

"Let him seek peace and pursue it."

1 Peter 3:11

We can minimize the hostility-producing tensions of the Christmas rush if we plan ahead.

List below all the things you need to get done today to make Christmas more peaceful for you and the ones you love:

1.
2.
3.
4.
5.
6.
7.
8.
9.
10.

Now look back at what you've written. What are the most important? They should be the first things you should do. Then, even if you run out of time, you will have the satisfaction of having completed the projects that matter the most.

I will actively pursue peace this year by planning ahead.

The Promise of Christmas—Peace

"And you, child, will give light to those who sit in darkness, to guide our feet into the way of peace."

Luke 1:79

This year, as we make out our gift lists for all those we love, we inevitably forget someone very important—ourselves!

If we could give ourselves anything we wanted for Christmas, what would it be?

A new home? A new car? A new love? A new job?

The greatest and most beautiful gift you could receive this year would be peace of mind. The gift of peace comes wrapped in a manger—the peace that results from knowing the love and forgiveness of Jesus Christ.

No matter what you are facing today, your Christmas can bring you peace of mind forever.

Do you feel the love and forgiveness of Jesus Christ? Take these moments now to come into His presence. "My peace I leave with you." (John 14:27)

> **I will give myself the gift of peace this year by following Jesus.**

The Promise of Christmas—Peace

"Have no anxiety about anything, but in everything by prayer and supplication with thanksgiving let your requests be made known to God. And the peace of God, which passes all under- standing, will keep your hearts and minds in Christ Jesus."
Philippians 4:6, 7

Jesus brings peace in the midst of turmoil. But it's up to us to do the maintenance work. You can keep peace in our lives if you:

P—PRAY for God's help and guidance as you face today and tomorrow.
E—ERASE your worries by dwelling on the hope of the manger.
A—ACCEPT realities that can't be changed.
C—COMMIT your limitations and expectations to God.
E—EXPECT only the best!

Through a peaceful time of prayer, do this now. Think of those worries, realities, and limitations, and let God bring to you this peace!

> I resolve to experience God's peace every day by Praying, Erasing, Accepting, Committing, and Expecting!

The Promise of Christmas—Joy

"And you will have joy and gladness and many will rejoice at his birth."

Luke 1:14

Many of you find Christmas to be a joyful season, but for some people it's a time of depression. Every psychiatrist, psychologist and pastor who counsels people, knows that this is a difficult season for many persons. Tragic memories come to the surface, bring back unpleasant and sorrowful moods. Their holiday festive spirit turns into the "Christmas blues."

I ran into someone the other day who said, "It's these Christmas tunes that get me depressed." And I suggested, "Why don't you switch from 'Christmas tunes' to 'Christmas tudes?'" He replied, "What do you mean?" I explained, "The Christmas tudes can give you joy if the Christmas tunes give you gloom. The four Christmas tudes are:

- GRATITUDE
- ATTITUDE
- ALTITUDE
- SOLITUDE

Beat the Christmas blues! Fulfill the Christmas promise of joy! Listen to the Christmas tudes!

I will tune into the Christmas tudes, and turn my blues into Good News!

The Promise of Christmas—Joy

"And the angel said to them, 'Be not afraid; for behold, I bring you good news of a great joy which will come to all people; for to you is born this day in the city of David a Savior who is Christ the Lord.'"

Luke 2:10, 11

A few years ago I wrote a little booklet on how to have joy at Christmas time. Actually I didn't write a thing. All I did was to put the letter A on one blank page; letter B on the next page and so on down the line. And I said this book is guaranteed to give you joy, but you have to finish writing it.

If you want to find joy in a time of gloom, all you do is practice GRATITUDE. Think of all the things you should be grateful for.

A- _____

B- _____

C- _____

D- _____

E- _____

F- _____

G- _____

H- _____

I- _____

J- _____

> **I have so many things to be grateful for! I have truly been blessed! Life is fantastic!**

The Promise of Christmas—Joy

"They shall obtain joy and gladness and sorrow and sighing shall flee away."

Isaiah 35:10

After you have practiced the Christmas tude of gratitude, amplify it with the second Christmas tude—ATTITUDE. The attitude of Christmas is one of being unselfish rather than selfish. That's what liberates you! It works wonders! When you are depressed it's because you are focusing upon yourself. Gloom, sadness, sorrow, lack of joy and depression are always the result of some self-centered thinking or feeling—"I didn't get what I wanted." "I didn't have my way." "I lost something that I had or things aren't going the way that I want them to go." But the Christmas attitude is just the opposite: "I'm not thinking about myself. I'm going to think about others."

Write down the name of those who could use your cheer, your help, or your prayers today.

_____

_____

_____

_____

By focusing on others, my sorrow shall turn into joy!

The Promise of Christmas—Joy

"Therefore, this joy of mine is now full. He must increase. But I must decrease."

John 3:29, 30

Benny Tee was one of my very good friends. He ran a retail shoe store near my home. One Christmas I asked him, "What is the favorite Christmas that you ever had?" He said, "That's easy to answer," and he proceeded to tell me his story. Two weeks before Christmas a poor man walked into Benny's store. Looking around at all the shoes, he asked. "Are you Mr. Tee?" and Benny said, "Yes." "I want a special pair of shoes for my son."

Standing next to him was an eleven-year-old boy dressed in shabby clothes. Benny looked down at the boy's feet and saw that he had club feet. His father explained, "The one thing my son wants for Christmas is a pair of shoes like the other kids. Could you make them for him?" Benny said, "Yes, but it will take time to order a special kind of leather. I can't promise they'll be done by Christmas."

The leather didn't come until the 24th. It took Benny until 4:00 in the morning of Christmas Day. But when Benny Tee lovingly delivered the special pair of shoes to the boy's home, he, Benny Tee, received the best Christmas gift of his life. *He received Joy!*

I will receive the gift of joy this year by giving of myself to others!

The Promise of Christmas—Joy

"For I have derived much joy and comfort from your love."
Philemon 1:7

Gratitude and attitude give you ALTITUDE! Altitude is the ability to suddenly break out, transcend and rise above your hurts, heartaches, rejections, problems and sorrows! Somehow you need that altitude. If you practice gratitude and if you have the attitude of giving to others, you will achieve the altitude. Suddenly you'll have joy! You'll rise to the point where you'll know that you are important! You break into space! You go into orbit! You gain altitude in spite of your problems. God is using you to help somebody. Nothing gives you more joy than knowing you are being used to help somebody.

Write how you felt when you helped the somebody on December 10.

_____

_____

_____

_____

Joy! It's mine to receive the minute I give!

The Promise of Christmas—Joy

"These things I have spoken to you, that my joy may be in you, and that your joy may be full."

John 15:11

One of my favorite people was David Nelson. When David was in high school, he incurred a disease that degenerates the nervous system. You can't walk or talk, but it doesn't affect the thinking, rational brain. Doctors thought David would have to drop out of school, but his classmates urged him to keep going on.

His classmates took turns reading his lessons to him because his eyesight was failing. When he was finally confined to a wheelchair during his senior year, they took turns carrying him up and down the steps to his classrooms. They wouldn't let David quit!

When the commencement time came and David's name was called, two football players picked up his wheelchair and lifted him to the platform. The entire student body jumped to their feet and applauded as if to say, "We made it, didn't we, David?"

David had discovered the "Christmas tudes." He found them in his living and relayed them to us when he left on his final commencement, to be with Jesus forevermore.

Jesus is our Joy! Today and for eternity!

The Promise of Christmas—Joy

"May the God of hope fill you with all joy and peace in believing."

Romans 15:13

The Christmas tudes: gratitude, attitude, altitude, and the final tude, SOLITUDE. How do you obtain that kind of gratitude, attitude, and altitude? Through solitude! You've probably been rushing so much in life that you haven't taken time to be alone with God and with Jesus Christ. I want to suggest something to you. Find a place where you can be protected from unnecessary interruptions and spend some time alone. I try to run every morning. This is my time of solitude. When I'm running with my eyes open, I am alone with God and I'm thanking Him for all of the blessings.

God can use us. He can direct us to the people who need our help. In offering our help to others, we are released from our self-centered thinking. And we find the joy that comes through giving as expressed in Acts 20:35: "It is more blessed to give than to receive."

God has a beautiful plan for your life. His plan is to use you to give Joy! How? By tuning into the Christmas "tudes."

> **I will take time today and every day to be alone with God and to feel the joy and peace of Jesus fill my entire being.**

The Promise of Christmas—Love

"For God so loved the world that He sent his only Son, that whoever believes in him should not perish but have eternal life."

John 3:16

What's the greatest need in the world today? The world needs energy, yes. But it needs something more than energy. Food? Food is urgently needed, but food isn't the desperate problem. What, then, is needed more than food and energy? My friends, it is love. I know people—and you do, too—who do not suffer from lack of material needs. They have food, clothing, and money; they have riches; they have physical health; but they do not have love! And they are constantly at war with themselves. They have problems with people and they have problems with God.

When Jesus came into the world at Christmas time, a spirit descended to planet earth that remains today and nothing can put that spirit of light out. That light is the Christmas gift of love in action!

Do you have the light of love in your life this Christmas? If not—it can be God's gift to you. If you have that love—give it to someone else.

> **I will remember to put Love on my gift list this Christmas.**

The Promise of Christmas—Love

"You shall love your neighbor as yourself."

Matthew 22:39

There is nothing that makes you feel so good as when you have the opportunity to do a loving deed for somebody. Christmas provides a reminder and an opportunity to do something generous in a display of love and affection to your fellow human beings. That's why many people discover the promise of Christmas—LOVE!

The greatest need in the world today is LOVE! Deep love! You can be God's channel. You can be God's instrument. The Christmas promise of love is not only God's promise to you, it's to everybody!

In one of the offices of the Tower of Hope is a banner which reads: "It's possible to give without loving, but it's impossible to love without giving." God's plan is to use you to give the love away. That's what the Christmas story is all about! His plan is to give His love to you and then you will give it away to others.

Who will you give love away to today? List five specific names:

_____

_____

_____

_____

_____

> **"It's possible to give without loving, but it's impossible to love without giving."**

The Promise of Christmas—Love

"Love your enemies and pray for those who persecute you."
                                        Luke 6:27

My gift for you today is an exercise of love that's guaranteed to work in your daily life. I learned this method from my friend, the late Dr. Frank Laubach, one of the great missionaries and international statesmen of the 20th century. I recall Dr. Laubach saying that he once had a difficult time loving some cantankerous person. And this really bothered him because he knew, as a devoted Christian, that he should love everybody. Well, he finally decided to face this problem openly and honestly during his prayer time.

He began, "Lord, you know that I am a human being and I am not perfect. I should love that person but I can't. But I don't want to stand in your way, so you love him through me." As he finished his prayer, he put one hand into the air with his palm open and said, "Jesus, come into the palm of my hand, flow through my arm, my shoulder and heart." Then stretching his other arm out and pointing at the imaginative person, he continued, "Jesus, I can't love him, but you can!" He enthused, "I waited and I felt Jesus flowing through my arm and filling my heart with love."

Who have you had trouble loving lately? Practice this exercise now. Repeat this prayer;

"Jesus, I can't love _____ but I don't want to stand in your way. Go ahead—Love _____ through me!"

Love is like all other exercise. The more you work it, the stronger it becomes.

380

The Promise of Christmas—Love

"We love, because he first loved us."

1 John 4:19

I shared the story of Dr. Laubach and his love secret (see December 17) in the pulpit one Sunday. A few days later I received a telephone call from a successful businessman who had been sitting in the congregation. Excitedly, he said, "Dr. Schuller, it works! It works! I went to work on Monday morning and who should show up outside my office but an obnoxious salesman who calls on me twice a year. This time I decided to try the Laubach love exercise.

"It was amazing. He seemed like a different person. He was really nice!"

I asked him, "Do you think he was different, or do you think you were different? Who really changed? Probably you were a different person!" And he got the point.

For as soon as you get out of God's way and allow Jesus Christ to literally flow through your life, you are going to be different! You will be changed! You will be affected! Then you will bring out the best in the other persons because Christ will actually be flowing through your life.

When we tap into God's love, we suddenly are able to see others as He does—
BEAUTIFULLY!

The Promise of Christmas—Love

"For this is the message which you have heard from the beginning, that we should love one another."

1 John 3:11

I shall never forget one summer when I was traveling with a small group in Greece. Included in our group was an 82-year-old lady. I called her "Sweetie." She was frail, tiny and thin, but she was such a brave trooper and didn't want to miss a thing. So, although she was very tired, she insisted on going along to the Euripedes Theater to see a Greek play.

No sooner had the play begun, than "Sweetie" started to fall forward. There were no backs on these seats. Before I could help, a local Greek peasant woman reached forward and took hold of the tiny narrow shoulders of Sweetie and slowly drew the tired body back until it leaned against her knees. She provided support for Sweetie for the entire play!

That's love! It is an international language. The two women never spoke a word to each other. But they used a different language—a language that transcends nations! The love of Jesus! It's universal and the need is so immense.

Love isn't love 'til you give it away.

The Promise of Christmas—Love

"Do you love me? Feed my lambs."

John 21:15

What does the world need? Love! No one displayed his love for the world more beautifully than Bob Pierce. It all started back in the 1940's. Bob was a missionary to China.

One day while he was there he ran into a woman he knew from Holland, Michigan, Tina Holkeboer. Now, Tina was one of those tremendous, powerful, independent, vigorous, bold women! And Bob Pierce was walking through town when he saw Tina. She was holding the hand of a little four-year-old girl. Tina said, "How are you, Bob? What are you doing these days?" "I'm preaching the gospel," he replied.

Then she picked up this little girl and said, "Here, Bob, catch!" And the small child was in his arms! "You preach about Jesus and love, now do something about it," she exclaimed. "Take care of this young child." "What do you mean?" he asked. "I mean just that," she answered. "She's yours!" "She can't be," he said. "Sorry," Tina explained, "I have six more just like her and I can't handle another child. You take care of her. Goodbye."

And that was the beginning of a movement called World Vision. Jesus came to bring love to all the world through you and through me.

Who can I feed with my love today?

383

The Promise of Christmas—Love

"For God sent the Son into the world, not to condemn the world, but that the world through Him might be saved."
John 3:17

Something happened at Christmas time and the world has never been the same because of it. What happened was not the birth of a new religion, but an eternal loving God revealing His real heart so that everybody would know what He's really like.

I shall never forget the Archbishop Fulton Sheen, who said, "If God had to reveal Himself to dogs, there would be only one way. He'd have to become a dog. If God wanted to reveal Himself to birds, He'd have to become a bird. When God wanted to reveal Himself to human beings, there was only one way—He had to become a human being!"

And this is what's meant by Christmas—God became a human person! And this person lives today and can come into human hearts! This Christmas receive Christ into your life and receive the gift of Christmas—love!

Jesus came so that you could realize at last that God loves you! Have you ever had better news than that?